BERLIN

1910-1933

BERLIN
1910-1933

Eberhard Roters

with
Janos Frecot, Sonja Günther
Joachim Heusinger von Waldegg
Ulrich Gregor and Arno Paul

TABARD PRESS

*This English translation is dedicated to the
memory of my grandfather and to the living
example of my mother. — M.M.*

Translated from the German by
MARGUERITE MOUNIER
German-language edition, *Berlin 1910-1933:*
Copyright © 1982 by Office du Livre S.A.,
Fribourg, Switzerland

English translation:
Copyright © 1982 by Office du Livre S.A.,
Fribourg, Switzerland

Tabard Press is a division of W.S. Konecky
Associates, Inc., New York, N.Y. 10011

All North American rights reserved by
William S. Konecky Associates, Inc.,
New York, N.Y. 10011

ISBN: 0-914427-03-2

Printed and bound in Hong Kong

CONTENTS

PREFACE

The idea for this book, proposed to me by the publisher, was to present an overall view of artistic accomplishments in Berlin during the Twenties. Initially, this was to cover only the realms of architecture and the Fine Arts. First attempts at broaching the subject already led to a decisive modification of our plans: it became obvious that, on the one hand, to restrict the time lapse to the Twenties would hardly correspond to all that went on in Berlin, that in order to do justice to artistic development specific to Berlin, the period of interest would have to extend from 1910 to 1933. On the other hand, to confine the presentation only to architecture and the fine arts could never render the development in Berlin coherent; the manifold connections and reciprocal influences alone necessitate the inclusion of theater and film. In fact, it was particularly in the artistic realm of film that Berlin had so much to contribute on the European level. It would have been tempting to include music and literature as well, but that would have been well beyond the framework of a book dedicated to the "visual arts". In order to guarantee an appropriate analysis of each field individually, encompassing their complex interrelations as well, we created a team of experts: this book is the product of our teamwork.

I should like to extend my heartfelt thanks to all my co-authors for their fine collaboration and to Mrs. Traude Stürmer for her organizational help in managing correspondence. My especial thanks go to the owners of the works of art, as well as to the legal proprietors of the titles, for their obliging permission to reproduce those pieces; and, last but not least, to Mr. Jean Hirschen for the inspiration to write this book.

Eberhard Roters

INTRODUCTION

During the twenty years from 1910 to 1930 Berlin, together with Paris and New York, was a metropolitan center for avant-garde art and culture in the West. Those two decades spanned the "heroic" era, during which Berlin's cultural industry developed traits that decisively influenced the international cultural outlook of twentieth-century industrial society. We have purposely coined the term cultural "industry", because there was such emphasis on productivity in all fields, whether in architecture, the fine arts, theater or film. This phenomenon was further encouraged by increased activity among the media, especially the press. Production reflected the impact of the Machine Age on human relationships, characterized by tempo, rhythm, dynamics, agitation and motoricity. Berlin, "capital of the Empire", a newcomer and Europe's youngest metropolis, was a perfect proving ground for those seeking a change, including researchers, amateurs, reformers and revolutionaries.

Berlin was a significant haven for cultural innovation because it attracted the very people who wanted to break away from the provinces and provincialism. In Berlin, as in Paris and New York, the arts relinquished their provincialism, including certain basic elements that distinguished the culture of one region from another, in favor of a more urban and cosmopolitan outlook. When the latter trend in turn influenced provincial capitals, a dialectical process was set in motion. Unlike other European countries, Germany's federated political structure could serve as a basis for delimiting cultural boundaries. Berlin became a creative and influential center for the international urban art that emerged from the Industrial Age, evolving from its beginnings, which encompassed whole civilizations, into metropolitanism. International art requires an industrial complex capable of sustaining it and therefore favors the development of the metropolitan centers that are so important to the modern cultural scene. Intellectualism is a major aspect of urban art of the Industrial Age; Berlin intellectualized art to serve its own purposes.

But it seems remarkable, at first glance, that this development in Berlin was not the outcome of growing economic prosperity, but that it blossomed despite the social and economic situation. The process began during the years from 1910 to 1913, at a time when the Kaiser's empire was already politically and ideologically on the decline. Then came the bitter and bloody years of World War I, from 1914 to 1918. From 1918 to 1933, the first German Republic went from crisis to crisis, and its existence was threatened internally even more than externally. Inflation was the inevitable consequence of postwar conditions triggered by the abortive revolution. And finally, after a relatively stable period of economic and political consolidation around the mid Twenties, the world was shaken by the international economic crisis. In order to allay the effects of the latter during the Weimar Republic, Brüning's cabinet put through a series of emergency measures which, given an already sorely tattered society and the attitude of a population unfamiliar with democratic proceedings, created a situation allowing National Socialism to consolidate its pernicious beginnings.

One can say that urban art in Berlin in fact derived its intellectual vitality from its opposition to economic and social developments. In the years between 1910 and 1930, Berlin art was essentially a product of social resistance; it could hardly have been otherwise, as contrast was an inseparable premise of its beginnings. The contradiction not only induced political and ideological debate, but asserted guidelines for the cityscape and for everyday life. As such, it implied heterogeneity, the coincidental alliance of unmatching elements, combinations between the incompatible: all of which were both discovered and fervently adopted. By reaction, urban art in Berlin took on forms that directly reflected efforts to come to terms with the substance of the contradiction. Stylistic methods were used to deal with the problem, so that, during the Twenties, montage was extensively used in Berlin in the fine arts, and in theater, film and literature. Not only photomontage, but montage as a whole, is Berlin's specific contribution to twentieth-century art. Berlin was a stage set: its citizens considered the buildings as backdrops, built as required and subsequently cleared away. The ensuing urban architectural eclecticism is a specific reflection of the society's heterogeneity. Contemporary cityscapes visually corroborate this stage-set attitude. The origins of urban contradiction are deeply buried in the city's history of emergence into a capital of the empire, an evolution that was so at odds with its subsequent growth into a metropolis that it could hardly be called harmonious.

As the capital of the Prussian Empire until the beginning of the nineteenth century, Berlin was still a residential city of, on the average, relatively provincial size and aspect. It was architecturally distinguished by its royal buildings representing phases in Baroque, Rococo, and early Classicism (see the city castle, the Charlottenburg Castle and the Potsdam buildings). The reigning Hohenzollern dynasty, driven to Mark Brandenburg in the first place by a historical stroke of fate that was almost coincidental, had undertaken for generations to bring together territories that had traditionally, linguistically and physically been most varied and far apart. These areas were united in the name of State supremacy in foreign affairs, to form Prussia, including the main districts of East and West Prussia, on the one hand, and Mark Brandenburg on the other.

Thus the dynastic configuration of the states was conducive to heterogeneity. Prussia, that artificial composite, was more an outgrowth of undivided power than of natural national origins, but it was to grow within the political vacuum of Central Europe, to which it was drawn all the more since the collapse of the Germanic Holy Roman Empire in 1806. In Berlin, a liberal, self-conscious middle class gradually emerged at the beginning of the twentieth century, stimulated to a large degree by the emancipation of German burghers of Jewish origin who had obtained recognition of their equal rights. In fact, all the immigrants who had, over previous years, come to Berlin when they were banished from other countries for their religious beliefs, encouraged Berlin's citizens to become open-minded, be it the Huguenots who fled from France or the Protestants who emigrated from Salzburg. Since then Berlin has been, and remains, a city of immigrants.

The fruits of this influx, supported intellectually by Berlin's liberal middle classes during the first thirty years of the twentieth century, were most impressive, as merely enumerating several names will attest: Moses Mendelssohn, Rahel Varnhagen, Heinrich Heine, Heinrich von Kleist, Alexander and Wilhelm von Humboldt, Christoph Friedrich Nicolai, August Wilhelm and Friedrich Schlegel, Karl Friedrich Schinkel, Ernst Theodor Amadeus Hoffmann, Friedrich Wilhelm Joseph von Schelling, Arthur Schopenhauer and Georg Wilhelm Friedrich Hegel.

Berlin's rapid population growth began when heavy industry, especially machine industry, was founded in that city. In 1841 the first German locomotive built in Berlin was put into service from the Anhalter station. From then on, Berlin became the manufacturing center for railroad cars and especially locomotives. The Berlin iron foundries and locomotive factories Borsig and Schwarzkopff attained worldwide repute. And as of the 1880's, when Siemens-Werke and Allgemeine Elektrizitäts-Gesellschaft AEG were founded, its also became an industrial center for electricity. In view of this industrial activity, Berlin attracted, as of the middle of the nineteenth century, all the jobless peasants, especially from Mecklenburg, and from the eastern provinces of Pomerania, East Prussia, West Prussia and Silesia. Over the years they contributed to the explosive demographic growth of a large-scale industrial proletariat. As of the 1860's, tenement blocks became a very characteristic feature of Berlin's cityscape.

The suppression of the 1848 Revolution was a traumatic experience for the liberal bourgeoisie, which can be traced back to the Biedermeier era. This was also the case in several other large cities of Europe, for instance in Vienna. But in Berlin the development was provoked by the particular circumstances that made Prussia the representative, at first unofficially and later officially, of the German Imperial government. Otto von Bismarck was the brilliant power strategist who managed the administration, and his conduct must be understood in the light of the demands made on him by his status as well as by the times. In 1866 Prussia sealed its decision to gain political supremacy in Germany by founding the North-German Confederation, after it conquered Austria, which until that time had been considered a stronghold of former imperialist concepts. The victory over the French Empire and the fatal foundation of a German Empire, with the choice of a Prussian king as emperor, were the turning points in Prussian-German power politics. Berlin, the political center of the dynasty, was already a metropolis that had grown too quickly, absorbed in the problems of its big-city status.

Until 1848, the Prussian court and the liberal bourgeoisie kept a mutually agreeable distance apart and yet were tied together by fairly frequent critical dialogue. That situation began to change as the city grew; an even greater discrepancy developed in 1871, when the German Empire adopted an imperialistic policy disguised as a throwback to former imperial concepts. The last Prussian kings destined to rule the German Empire already considered their authority as a holy mission. Hence the last German emperor embodied, in tragi-comic fashion, the misalliance between

modern industrial imperialism and imperial divine right, as well as the conflict of roles implicit in that duality.

And so the crucial dialogue with the liberal bourgeoisie no longer existed. It was replaced by the fight for power, carried on by the administration through a repressive series of laws and prohibitions. The same methods were applied by the Imperial government to abort claims to emancipation made by the industrial proletariat.

Around 1900 Berlin society could be classified for the most part as follows:
– the Imperial family and court society, who were nationalistic and utterly conservative, and therefore reacted energetically against any hint of liberalism. Since the Kaiser was interested in the arts, he was able to detect the revolutionary aspects of the new tendencies; he was responsible for coining the term "gutter art";
– the middle classes, who were oriented towards national conservatism, and therefore loyal to the Kaiser inasmuch as it was in their political interest. In his book *Der Untertan* ("Man of Straw"), Heinrich Mann impressively portrays the type of social climber this group produced;
– an industrial proletariat, who were the major element of Berlin's population. They had fought politically over the last ten years against oppression and were at last able to celebrate their first victory when the representatives of the Social Democratic Party obtained a majority in the Reichstag and could push a series of socialist laws through the legislature;
– and finally, the ideologically contradictory petty bourgeoisie who, however, included the critical Berlin intelligentsia at its summit. The latter kept up the intellectual traditions of Berlin's liberal middle classes, and their representatives played a leading part in the opposition: a role which enticed them and which they assumed openly. As the public adversaries of the Imperial family and its ideology, they formed an intellectual vanguard. The friction created by confrontations gave impetus to their wit, sarcasm and irony.

Wit, sarcasm and irony virtually define Berlin's intellectual life. The city was fittingly uncomfortable; it was like a new flat, half furnished with ill-assorted equipment, drafty because of all the open doors. In 1910 in his book *Berlin – ein Stadtschicksal* ("Berlin – The Destiny of a City"), Karl Scheffler describes Berlin as a city condemned to the throes of becoming, and never being. But this very quality is what attracted creatively critical minds and was the reason they came to Berlin: in order to carry on debates and discussions, to disagree with each other, to argue and then come to an agreement. This was the background and basis for Berlin's tremendous creativity in the years from 1910 to 1930.

E.R.

I CITY, ARCHITECTURE AND HABITAT

Janos Frecot and Sonja Günther

Berlin became an important European metropolis quite late. In the area extending outwards from the Mediterranean, many settlements grew as appendages to monasteries and the residences of bishops and princes; the earliest along the military roads of the Romans and, later, following in the footsteps of the Christian missionaries, i.e. north of the Alps, through France, southern Germany, up to the North Sea, and further up to Ireland and Scotland, on to Scandinavia and Russia. At the time, however, the area later to become Mark Brandenburg, the core of Prussia, was still in a nearly prehistoric twilight state. The foundation of the city of Berlin has traditionally been considered as having

1 Aerial view of Leipzigerplatz and Potsdamerplatz. The Potsdamer Railroad Station (left), large hotels and entertainment establishments, as well as ministries, embassies, offices and department stores surrounded the busiest square of prewar Berlin: 1931

13

taken place in 1237; recent research sets that date from fifty to seventy years earlier.

If one were to draw a horizontal line through Europe, from Amsterdam to Warsaw, and a vertical line from Copenhagen to Venice, their point of intersection would give the approximate location of Berlin. Until Germany was split up as a consequence of fascist ambitions to rule the world, Berlin was indisputably one of Europe's commercial centers, in a median position between East and West Europe, the first station on the road from Scandinavia to the south or from East Europe to the west. Even nowadays, despite Germany's partition and West Berlin's insular situation, the trains of the intercontinental railroad union on the line Leningrad-Warsaw-Paris-London go through both parts of Berlin, so that one can travel from one or the other of the Berlins to Warsaw, Prague, Vienna and Copenhagen without a change-over, as well as to Amsterdam or Paris.

The city's climate is determined by its situation in the north German Lowlands and its proximity to the North and Baltic seas: on some stormy spring or fall days, it is as if one were breathing in fresh sea air that has blown straight across the sandy flat country, to refresh the citizens of the city. Then we remember that the air of Berlin, was once very praised.

The lands surrounding Berlin are poor in mineral resources. Further south, in the Lausitz region, soft coal is produced; and in Rüdersdorf, on the city's eastern outskirts, there is a rather large limestone deposit, which is fast running dry. The more noble construction materials are absent from the city's aspect; since time immemorial, the city has been built up out of bricks. Some of the old churches were built of fieldstone.

The Mark is sandy and lacks topsoil; seas, bogs, and sluggish rivers weave through the area. As the eye gazes across the land once flattened by enormous glaciers, it is arrested by the occasional dune-like sandy hillocks and the hills of sand and debris from the glacial age – the moraines. All in all, the landscape is peaceful, neither sensational nor touristic, but of a hidden beauty discernible only at second or third glance.

Centuries of cultural barrenness and eco-

nomic penury have left traces, still visible nowadays, on the face of the city, or rather on the unequal halves of both West and East Berlin; almost nothing was spared by the city's history, hardly a castle, church, royal palace or bourgeois home. Berlin became a city of the nineteenth and twentieth centuries, and the change was so enormous that the few remaining older buildings – the Marienkirche, the citadel, the Charlottenburg Castle and the village churches – seemed outlandish and discordant in their shattered environment.

The site of Berlin's foundation was not chosen with an eye to a bishop's or prince's seat, but in view of the existing ford, in the midst of forests and swamps, over the Spree River. The twin city of Berlin and Coelln grew on and next to an island between the river's arms, at the narrowest point of the Warsaw-Berlin lowland valley, where dry projecting sand bars came closest to each other, only a few meters above the lowlands.

Over the centuries, the city grew slowly. Nearby, Köpenick and Spandau could claim equal status for many years, and it was only

2   The Spree River between the Reichstag and the Friedrichstrasse Railroad Station. The fruit barges were part of the image of Berlin, a river and canal city; they brought wares in directly from the country, from the producers to the consumers: around 1930

3 The Anhalter Bahnhof, the largest and most beautiful of Berlin's railroad terminals, where tracks of train lines from the south, southwest and west met. The rail overpass over the Landwehr canal (visible on the photograph) was a famous site: the canal, street, railroad and elevated train bridge (from which this photograph was taken) met in one spot on four levels: 1932

4 Along the railroad, the fire walls and end walls were rented as billboards; beside them, a factory yard, the buildings faced with glazed brick: around 1930

when Prussia expanded, on the basis of its military exploits, that Berlin became important as a royal residence. (Nevertheless, it was decided that the coronation of the princely elector as King in Prussia would take place at Königsberg in East Prussia.) Frederick II not only conquered the land but also set out to colonize the interior: he had the swamplands drained and built up canals that became the basis of a widely ramified north German water-road network, with Berlin at its center. The large-scale industrialization of Berlin was launched with the completion of the railroad stretch between Berlin and Potsdam in 1838. Borsig began building locomotives, and Berlin steadily became one of Europe's industrial metropolises. In 1866 it became the capital of the North German Confederation, and in 1871 of the German Reich. It was not only the beginning of the famed and notorious period of promoterism, when corporations went bankrupt as fast as they were established; but at this time also, Berlin emerged as the political, commercial and cultural center of the Reich territories, including the older cultural entities of Saxony, Swabia and Franconia. As such, Berlin greatly detracted

from the significance of former regional centers, which reacted grudgingly against the parvenu, giving rise to home-grown feelings of hostility against big-city tactics, and thus providing the emotional basis of political frictions that were to last until the Nazi era.

If one were to compare a city map of around 1860 with one of 1900, not all the changes would represent the natural outgrowth of the city's development. Berlin was surrounded by numerous villages, cut off from the city by the circular railway built during the 1870's; the railway was the equivalent of a city wall 10 to 15 kilometers wide around the city. A densely overbuilt city of four- to six-story apartment houses — oblong buildings with side wings and courtyards to the rear — grew within that "wall". And although the former farm villages outside that circumference became large industrial towns within a few decades, a vacant area of "forgotten land" remained from the original separation and is used nowadays as garden allotments, railway and industrial land, camp sites and recreation areas.

Further comparison of a city map of around 1900 or 1910 with that of one of

15

1920 or 1930 brings to the fore the fact that the spaciously planned lay-out and creative formation of Berlin came to a halt even before 1914. Although an act of administration enlarged Berlin by creating Greater Berlin in 1920, provoking the consolidation and development of traffic arteries and functional land allotments, there were hardly any additional changes.

As the capital of the Weimar Republic, Berlin was a city of four million inhabitants, covering an area the size of the entire Ruhr territory, with houses, streets, forests and seas. As an industrial capital, Berlin produced almost everything from machinery, to chemical and electronic equipment, precision and fine-mechanical products. It was the commercial center of northern Europe, a transit city, and the first stop for the many emigrants who, for economic and cultural reasons, left Russia, the Baltic provinces, Poland and Hungary. For a hundred years it had harbored one of Europe's largest Jewish settlements. And for fifty years, it had been undeniably the political and economic center of Germany. Berlin was also the center of the German

5 City map of the railway (*Ringbahn*) encircling downtown Berlin and adjacent suburbs, an annex to a street plan: 1925

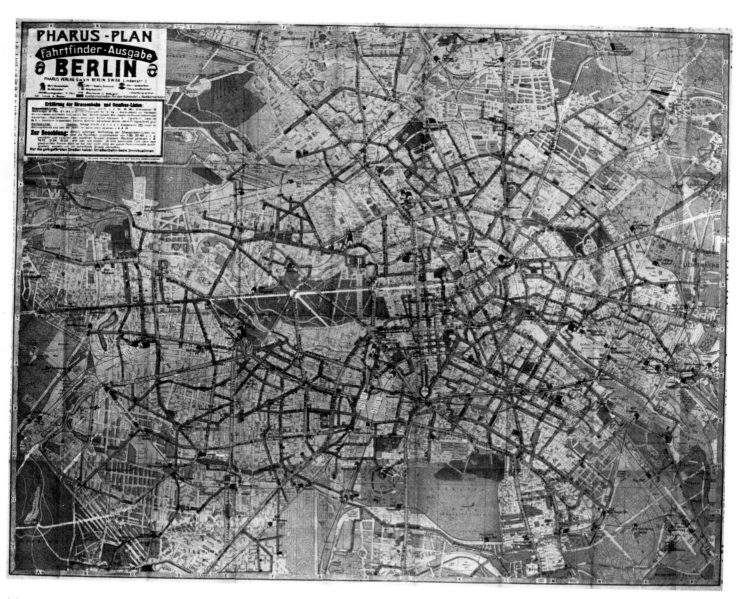

press, although the headquarters for other types of publishing remained in Leipzig. Despite the city's efforts to surpass in rank the older cultural centers such as Dresden or Munich, the Bauhaus was set up in Weimar rather than Berlin; nor did Dresden, Cologne or Hanover lose any of their significance. Berlin never managed to induce a centralization of Germany comparable to what Paris has accomplished in France. (And Munich became the "trend capital", linked to Vienna by channels of communication.)

Since the turn of the century, Berlin had been seeking its own approach to new forms of construction for apartment houses as well as for factories and commercial buildings. Tradition was no obstacle – nor was it of much help. The city maintained its earlier irregularities in the unkempt juxtaposition and confusion of its cityscape. Instead of developing in concentric circles, expanding step by step from a central point as did many other cities, Berlin erratically overran villages and small towns, without always digesting them first. The face of Berlin is not homogeneous; rather, at least until the war, it offered many different views. But that face of the city has often been obliterated by bomb damage during war, as well as by demolition and reconstruction during postwar years.

Already by 1900, little remained of medieval Berlin; Baroque Berlin was represented by several residences and palaces, and the outlines of the fortress glinting here and there through the street layout. Frederick the Great's Berlin was torn down piece by piece by William II, who rebuilt it with business buildings. The reputation of bricks as a new construction material, due to Schinkel and his school, gained recognition quite slowly. The city castle, Museum Island and Forum Fredericianeum, Unter den Linden, the Charlottenburg Castle and Potsdam represented centers of Prussian domination and culture. Heavy industry developed along the Dahme, Spree and Havel rivers and along the canals; highly specialized products, often of worldwide repute, were produced by the manufacturing companies in the industrial yards of the downtown working districts. Suburban settlements soon stretched far out into the country, in all directions along the many spokes of the railroad lines. Fashionable colonies of villas grew up far away, in villages idyllically located amid seas and forests. It was here that the descendants of the founders of the old garden suburbs of Berlin – the Tiergarten and Kielgan districts, Westend, Lichterfelde, Friedenau and Wannsee – retired from business pressures.

Berlin was never a city of aristocrats known for being patrons, as was Paris or Vienna. This was because the countryside was too poor to generate a rich and cultivated country nobility capable of assuming a glitter-

6 The Karstadt Department Store on Hermannplatz was built in 1929 by Philip Schaefer; it went beyond all conventional standards of architecture in Berlin to that date, both in its style and in the construction site chosen—an old city square. The American styling made the building appear taller than it was: 1929

17

ing role in the city. Prussian nobility served as officers and officials. It was the industrial and civic barons who first built themselves palaces – in the center of the city, for a short time, and later in the form of palatial villas and country houses.

The host of employees and workers lived in apartment houses and aspired to a little house in the suburbs, or at least a *Laube* ("garden shack"). The workers' weekend houses were located in garden colonies, which popularized the term *Laubenpieper* ("garden shack chirpers") used in the caricatures, songs and films of urban folklore.

Between 1900 and 1939, Berlin's participation in international architectural developments did little to alter its own cityscape. The major architectural achievements of the 1920's, such as factory buildings and housing developments, were located on the outskirts of the city. The new tempo of automobiles, rather than the city railway, trolley and elevated train, made a far greater impact on life and opinions in Berlin and was certainly more influential than the occasional tokens of Functionalist style sprinkled across the city's

7 Workers on strike in front of the gates of the AEG on Brunnenstrasse in north Berlin: 1932

8 Alexanderplatz: an architectural collage. In the foreground, two business premises and office buildings by Peter Behrens; behind them, built over the former moat, the commuter train.
Turn-of-the-century stores along Königstrasse are dominated by the tower of the Roten Rathaus, a rough brick structure erected in the 1860's: around 1932

18

9 During the Thirties, Berlin's electrically operated *S-Bahn* ("fast train") was considered the most modern and efficient high-speed railway in the world. Its lines, surrounded by those of the *Ringbahn*, stretched out into the suburbs and country towns on the outskirts of the metropolis: 1927

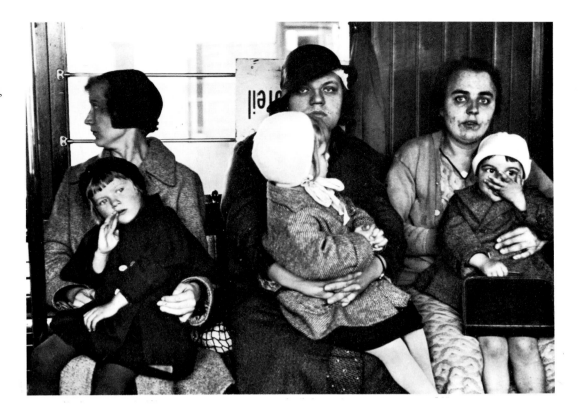

10 A last look in the billfold before an excursion on motorbike into the green countryside: 1930

downtown area. Individualists, car drivers tend to withdraw from participating in urban collective life; they become estranged from the city, which they gradually consider with indifference and even hostility. Their only concern is the fastest route from one point to another. To them, the city's historical development, with its projections, edges and bridges, is nothing but a bothersome brake to their projects.

In the 1920's, when architecture became interested in building developments in the countryside on the outskirts of the city, it wrote off the city and left it to its traffic planners. Fascist architecture wrote off the city as well, considering it merely as an available area for showrooms and parade axes. National Socialist enemies of the city developed two strategies reflecting their internal cleavage — and both were to the city's detriment. Their backward-oriented, romantic social approach, on the one hand, and their futuristic obsession favoring technology, on the other, encouraged people to leave the city and to settle on native homestead soil or helped to spread the notion of the car as a popular means of transportation. It was only during

the Adenauer era that both dreams could be fulfilled, in the Lückeplan (1960), which abolished government control of the building industry, and in the boom of the automobile industry.

Ever since, big cities — even those less damaged by the history of their self-inflicted faults — hardly have a choice between a glorious downfall under the veneer maintaining the cityscape, or the anarchy of land and housing speculation.

J.F.

The City around 1920: The Promises of Technology – International Aspirations

Political Factors

Building activities in Berlin in the Twenties were shaped by factors reflecting the defeat suffered in World War I. Internationalism was to supplant the nationalism that had been decisive during the Kaiser era. Certainly, the heritage of nationalism was a heavy load for

11 Memorial in Berlin to Rosa Luxemburg and Karl Liebknecht; designed by Ludwig Mies van der Rohe: 1926

the young generation to bear, but they were nevertheless courageously determined to begin anew. And, despite enormous failures, their ambitions were partially fulfilled.

Outward appearances during the Twenties – the functional architecture, the elegant interiors, and a lifestyle that seemed above petty-bourgeois concerns – were bound to be misleading from the start. Before the brilliant era of the "golden Twenties", there had been endeavors to avoid the horrors of war by international solidarity. As of 1915 already, the left wing of the SDP ("German Social Democratic Party") fraction had voted to reject war credits. Peace conferences had taken place in Switzerland (1915 and 1916) and in Sweden (1917). But pacifism had not succeeded. The only issue of *Die Internationale*, published by Rosa Luxemburg, Franz Mehring and Karl Liebknecht, was confiscated; Liebknecht, barred from the SDP for his pacifist activities, was sentenced to two years in a penitentiary. In 1919, officers of the radical Right instigated the vicious assassination of Luxemburg and Liebknecht. The 1918 November Revolution, which took place mainly in Munich and Berlin, had in fact led to the proclamation of a Soviet Republic that was, however, re-defeated after the fighting; the Spartacist revolt in Berlin was squelched. The tangible result was the democratic-republican form of government of the Weimar Republic, proclaimed in 1919. The same year witnessed the creation of the German Workers' Party as well, which was later to become the NSDWP ("National Socialist Democratic Workers' Party").

The Twenties bore the parallel imprint of progressive internationalism and petty-bourgeois nationalism. In Germany, this was especially evident in Berlin and Munich, but whereas Bavarian nationalism was an important element in Munich, Berlin developed into a metropolis during the Twenties. The variegated mixture of all the arts was important to this development; it burst forth like a display of fireworks, allowing Berlin, like Paris, to appear in an international light. Berlin's international standing was also the product of the unison between the arts and everyday life: film and photomontage, socially critical theater and jazz, all were as much a part

of modern life as architecture. Architectural interest in housing developments, as a means of procuring living quarters for a wide portion of the population, was a first step towards its integration into everyday life. It was the utopists of the Gläserne Kette – Wassily Luckhardt, Hans Poelzig, Hans Scharoun and Bruno Taut – who, upon realizing that their dreams of a new city encompassing all aspects of life were impossible to fulfill (given the political situation) were finally obliged to carry out only a partial realization of them.

All the cultural and technological innovations could have contributed to improving the general public's quality of life, had they not been misused as mere decorative elements to promote sales. The contrast between Utopianism and Realism was typical of Berlin in the Twenties and served as a catalyst to the city's spirited vitality. The activities of the Gläserne Kette and in the realm of housing reforms remained ideals only. The promise of innovations and technological joys was to remain superficial and illusory as long as the world of the Twenties refused to go beyond the counterfeit, glittering surface of a better life.

Employment

The German defeat brought about a deep crisis in the German economy after 1918. The Treaty of Versailles had sentenced Germany to make reparations in the form of a sum that seemed impossible to assemble, and the inflation of 1923 brought an already unbearable situation to a climax. The famous Twenties were also years of unemployment and of shortages in housing and food. Those who returned from the war, a great number in a hopelessly disabled condition, could find no work. For many, the daily trip to the Arbeitsamt (Employment Office) was part of everyday life, and anyone who found a temporary job could consider himself lucky. Numerous workers were reduced to the state of *Lumpenproletariat* ("shabby proletarians"). They had no permanent residence, since they could not pay rent on a regular basis. Families fell apart, with no home to hold them together. Crime and prostitution were symptomatic associates of the economic crisis.

Berlin became a social disaster area because it was overcrowded by urban workers. The ill-paid workers were in such a precarious economic condition that pay cuts or illness most often totally shattered their lives. Their pay could barely sustain them from week to week. The hopelessness of their situation led to the collapse of family life, to alcoholism or suicide. Political parties and labor unions were powerless to help them. Strikes of little avail were directed against the unscrupulous circles of high finance, where an elegant style of life prospered during the Twenties: a life the 'little man' knew, at best, from advertisements or the movies.

Leisure Activities

Not only was the employment situation hopeless around 1920, but no programs existed for leisure time either. No institutions had been built, as they were to be in the later Twenties, to provide relaxation and recreation for workers, that is to say, to keep them in shape for work. The main concern was to stabilize employment and housing conditions. Sports and play outdoors, new dances to snappy music, public channels of communication – none of these existed yet. Leisure time around 1920 was the same as it had been in 1910: a walk on Sundays, a visit to a garden restaurant, taking care of one's wardrobe and apartment, perhaps a visit to a Party meeting as well. The new technically oriented man still had to be programmed on the basis of the newly emerging ideologies. But before we present examples of these new ideas in architecture in Berlin, we shall briefly consider the beginnings of the Industrial Age.

Early History of New Constructions – Spread of an International Doctrine

Berlin's Commitment to International Events

Innovations in the realms of urbanism and architecture during the 1920's were intellec-tually prepared at the turn of the century, notably during the big World's Fairs affording an exchange of ideas on an international level. The most important of those fairs was the World's Fair of Paris in 1900, where the novel design of the *Jugendstil* ("Art Nouveau") went on display. The new style was either criticized or frankly admired; it was approved in terms of its functional and material suitability, or was judged old-fashioned and relegated to the nineteenth century.

Berlin's contributions to the Fair were disappointing and a far step behind the other exhibits: two interiors and two small staircase niches were all that Berlin entered into the competition in Paris. Alfred Dunsky, Karl Hoffacher and Julius Zwiener, as well as Hermann Werle and Max Bodenheim, were responsible for the interior arrangements. [1] The wall panelling of the "Florida cedar cabinet" was designed by Hoffacker; Zwiener created the funiture: Rococo imitations designed for Kaiser William II! The exhibition committee's choice of contributions to represent Berlin in Paris fell on furniture that, despite first-class execution, nonetheless had been classified by progressive art critics as long outdated and antiquated.

Karl Hoffacker, an architect and publisher of the *Kunstgewerbeblatt*, had tried to save appearances by presenting his interior as a Jugendstil imitation of Van de Velde. Werle and Bodenheim were slightly more successful imitators in their "two cozy German fairy-tale nooks", as their staircase niches were described. [2] But none of the Berlin artists represented in Paris were on a par with Henry van de Velde, who decisively influenced Berlin's Jugendstil as well. In his book *Renaissance im modernen Kunstgewerbe* (1901), Van de Velde asserts: "The rebirth in the art of our times implies a jump forward by the mind and heart. It is a jump towards assimilating newly acquired facts and promoting the utilization of materials recently placed at our disposal". [3] It was Van de Velde who shaped that turn-of-the-century rebirth, not only in Berlin but, for several years, throughout Europe also. In Berlin, his designs for interiors – the Havanna Company salesroom and the Hohenzollern Kunstgewerbehaus (both of 1899), as well as the Haby hairdressing salon (1901) – are

12 Interior decoration of the Hohenzollern Kunstgewerbehaus in Berlin, designed by Henry van de Velde
The Functionalism of the Twenties has its roots in *Jugendstil* (Art Nouveau). At the turn of the century, the new shapes are organic; Arts and Crafts have fused.

unforgettable records of the style of art around the 1900's. No one could deny the fascination of his smoothly curved interior forms, rendered as if they had developed organically. The Berlin Jugendstil was Henry van de Velde's style.

Just about 1902, a tendency favoring rectilinear forms appeared throughout Europe. "The misunderstood Jugendstil and its horrible sinuosity" was surpassed,[4] because its stylistic features could only be produced by hand, which made the style too expensive for normal use. The new angular contours of furniture were better adapted to industrial and mass production. Van de Velde had fallen out of fashion.

The World's Fair in St. Louis of 1904 was central to this new trend. As the Berlin architect Hermann Muthesius reported from America: "The extravagances still visible at the last Paris World's Fair had disappeared,

13 Presidential study in the government buildings in Beyreuth, by Bruno Paul, displayed at the St. Louis World's Fair: 1904
The purified style prior to 1910 was a model for later mass production.

and the delights of their capricious lines were replaced, in almost all cases, by endeavors to achieve high-class, artistic and homogeneous spatial effects in interior design". [5]

Berlin was well represented in St. Louis with ten interiors at that international exhibition. Above all, it is worth mentioning the Berlin artists' club, Werkring, which included Anton Huber, Alfred Grenander, Arno Körnig, Curt Stöving and Rudolf and Fia Wille as members. [6] The group could not keep up with someone like Bruno Paul of Munich, whose designs were awarded prizes in St. Louis, but Muthesius was nevertheless able to describe Grenander's room as infused by "charming grace". [7] The Berlin artists had endeavored to meet international standards of fulfilling a functional purpose and choosing suitable materials.

New Functional Trends in Architecture

At the turn of the century, the new style applied especially to interior decoration. Architecture, at the time, was only affected (as far as a few facades were concerned) in that the antiquated decoration, fashionable until that time, was replaced by curves derived from Jugendstil. It was only around 1910 that a new trend caught on in building: architects tried to translate rectilinear shapes into construction forms and to conceive layouts in functional terms. This new development in design was a product of the foundation of the German Werkbund ("work association") in 1907. Their motto was "the promotion of the fruitful collaboration between the Arts, Industry and Crafts, to their mutual benefit". Thus the new trend was openly declared and set up its first program, although the statutes were not published until 1908. [8]

Trend leaders at the time, among Berlin architects, included Peter Behrens, August Endell, Hermann Muthesius and Bruno Paul.

In 1909 the AEG-Turbine factory was completed, according to plans drawn up by Behrens. In view of our contemporary knowledge of architecture in the Twenties, the building may not seem altogether functional, but it was intended at the time as the

first embodiment of Functional concepts. Behrens was the industrial architect and designer for AEG, and his buildings translated Werkbund ideas into reality. Painters and draftsmen wanted their art to serve industry "to their mutual benefit", as the Werkbund had proclaimed in 1908. [9] Artists equipped ships, drew up coupés for railroad cars and were active in designing household machines. [10] Bruno Paul, another artist whose work was to influence stylistic developments in Berlin, came to that city in 1907, the same year as Peter Behrens. He also belonged to the Werkbund and, as such, worked along the same lines as Peter Behrens, although the visible results were quite different. His first house in Berlin, Haus Westend in Charlottenburg's Ebereschenallee, is characterized above all by the straight lines and functionalism of Classicism. It is a highly elegant house, with a generously conceived layout and an exterior conveying refined austerity and elegant restraint. Form and function fall under a common denominator, incorporating the well-defined program of the Twenties. [11] In his description of the years around 1910, Julius Posener comments: "The age of

14   AEG Turbine Factory, by Peter Behrens, Berlin: 1909 First functional elements in industrial architecture

24

William II was a turning point, and if architectural innovations at first appeared in conventional forms and, moreover, at the same time in manifestos concerning the conventional, that was due to the fact that architecture cannot shed the social context that is the only area where it can be effective, as long as the society it serves remains intact". [12] "Innovations... in conventional forms" can be seen in the work of two more artists active in Berlin at the time: Hermann Muthesius and August Endell. "Muthesius's work belongs to the era of William II... even after 1918". [13] Yet he contributed something new to Berlin: the country-house style popular in England, which became the basis of the organic and asymmetrical architectural layouts of one-family homes in the Twenties. The country houses built in Berlin by Muthesius had a long-lasting influence. August Endell is the last name on our list of architects of importance in Berlin around 1910. He was born in Berlin but active in Breslau and Munich as well. Around the Jugendstil era he belonged to the circle of Munich's avant-garde artists, and it was in that city that he built one of the most important artistic creations of the turn of the century: the Elvira Photo Atelier. The construction elements were subordinated to the famous, strange dragon motif decorating the facades. The windows and doors were no longer part of the architectural whole, but served as a background to the ornamentation, accentuating it.

August Endell's work typifies the architecture of the 1910 period best: the starting point for his work was a theory. He had studied philosophy and assimilated the teachings of Theodor Lipps concerning the "theory of insight, according to which esthetic sensitivity allows the subject self to shift over to the artistic object". [14] Stimulated by his friendship with the sculptor Hermann Obrist of Munich, Endell translated the theory into action and created the Elvira Photo Atelier. Until then, architectural ornamentation had been considered as an attribute of Historicism. But now the applied arts acquired a new substantive form, that was voluptuously perceptible. The transformation of the contents of Jugendstil ornamentation and architectural style into a Functional form occurred around

1902, because, as we mentioned earlier, Jugendstil forms could only be produced by hand. The trend in the twentieth century, however, favored machines, technology and mass production. The German Werkbund, to which Endell adhered in 1913, was concerned with this trend. Endell related to the new theories in art, crafts and industry, and strove to live up to them in his architecture. He planned and built a series of constructions in Berlin around 1910, including the Mariendorf trotting racetrack, which is of special note. Architecturally, this voluptuous realization corroborates Endell's claims of 1900, but it is also functional because it has a purpose to fulfill, and it represents a harmonization of form and construction.

First Proposals for New Housing

New forms in the 1900's began to be developed in connection with interiors and only gradually came to be applied to the realm of construction. Thus, during the period around 1910, innovations were first conceived in the field of furniture, where a program for the Twenties began to take shape. The most famous names in Berlin during the era preceding World War I once again include Bruno Paul and Peter Behrens. Their projects, based on harmonizing construction and function, were way ahead of the times. In 1906 Karl Scheffler could still describe a Berlin apartment in the following terms: "An endless, narrow and totally obscure corridor stretches out ahead, and we have to grope our way past the hallstand to a door. Then we enter the front room. What sumptuousness! Harshly painted ceilings, admittedly senseless, hideous and foolish, but 'rich'. An elaborately over-decorated tiled stove, smeared with gilt-bronze paint and huge double doors crowned right up to the ceiling – four of them in one room – their joints parting, their fillings bursting, closing poorly and made of a wood so poorly treated that the resin of the knotholes seeps through the layers of oil paint. The leftover wall space is covered with glossy gold wallpaper". [15]

Bruno Paul's "unit-furniture program", exhibited for the first time in Berlin in 1908, was intended to improve the above-mentioned conditions. It was practical, handy, combinable and solid; in short, it fulfilled all the demands that are made, even nowadays, on such a program. The separate units could be arranged in series according to requirements and thus be adapted to furnishing small- to medium-size apartments.

The catalogue of the Vereinigten Werkstätten für Kunst im Handwerk, Munich, which produced the program, specified that unit furniture "is not a new addition to the countless stylizations of the last forty years: the Renaissance, Gothic, Empire, Rococo, Egypto-Grecian-Assyrian styles, the Louis XVI and Jugendstil gadgetry. We want to pave a new road for those who seek to furnish their homes tastefully at a modest cost; [with respect to] those rooms in which our women spend most of their time, those which most influence our children in their formative years, and where we relax and recuperate from our daily work". [16]

In this context, Jugendstil was also classified as a fashionable art trend; it was con-sidered outdated, too expensive and individualistic. And although Bruno Paul's unit-furniture program was based ideologically on the Jugendstil, it rendered economic production feasible, since it was manufactured in series and according to the *Baukastensystem* ("modular-design principle"). This meant that the factory-produced unit pieces could be fitted into different furniture combinations according to a variety of requirements. The basic elements were plywood boards that could be supplied selectively in terms of the total price of installing a room. Components could be added, and their narrow width and rectilinear shape afforded a greater variety of possibilities for placement. Moreover, and it was something new at the time, furniture was no longer intended for a specific room. For instance, parts of the library furniture could be adapted to the dining-room units. The same models of chairs were offered for the bedroom and for the boudoir, and a sideboard conceived for the dining room could be transformed, according to the modular-design principle, into a washing stand for the

15   Group of chairs from the unit-furniture program designed by Bruno Paul: 1908

26

bedroom. This system, which was first conceived by Bruno Paul, was to become the basis of Bauhaus projects a few years later.

However, the program was not inexpensive. Although ornamentation was eliminated, the group's aim remained that of pleasing the middle classes, since their products were too expensive for the lower classes. Debate concerning moderately priced and attractive home furnishings had begun at the turn of the century and reached a climax in about 1910, when the Berlin Gewerkschaft instigated a procedure unheard-of in the history of furniture production. They created the so-called "Commission for Model Workers' Apartments", whose members included Gewerkschaft people and the chairmen of the "Association of Working Class Girls and Women", as well as Paul Göhre, a Social-Democratic member of the Reichstag. The commission's purpose was to find out what furniture really appealed to workers, what criteria molded their opinions of furniture programs and, above all, to attract the working classes away from antiquated ostentatiousness and towards unassuming rectilinear and functional forms.

One of the first furniture programs for a worker's household was created by the Berlin painter Hermann Münchhausen and displayed at Gewerkschaft headquarters to be appraised by the prospective customers. Peter Behrens, the well-known AEG architect and industrial designer, was requested by the commission to draw up a second program, taking into consideration all the transformations proposed by visitors to the exhibit. Whether or not the results fulfill modern-day expectations — that such furniture be unassuming and attractive, inexpensive and solid — remains a matter of opinion.

"A citizen can do more for the development of his native country by the way he purchases than by getting excited over elections. That should be understood. But it will only be understood when the Germans become politicized, that is, when the citizen does more than merely dabble in politics from time to time; when he keeps his political duty in mind at all times, estimates every transaction in political terms. And purchasing should be among his foremost concerns."[17] That was

the opinion of Robert Breuer, another member of the commission, no doubt in the hopes of politically activating the workers in conjunction with the sale of furniture programs through the Gewerkschaft's headquarters. Very few workers bought any pieces of the workers' model home furniture, but the endeavor was unique in a two-fold sense: both because it was the first time a target group was consulted for a project, and because it was to become the basis for the inexpensive furniture programs of the Twenties. More exactly, everything that was mass-produced was modeled, consciously or unconsciously, on the Gewerkschaft furniture of Hermann Münchhausen and Peter Behrens. It should be noted however, that the Bauhaus originally thought along different lines; its ideological basis was a classless society, for which the inexpensive products of mass production were intended.

In 1910, too, the Brussels World's Fair took place. It should have been an occasion to present endeavors in the field of ideas described above on an international level. But in Brussels, internationalism was equated with incorporating German products into the competitive world market. Max Osborn's report from Brussels was as follows: "If one considers that the entire contemporary movement in the arts basically favors trends and structural forms that should have so much to gain by being presented in the architecture

16   From the furniture program for workers designed by Hermann Münchhausen, displayed at Berlin's Gewerkschaftshaus: 1911
New design for the low-income groups.

and set-up of an exhibition, then one is doubly shocked by the empty bleakness and frills of exterior and interior constructions, by the amazing helplessness [one feels] at the hundredth rehashing of the *déjà vu*, by the countless crimes against the entire spirit of good taste that one is obliged to swallow at every glance.... The barbarisms committed here are a crying shame". [18]

If the 1910 Brussels Fair was disappointing, the Cologne Werkbund Exhibition of 1914 was a balance-sheet of all that had been accomplished since 1900 and of the trends that would survive World War I. In this respect, Henry van de Velde's Werkbund-theater should be mentioned: the organic forms of a purified Jugendstil represented a translation into exterior architecture of the contours that, until recently, had been restricted to interiors. Worth noting as well: the office building, machine hall and Motor-Deutz pavilion by Walter Gropius, which already foreshadowed the functional and constructive architecture of the Twenties. Bruno Taut's glass house should be classified between the two works mentioned above, as a real accomplishment of the year 1914. It combines Traditionalism with Functionalism, the free play of the decorative with the appropriate materials, the ideal with reality.

Reconstruction Programs after World War I – Unattained Goals are Defined

The Ambitions of the Bauhaus

The Staatliche Bauhaus opened in 1919 in Weimar. This school re-formulated the claim that crafts should be the basis for creation: "Architects, sculptors, painters – we must all go back to the crafts. For art does nots exist as a 'profession'. No essential difference exists between artist and craftsman. The artist is an enlightened version of the craftsman. By the grace of God, those rare moments of revelation exist, beyond the artist's will, when a work of art unconsciously springs forth from his hands; however, a foundation in craftsmanship in indispensable to every artist and represents the well-spring of creativity". [19] Those words were written by Walter Gropius, the founder of the Bauhaus, in the "Bauhaus Manifesto". Even the choice of the institution's name was based on an ideological conception of handicrafts, since the word *Bauhaus* is derived from the medieval *Bauhütte* ("association of craftsmen").

As a result, early Bauhaus products appeared overly craftsy: *Stollenkonstruktion*

17 From the furniture program for workers designed by Hermann Münchhausen, displayed at Berlin's Gewerkshaftshaus: 1911

18 Kitchen from the furniture program for workers by Peter Behrens, displayed at Berlin's Gewerkschaftshaus: 1912

19 Kitchen of the model house
Am Horn, exhibited in Weimar,
under the auspices of the Bauhaus
Week: 1923
The house was designed by the artist
Georg Muche; Adolf Meyer and
Gropius's workshop were
responsible for its construction.

and woven chairs that were decorative merely by the choice of combinations of colors and materials. In fact, around 1922 the Bauhaus was in touch with the Dutch group De Stijl which advocated right angles, elevating industrial realizations to the level of the artistic. Not only did Arts and Crafts form a symbiosis, but industry would henceforth play an important role as well. Under the auspices of "Bauhaus week" in 1923, the trial house Am Horn was displayed. It was this first practical suggestion for new housing that the young group chose to present to a wide public. Community life was the clearly expressed ideal serving as a basis to the layout: a large living room occupied the center, designed to receive daylight exclusively from skylight windows, thus focusing attention on indoor activities, that is, on the inhabitants themselves. Separate rooms for particular activities were grouped around this large room, so that, for instance, the kitchen was designed as the "housewife's laboratory", in the sense that "surplus room size and impractically arranged fittings lead to constant overwork.... As long as women cannot be relieved of this burden

by abolishing individual households, by a general acceptance of large cooperative apartment houses, we must strive to steadily improve spatial arrangements and the household organization of one-family dwellings". [20]

This implied a new housing program, which gradually could have become a political ideal as well. The communal style of life contributed to a new social organization, that did not forcibly suppress individualism but left it available as a free choice.

Walter Gropius was in charge of the Bauhaus from its foundation until 1928. His successor was the Swiss Hannes Meyer, who claimed that technology should serve the workers, and that they, in turn, should benefit from all the possibilities that recourse to machines could so auspiciously have offered them. In 1926, he publicized a brochure entitled *Die Neue Welt*, which was nothing short of a hymn to the Twenties. The text explained: "The community rules the individual.... As long as we do not confront the problems of urban construction with the total impartiality of a factory engineer, we are strangling mundane life in the modern city by our idolatry of ruins and our conventional conceptions of street axes and focal points.... The degree of our standardization is an index of our social economy.... New art work is collective and destined for all, no collector's pieces or individual privileges.... And personality? Feelings?? Soul??? We plead in favor of a cleancut divorce. All traces of the following are to be relegated to their very own spheres: eroticism, love of Nature, human relations". [21]

Meyer's vision of a "New World" was to remain a utopia. The Weimar Republic era was too short-lived, and not persuasive enough in the face of a reaction — reinforced during the Twenties — in favor of allying national trends with high finance.

When Ludwig Mies van der Rohe took over as director of the Bauhaus in 1930, Meyer's political claims were about to stifle in Formalism. Housing improvements based on improved real estate policies and the emergence of standards to reduce product prices were to no avail in a society whose economic interests were more of a liability to realizing the program than an indispensable asset.

29

20 Drawing showing the wide strips of greenery between the ten-story, high-rise apartments, built in rows, designed by Walter Gropius: 1929

The German Werkbund Defines its Goals

The products of German-Werkbund activities during the Twenties were displayed in a series of international exhibitions, including two that stood out above the others: Die Wohnung ("Housing") in Stuttgart in 1927, known as the "Weissenhof Development", and Die Wohnung unserer Zeit ("Housing of our Times") at the Deutsche Bauausstellung in Berlin in 1931. Others included the Deutsche Gewerbeschau-München ("German Trade Show – Munich") in 1922, the touring exhibition Die Form ohne Ornament ("Forms without Ornamentation") in 1924, Wohnung und Werkraum ("Living and Work Space") in Breslau in 1929, as well as Film und Foto in Stuttgart in 1929, and the contributions of the German Werkbund to the Exposition de la Société des Artistes Décorateurs in Paris in 1930.

Since the Gewerbeschau in Munich in 1922 was one of the first recorded displays of Werkbund work after World War I, we shall allude most particularly to this still rather traditional exhibition, where art continued to be defined in terms of craftsmanship. In fact, at the Werkbund convention in Munich in 1921, that is to say, a year before the show was to open, the participants agreed unanimously that the forthcoming trade show should be a "cultural testimony to solidity and authenticity". [22] The architect Bruno Paul who, in the meantime had become active in Berlin, was among the most important of the show's artists. Although his new architecture was to make a great impact on Berlin's image over the following years, in Munich he was still devoted to traditional craftsmanship. The public in general was not yet familiar with the accomplishments of the Weimar Bauhaus, nor had the Werkbund sufficiently assimilated industrial production methods.

The Werkbund's Walter Riezler wrote a most aptly descriptive preview to the coming trade show: "We can expect the Gewerbeschau to offer a rich and clear picture of the contemporary situation.... But there is one thing we cannot expect: that it already confront the public with the 'style of our times' as a directly convincing, integrated whole". [23]

Three years later, in 1925, a novel French influence came to the fore as a result of the Exposition Internationale des Arts Décoratifs et

21 The pavilion of Christofle and ▷ Baccarat at the Exposition Internationale des Arts Décoratifs et Industriels Modernes, in Paris: 1925

22 The Werkbund Exhibition ▷ "Die Wohnung" in Stuttgart at the Weissenhof Development: 1927 First concrete attempt to build in accordance with Werkbund concepts

Industriels Modernes that opened in Paris. Some of the same artists who continued to work in turn-of-the-century style were represented at this elegant show by bizarre, glittering, dazzling, crystal-like pieces. Exclusiveness was a trump-card in Paris; France was luxuriating in a mood of triumph and was more radiant than ever. It was the birth of Art Deco style, for which there was, as yet, no German equivalent. No German products were exhibited in Paris; the country was in the throes of employment, food and housing problems. It was no time for a brilliant presentation of the social scene, and no international show had ever been set up to represent dire reality.

It was only in 1927 that the first suggestions for new housing were produced by the Werkbund circles, marked by the completion of the Weissenhof Development. Peter Behrens, Walter Gropius, Ludwig Hilberseimer, Ludwig Mies van der Rohe, Hans Poelzig and Bruno and Max Taut, all of whom already had decisively influenced Berlin's cityscape or were to do so in the future, were among the most important architects of the Stuttgart exhibition. As a realization of the Werkbund program, the Weissenhof Development was a unique accomplishment of the exhibition. Mies van der Rohe, who had drawn up the development plans, wrote in the exhibition catalogue: "It is not superfluous today to point out that the problem of new housing has to do with the art of building, despite the technical and economic aspects involved.... From this point of view and, despite the 'rationalism' and 'standardization' that are the legitimate catchwords of our era, I considered it necessary to free the work destined for Stuttgart from biased and dogmatic elements".[24] Hence Stuttgart played a decisive role in freeing construction from biased standards, and this paved the way for new results.

Besides the Stuttgart exhibition, the Werkbund contributions to Paris in 1930 and to the Berliner Bauausstellung in 1931 were outstanding examples foreshadowing the programs of the Twenties. "Housing for our times does not yet exist," was asserted by Mies van der Rohe, in the program for the Berlin Exhibition. "But changes in living con-

23 Deutsche Bauausstellung in Berlin: 1931
Gym with swimming pool, by Walter Gropius, in a community high rise

ditions encourage its realization. The prerequisite for this realization is a clear analysis of actual living conditions."[25]

The "housing for our times" was displayed at the Berlin Exhibition in the following manner: Mies van der Rohe had designed an inimitably elegant house on one floor. Light partitions were set up in frames; large glass walls connected the interior with the exterior, creating a harmonious whole of architecture and nature. The furniture likewise appeared lightweight; everything was to be clear and transparent, discretely subordinated to life. Such were also the characteristics of the Sportsman's House designed by Marcel Breuer and Gustav Hassenpflug. Partitions were almost totally absent and replaced by the furniture itself. The Four-Room House by the brothers Hans and Wassily Luckhardt seemed a bit more compact. But the so-called Boarding House by Robert Vorhoelzer, Max Wiederanders, W. Schmidt and Christian Hacker of Munich was the most brilliant achievement of the Berlin Bauausstellung. The communal rooms were located on the ground floor, under the separate apartments of different sorts. "Every apartment has a small electrical cooking cupboard to make warm snacks, whereas real meals can be prepared as part of the boarding house system itself".[26]

24 Heidehof Development by ▷ Paul Mebes and Paul Emmerich in Berlin-Zehlendorf: 1924
The garden-city movement tried to bring an illusion of bucolic nature to the doorsteps of the big city.

25 A double house for workers by ▷ Hermann Muthesius, at the Sparsame Baustoffe Exhibition, Berlin: 1919

The 1931 projects at the Bauausstellung in Berlin inspired a longing for an easier, better, light-flooded way of life, where everything disrupted into disharmony by social constraints once again merges into an integrated whole: leisure time and work, individualism and community, art and life. "What does the hour of happiness know of the hour of distress? Let us take care that our living quarters be suitable to both. Man is not specialized; he is versatile and generous. His housing should share those traits of character."[27]

The "Garden-City Movement" and Heinrich Tessenow

The "garden-city movement" is quite a contrast to the "versatility and generosity" described above, to community life and to individual development within the context of group life. It contrasts with Hannes Meyer's "New World" as well, where the "community" should rule the "individual" and art should be a "collective work", destined for all. If the movement did produce some nice results, it nonetheless implied a retreat from the varied wealth of possibilities offered by a big city, in favor of the idyllic countryside. Technology, praised during the Twenties, in the hopes that it would free mankind from misery and oppression, was considered fatal by the followers of the "garden-city movement". The founders of the movement wanted to entice people away from the city's tensions, from the havoc wreaked by technology, from the conflicts induced by politics. Family life and peace and order were at the top of their list of priorities for happiness. The ideal housing was a small one-family house set in nature and, if possible, having some connection with traditional handicrafts.

The same ideas of saving man by shutting him off in the bucolic countryside continues to impress certain architects and city-planners, although it soon became obvious that the garden-city mode of life was only accessible to a few and that industrial development could not be stopped.

Heinrich Tessenow, one of the founders of the movement, became a professor at the technical college of Berlin-Charlottenburg.

33

At the same time he took over the direction of a master workshop at the Berlin Fine Arts Academy. He was thus in a position to impregnate building activities in Berlin with his ideas. Around 1910, he played an important role in the planning of the Dresden-Hellerau garden city, where he built workers' and petty-bourgeois homes. After World War I, he founded and directed a handicrafts association in Hellerau. Tessenow's concept of a new mode of life was a form of return to craftsmanship, in the sense of recreating the medieval families of craftsmen, who lived and worked together under the direction of a master. The idea was to resuscitate idyllic village life. Tessenow described his ideas on housing in the following terms: "In this big world, our housing represents but a small meeting point of almost all the streets, but it is most obviously linked to the whole world by infinitely many threads. On the basis of our housing we can understand the world quite well and, on the other hand, the world understands us. When we neglect our housing, build and cultivate to a minimum, or if housing is barely inhabitable, then we are bound to have very little understanding for the world in its entirety, as we will be misunderstood by that world. Therefore, also, any reliable history of a civilization includes, to a large extent, a history of the housing that belonged to it, and when housing records can no longer be clearly traced, its history virtually comes to an end. Real history generally begins where the livable begins, just as our personal life history really begins when we make a home for ourselves." [28]

Tessenow's projects did not relate to real conditions, but represented artificial petty-bourgeois housing dreams. Peace and order were to reign in his little houses nestled in the wine leaves and executed with first-class craftsmanship. One "makes a home for oneself" far from production standards and labor divisions, high finance and banking.

In 1928 Tessenow built the Am Fischtalgrund Development in Berlin-Zehlendorf, consisting of row houses 6 meters wide with connected garden sheds in front of small gardens. Tiny villas for workers, financially inaccessible to all but a few of them. Tessenow's ideal of a better life was a far cry from

that of the 1931 Bauausstellung in Berlin and from those happy inhabitants of the Boarding House, where the lively communal rooms were filled with freshness, pep and political activities.

Realities of Urban Life – Unemployment and Material Poverty despite New Realism

Housing

The programs for the Twenties were varied and imaginative. In their desire to satisfy all classes of society, they were obviously destined to remain utopic. Despite all the efforts on behalf of new housing, despite years of proposals to rearrange political priorities, and consequently those of architecture and cityscaping, the housing shortage remained as acute as ever. By 1928, living conditions in Berlin could still be described as follows: "Conditions are altogether wretched. Frequently six or more people sleep in the same room; man and wife and one or two children in the same bed. Bed linen is often missing, washing facilities consist of the kitchen sink and, despite all the housing misery, the kitchen is rented out as sleeping quarters for overnighters.... It had been decided, before the war, that attics and unhealthy cellar dwellings were not to be admitted as living quarters. But nowadays, countless families live in unheated attics without lavatories, in damp and deep cellars, in primitive woodsheds on garden allotments, insufficiently protected from winter storms, humidity and cold, and with sanitary installations that are a crying shame." [29]

The Villa Sternefeld, built in 1923 according to plans drawn up by the architect Erich Mendelsohn and the first Functionalist house built in Berlin, thus offered a great contrast with that deplorable state of affairs. According to the new programs for the Twenties, villas for individual use would no longer be included in new city planning: collective life in groups should be the model and even architecture should base its projects on this

34

26 Villa Sternefeld by Erich
Mendelsohn, Berlin-
Charlottenburg: 1923
A new life style for the privileged
classes—the villa

27 Haus Poelzig by Marlene
Poelzig, Berlin-Westend
Terrace and pool in front of the
children's bedrooms

28 One of a group of houses on
Schorlemerallee in Berlin by Hans
and Wassily Luckhardt and Alfons
Anker: 1929
Terrace and front garden

ideological premise. The Functionalist elements of the Sternefeld house are purposefully confined to a formalistic interpretation of the new exterior and of the original layout. Otherwise, it makes an austere impression for a villa, totally unadorned and lacking the pompous attributes of comfort. The severity of the cubic structuralization is relieved by the construction's stately proportions and noble materials. The house and garden are connected by generous glass surfaces that replace the conventional confining walls. Spacious terraces lead to the garden. An architecture flooded with light right out of the utopists' dreams. The rooms are disposed in a smoothly flowing fashion and sparsely furnished, in line with the original intentions of those who had developed the program for the Twenties — although almost all of them had been thinking in terms of communal life. The inhabitants of the Sternefeld house led a grand life aided by domestic help. The house had been individually tailored to the owner's demands, an owner who had to dispose of financial means adequate to maintaining the building. Norms and standards would have been out of place here, with the possible exception of the simple Bauhaus furnishings which, designed to a standard, had been adopted only by the intellectual upper classes during the Twenties.

Many villas similar to the Sternefeld villa were built in Berlin. Marlene Poelzig built her family a house flooded with light and very simply furnished, showing distinct traces of her familiarity with the buildings of the Weissenhof Development in Stuttgart. The generous glass surfaces of the Poelzig house look out onto the surrounding countryside. The same fusion of architecture and nature emanates from the Am Rupenhorn houses by Hans and Wassily Luckhardt, and Alfons Anker (1928). The architects sought to achieve the appearance of restraint and modesty advocated by the new housing programs. Besides the two houses described above, the equally attractive houses built by Luckhardt and Anker in the Schorlemerallee (1929) are worth mentioning: light, unpretentious, simple materials for the exterior, and a well-conceived layout. The Haus Lewin on Fischerhüttenstrasse, built by Gropius in

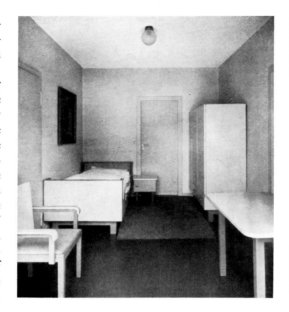

1928, belongs with the most important villas of the Functionalist trend in Berlin and shares the same characteristics in terms of historical architectural classification. Functionalism is restricted to the shape of the building and to the way the materials are handled.

Alongside the Berlin villas that structurally paid such a great tribute to Functionalism, others were built during the Twenties with antiquated ornamental elements and conventional layouts. A group of English country houses as well as individual works of Expressionist style also appeared. Naturally these houses were also destined, like castles in extensive parks, for the upper classes and presented very ostentatious interiors reminiscent of former times. In the years 1922 to 1924, Hermann Muthesius built a gorgeous villa, with a view of the Havel Lakes, for the businessman Willi Kersten, in Berlin-Charlottenburg. On walks through his huge property, the proprietor could make use of telephone columns, set up out doors, to receive calls or give orders to his employees.

Oscar Kaufmann's Art-Deco villa on Oberhaardter Weg (1922-23), built for the director of a paper factory, also resembles a little castle. The Baroque arrangement of the layout gives the building a bizarre appearance. Heinrich Straumer's English country houses, in the style of the early villas by Muthesius, fit remarkably well into the Mark

33   Weekend house, Robinson, by Fränkel and Kretschmer at Das Wochenende Exhibition, Berlin: 1927
The dream of owning a house made possible for the "little man" too

34   Haus Hagen, by Otto Block and H. Ebert in Potsdam
Expensive idyll on the outskirts of the big city

35   Onkel-Toms-Hütte ("Uncle Tom's Cabins") Development by Bruno Taut, Martin Wagner, Hugo Häring and Rudolf Salvisberg, Berlin-Zehlendorf: 1926-32

36   Onkel-Toms-Hütte Development by Bruno Taut, Martin Wagner, Hugo Häring and Rudolf Salvisberg, Berlin-Zehlendorf: 1927-32
New housing for workers and employees in row houses (photograph of a reconstruction drawn by Helge Pitz)

landscape of the southern and western Berlin suburbs, but since they too are destined for the privileged classes, they have as little to do with the programs conceived for the Twenties as the cubic villas considered representative of New Realism.

The villa for the 'little man' remains to be considered: the weekend house. Many proposals were forthcoming in this respect as well; for at least several hours of their free evenings, workers were to have the feeling of participating in the comforts of New Realism.

The villas of the Twenties in Berlin are lovely individual examples of new architecture. They are unique testimony to a style which, in aspiring to meet the times, produced not only Functional, Historicist and Expressionist results, but results that were above all expensive and exclusive. The villas did not accomplish any social innovations.

A great many housing developments were built in Berlin during the Twenties, effectively incorporating norms, systemization and standardization. Much care was taken in drawing the detailed floor plans of apartments, producing norms that have remained valid to date. The largest room was the living room, which served as reception room, boudoir and den, children's playroom and salon for company, all in one, whereas villas provided separate rooms for each activity. The next largest room was the parents' bedroom, followed by the children's rooms. The built-in kitchen was entirely automated and had a dining corner, so that no domestic help was needed to serve at table – thanks to the utilitarian floor plan, the housewife could take over that job. Good architecture, living up to the new standards, was guaranteed by the renowned artists who collaborated in creating the program in the first place.

Only the most important housing developments built in Berlin during the Twenties are listed below: the Hufeisensiedlung Britz in Neukölln, to plans by Bruno Taut and Martin Wagner (1925-27); the Onkel-Toms-Hütte Development in Zehlendorf (1926-32) by Bruno Taut, Hugo Häring and Rudolf Salvisberg; the Wohnstadt Carl Legien, Prenzlauer Berg, to plans by Bruno Taut and Max Hillinger (1929-30); the Weisse Stadt in Reinickendorf (1929-30) by the architects Rudolf

Salvisberg, Wilhelm Brüning and Bruno Ahrends; the large housing development Siemensstadt in Charlottenburg and Spandau (1929-31) by Otto Bartning, Fred Fornat, Walter Gropius, Hugo Häring, Paul Rudolf Henning and Hans Scharoun. [30] The norms shaping construction of developments were also applied to the interiors and furnishings; down to the smallest utilities, everything was standardized. In 1930 in a brochure entitled "How Should I Furnish my Home?", Wilhelm Lotz wrote: "Only buy what best fits your needs. Some items might fit in with a larger household but be an unnecessary encumbrance in a smaller one.... Buy whatever is practical and works well." [31]

Standardization had originally been intended to make life easier, to free people from unnecessary nuisance jobs and leave them more time for activities and collective projects. But it was misappropriated for purposes contrary to its original intent and stifled with petty-bourgeois ideals. Victory for the "garden-city movement" in the broadest sense? Retreat to the one-family house and family intimacy as a basis of order, morality and peace? Resignation instead of activity? That was certainly not the idea behind all that was said at the beginning of the Twenties. What did remain was a new architecture and

a new cityscape of housing developments set in nature. These new housing models remain today as prototypes on an artistic level.

Large-Scale Public and Private Buildings

The influence of the new forms in architecture was not limited to housing alone; many large public and private buildings also clearly rejected the traditional. Innovations in construction were made possible by the discovery of new materials, which in turn led to new structural concepts. The projects of the Gläserne Kette were among the brilliant triumphs of the Twenties. Glass as a construction material afforded unexpected possibilities, and in 1920 Adolf Behne wrote: "No material can surmount matter as well as glass. Glass is a totally new, pure material, in which matter has been melted down and recast. It is the most basic of all the substances available to us. It reflects the sky and the sun, it is like clear water and offers a rich variety of truly inexhaustible possibilities in colors, forms and characteristics, that can leave no one indifferent". [32]

And Paul Scheerbart, the visionary poet of utopic urbanism, wrote rhymes such as:

Das Licht will durch das ganze ALL
und ist lebendig im Kristall
("Light penetrates everything and comes alive in crystal")
or *Das Glas bringt alles Helle,*
verbau es auf der Stelle
("Glass brings all that is light,
Make use of it on the spot").

Wassily Luckhardt, Hans Poelzig, Bruno Taut and Hans Scharoun created utopic designs for festival halls and theaters, which looked like monuments to a thousand victories. The projects were significantly entitled: Alpine Architektur, Glashausproblem, Vivat Stella, An die Freude.

Poelzig created the Grosses Schauspielhaus of Berlin in 1919, on the basis of one of his designs in that "joyous" vein. The interior produces the same impression of the triumphant as the designs of the Gläserne Kette. However the principle of intensification was reversed to accentuate all that was static and cumbersome, yet without sacrificing the effect of lightness. Poelzig's theater was not just a formal translation of the concepts of the Gläserne Kette into practical building, for the interior was also in tune with the times, in that the festive and joyous elements are intensified into a hymn to architecture.

Almost ten years after Poelzig's Grosses Schauspielhaus, Mendelsohn built the Universum Cinema in Berlin (1927-28). Films had made a place for themselves, next to plays, as works of art quite a time ago, but it was an innovation for a renowned artist to design a cinema as a work of art. The semi-circle inside is clearly translated onto the exterior. Shops and restaurants along the streets beside the movie house join the building, optically and functionally, with the cityscape. A characteristic of Mendelsohn's architecture is the avoidance of angular forms, which allows his large buildings to relate to existing constructions. The crossroads seem friendlier that way, the corners of the houses seem softer, and the big city seems more intimate and closer to its inhabitants.

In addition to theaters and movie houses built in Berlin during the Twenties, other large constructions were erected such as swimming pools, racetracks, commercial buildings and labor-union headquarters. And many restaurants, cafés and dance halls were renovated. But all the investment capital, concentrated in large individual companies, needed new administration buildings too so that the new constructions also included insurance buildings, banks, department stores and office buildings. These were symbols of the power of high finance and often looked like palaces: palaces in keeping with New Realism or still imbued with traditionalism. Some of the reception rooms were richly decorated to excess; the most expensive materials projected a pompous image of the company.

Renowned artists were commissioned to build industrial buildings as well. The Kathreiner Hochhaus was finished on Potsdamerstrasse in 1929, according to plans drafted by Bruno Paul. Despite the building's relative massivity, the architects managed to integrate it into the cityscape by carefully studying the

40 Portal of the Kreuzkirche by Ernst and Günther Paulus, Berlin-Schmargendorf: 1930 Expressionism, a style characteristic of the Twenties

41   Grosses Schauspielhaus by
Hans Poelzig, Berlin: 1919

42   Universum Cinema by Erich
Mendelsohn, Berlin: 1927-28
Quintessential architecture of the
Twenties

43   Mosse-Haus by Erich
Mendelsohn, Richard Neutra and
Rudolf Paul Henning, Berlin: 1923

44   Office building by Max Taut
for the Allgemeiner Deutscher
Gewerkschaftsbund, Berlin:
1922-23

structure of the facades and the body of the twelve-story building. The facades are patterned horizontally and faced with travertine. Everything looks perfect, well thought out and solid.

Work and Leisure Time

The lively building activity in Berlin during the Twenties may give the impression that everyone took an active part in public life and could have taken a stand on all the political questions or influenced decisions. A burgher was expected to become a world citizen, imbued with the international mood. How-

45 Clubhouse at the Avus racetrack by Edmund Meurin, Berlin: 1923
Expressionist elements in the architecture of the Twenties

46 Shell-Haus by Emil Fahrenkamp, Berlin-Tiergarten: 1931

47 Kathreiner-Hochhaus by Bruno Paul, Potsdamer Strasse, Berlin: 1929
One of the first high rises in Berlin

48 Workers—drivers in the parking lot of the Kindl-Brauerei, a brewery in Berlin

49   The small-scale, private
entrepreneur—an ice-cream cart in
Berlin's Tiergarten district: around
1930

50   On the train: title page of *Die
Dame*, 2, no. 21 (1925-26)

51   The nicest part of an
automobile excursion: title page of
Die Dame, 2, no. 18 (1926-27)

52   The thrill of new technical
design and of a faster-than-ever
means of locomotion

53 Sports room of the Haus Hagen by Otto Block and H. Ebert, Potsdam
Sports was a leisure-time activity for the upper classes.

54 The Wannsee Strandbad, a pool on the beach, was built according to plans by the architects Martin Wagner and Richard Ermisch: 1930
The slogan of the new times—"Youth and Health, Sun, Sand, Water and Wind"—was to be doomed within three years.

55 Winter garden of the old
Reich's Chancellery by Leonhard
Gall, Wilhelmstrasse, Berlin: 1937

ever, during the Twenties, this was a misleading delusion of magazine romanticism, for everyday life was in fact harder than ever. Employees and factory workers lived in constant fear of being dismissed, the self-employed of lacking work, the tenant of having his lease revoked. The "golden Twenties" existed only in publicity, movies, and popular songs.

Standards of living in general belonged to the concerns of the new programs: practical clothing was a symbol of the employee's independence, women's short haircuts symbolized their emancipation and travel symbolized liberty. Technological progress offered new possibilities for getting from one place to another more quickly. Travel by plane, boat, train and car was promoted. New plane models for passenger transport were developed, and reports of trips to faraway places were publicized. Passenger boats were built and furnished exclusively with luxury cabins. The railways received more sleeping and restaurant cars, and many new models of automobiles emerged on the market.

Architecture was not the only field where the principles of sun and nature, light and air were proposed to counterbalance the gloomy housing misery of hidden courtyards. Sport was considered an important leisure-time activity; vigor and gaiety were to relieve the worker of his dreary everyday life. "Life, an organic growth, is a dialectical process that determines both *ja* ['plus'] and *nein* ['minus']. Everything that comes into being is part of the social living process, is a consequence of specific facts and in turn influences existing intents. An ideology, a point of view, a meaning and a relationship develop on the basis of what is thus created and, in turn, spread to the existing." [33]

This dialectical process, formulated in 1929 by El Lissitzky, became progressively more obvious in the Twenties. For all that was suggested after 1900 as a program (and which was effectively accomplished after World War) was transformed into new theories and programs within the political context of the Weimar Republic. The first setback already occurred, however, when the

56 Antiquated pomp still
characterized the interior decoration
of a businessman's home during the
Thirties.

Deutsche Arbeiterpartei, later the NSDWP, was founded in 1919. Hitler's *Mein Kampf* appeared in 1925. Under those circumstances, the goals that had been set could be attained only within limits. Nevertheless, certain trends that had developed in the realms of art and architecture were partially appropriated as of 1933, though transformed into the contrary under the first symptoms of National Socialism.

The National Socialists Come to Power: End of the "New World" Dream. Petty-Bourgeois Ideologies Transform the Theories of the Twenties

The National Socialist pogroms on the occasion of the burning of the Reichstag in 1933 led to the political exclusion of the opponents of the NSDWP. The first concentration camps that interned those who stood in the way of the National Socialist take-over were built. All parties in the Reichstag, with the exception of the SDP fraction, voted to approve the law investing authority in Adolf Hitler. Communists and some members of the SDP were kept from voting by being placed under arrest. And thus began the terrorist domination of the Third Reich.

Nothing original developed in either architecture or cityscaping under the Third Reich. Existing elements were arbitrarily sorted out as worthy or not of the stamp of approval of some huffy philistines. Manipulation was accomplished in wide circles, and there was no resistance from those concerned. Petty-bourgeois ideas were promoted to the level of a State ideology. Elitist life styles were reserved for the upper classes, then as before, and the masses were manipulated into accepting the fact. Progressive artists and architects were obliged to emigrate. They were left with the bitter realization that individual engagement can only be successful when it has a link with those concerned.

S.G.

II PAINTING

Eberhard Roters

Expressionism

The beginnings of German Expressionism in Berlin coincided with a series of events, all of which occurred during the years 1910 and 1911.

On March 3, 1910, the first edition of Herwarth Walden's weekly, *Der Sturm*, appeared. Exactly one year later, in March, 1911, Franz Pfemfert issued the first edition of the weekly *Die Aktion*. Both competing journals considered themselves as rallying points of a cultural revolution and, for the first time, a common forum was available to young authors and artists of the avant-garde. In 1910 as well, Ernst Ludwig Kirchner came to Berlin for the first time; he lived in his friend Max Pechstein's studio and remained there for quite some time. (Pechstein had already moved to Berlin from Dresden by 1908.) In October, 1911, Kirchner moved to Berlin permanently; that winter his comrades in the Brücke group from Dresden (Karl Schmidt-Rottluff and Erich Heckel) joined him there.

The metropolis attracted young artists for obvious reasons; by that time, Berlin had already acquired a reputation as an art city open to innovations. Since its foundation at the turn of the century, the Berliner Secession movement, under the presidency of Max Liebermann, had successfully triumphed over the academicians. Its success was all the more impressive in that it meant countering the Kaiser and court society as well.

Berlin harbored galleries open to contemporary art: Fritz Gurlitt's gallery, which was to represent Max Pechstein; Paul Cassirer's, J.B. Neumann's and others. The press in Berlin published art reviews that were read throughout the Empire. Berlin's art public was the most open-minded of all; they were also the hardest to please, the most sceptical and critical. In a nutshell, Berlin was on the go. Artists hoped for recognition there, hoped to find buyers and to acquire fame. The city was a touchstone for their breakthrough. The Expressionist trend linked up with the rhythm and motoricity of the big city, bringing something new into being – Urban Expressionism – a transformation that was not inherent, that was actually in contradiction, to the style's basic impulses.

German Expressionism originated in the provinces: the art of the Blaue Reiter circle of artists came from the Bavarian towns of Sintelsdorf and Murnau-am-Staffelsee. Paula Modersohn-Becker's painting from Worpswede, Christian Rohlf's from Soest in Westphalia and Emil Nolde's from the little coastal village of Seebüll in Schleswig-Holstein. In 1905, several young painters in Dresden founded the *Brücke* ("Bridge") group of artists, a group that included Max Pechstein, who joined them in 1906 and was the only one of the members who was not self-educated. They all moved to the country in the hopes of finding simplicity in nature. They used to bathe in the nude in the Moritzburg lakes, which caused a terrific scandal in the light of contemporary moral codes: a local policeman, complete with a spiked helmet, arrested the artists and their models. The energy of the Brücke artists' early enthusiasm for colors and shapes came from their back-to-nature drive, which was a reaction against

57 Max Pechstein: *Am Strand von
Nidden* (1911), oil on canvas,
50×65 cm. Berlin, Staatliche
Museum Preussischer Kulturbesitz,
Nationalgalerie
In the little East Prussian fishing
village of Nidden, Pechstein created
his gaily colored tributes to life in
Nature. The stylization of the girl's
head seems to foreshadow his
encounter with the South Seas.

58 Ernst Ludwig Kirchner: *Die* ▷
Strasse (1913), oil on canvas,
120.6×91.1 cm. New York, The
Museum of Modern Art
Kirchner's street scenes with large
figures embody the high point of
Urban Expressionism in Berlin.

54

industrial society and the cities that were its trademark. The popular slogan of the Brücke Expressionists, who inscribed their banner with Horace's *Odi profanum*, also stood for originality, in the sense of a return to sources, to authentic unspoiled sensitivity — a catharsis, an act of purification. The artists sought to reflect nature's lack of sophistication and the strength of its simplicity, newly discovered artistic virtues inspired by non-European, primitive races.

The move to Berlin, a metropolis, was in direct contradiction to the flight to the countryside, born of the Brücke artists' longing to return to their origins; now, the artists were responding to the opposite impulse. The encounter between the Expressionism of the Brücke artists and big city life was comparable to an effervescent reaction, in which Expressionism was to lose its innocence. The style inevitably linked up with the city's atmosphere and absorbed its rhythm, motoricity, tempo and exaltation. These essential features made of Urban Expressionism a stereotyped art, which became so differentiated from its former association with nature as to reach a breaking-point. The artists, nonetheless, continued to seek their motifs in nature, but the stylistic symptoms of the breaking-point were to remain.

The Brücke artists moved to Berlin just after their first great success: the 1910 Brücke Ltd. art show at the Arnold Gallery in Dresden was a breakthrough. Characteristically, the first member of the group to come to Berlin was the one whose innate talent came closest to their ideal, the well-spring, that is Max Pechstein. He was considered a nature-boy and that was the way he behaved, thus attracting the attention of the distinguished cultural bourgeoisie of Berlin, who secretly would have liked to imitate his manners. Pechstein, the "nature-boy", had a most uncomplicated mentality. He came to Berlin in 1908 simply to sell his paintings and to become famous soon — which is exactly what he succeeded in doing. However, his paintings are hardly touched by urban life. He painted Baltic Sea motifs, the fishermen and the little fishing villages, all of which had been his paradise until he left for the South Seas in 1914.

In 1910, Ernst Ludwig Kirchner, a far more complicated fellow member of the Brücke, came to join Pechstein in Berlin. Kirchner tended to be nervously over-sensitive, on the verge of neurasthenia; in fact he was later to become deeply neurotic. He combined this aspect of his personality with intellectual shrewdness and perspicacity. These were qualities that enabled him to adopt and portray city life with every fibre of his being. The works he produced in Berlin from 1910 to 1914 are typical examples of German Urban Expressionism, especially the famous street scenes. The large-scale, dense street scenes depicting prostitutes and women of dubious repute, followed by a flock of elegantly dressed gallants, are shady street ballets. They are composed of brush strokes spun out like so many pointed beams interacting to form the color structure, a transcription in painting of ecstatic nervousness. Kirchner's street scenes are like colorful stroke-storms that release enormous psychic tensions. He not only captures the symptoms of urban tempo, i.e. its rhythm, dynamics and motoricity, but he also uses them to develop a staccato technique that underlines the rhythmic haste to such a degree that it comes alive to an observer today and stimulates the latter to participate in the experience.

The way the artists chose to cope with city life greatly influenced their personality and hence their style. This was most obvious in Ernest Ludwig Kirchner's Expressionism, but it was also true of the friends who followed him to Berlin and whose style began to change in that city. In Dresden, their painting had covered the canvas with an interplay of freely flowing colors that reflected Fauvist style. But in Berlin, the structure of their compositions acquired a crystalline clarity, through outlined contours that stabilized the design. Karl Schmidt-Rottluff's terse imagery is intensified to convey massive cubic strength, by the artist's use of energetic contour lines to capture great contrasts between the planes of color. The decidedly sculptural effect of his forms is the result of the cubic composition of the contours, which, however, has less to do with French Cubism (with which Schmidt-Rottluff's work was hardly concerned) than with his independent interest in primitive African wooden sculptures.

59 Ernst Ludwig Kirchner: *Friedrichstrasse, Berlin* (1914), oil on canvas, 125×91 cm. Stuttgart, Staatsgalerie
The nervously vibrant rhythm of Kirchner's brushstrokes produces a street ballet of erotic tension, combined with appealingly morbid elegance.

56

The tendency to create cubic forms in painting simply by outlining the tensions within the pictorial framework is the result of a keen interest in wood engraving. The Brücke artists carved the motifs of their woodcuts directly into the grain of logs, using a simple knife and without making any preliminary sketches. The resistance offered by the material (which had to be overcome) produced a monumental effect that underscored the simplification of the figurative imagery; therefore, the graphic technique in which the Brücke artists expressed their style most appropriately was wood engraving. Some of the shapes and symbolic forms they discovered there were adapted to other technical media, especially to painting.

In a fashion similar to Schmidt-Rottluff, Erich Heckel's style during his Berlin period reflects a manifest tendency to crystallize shapes. But in contrast to Schmidt-Rottluff, Heckel's paintings are not Cubist in effect. His acutely angular, elongated shapes convey the brittleness of glass and its fragility. One of the basic patterns appearing in his compositions is a pointed triangle set on its tip. Heckel's art during his Berlin period reflects the artist's progressive withdrawal. The French label German Expressionism "Gothic"; this could apply especially to Heckel's artistic production during his Berlin period. The tender, pointed and elongated figures, with their calm faces, really do seem to have an inner relationship to wooden sculptures of the thirteenth and fourteenth centuries.

Their conversion to urbanism did not keep the Brücke artists from continuing to seek the paradise of their origins in the freedom of Nature. They spent summers together or alone, painting in Nidden on the Courland offshore bar, on the island of Fehmarn in the Baltic Sea or in Dangast on the Jadebusen Bay. Their coastal landscapes and bathing scenes are testimony that, in the final analysis, the style of their Expressionism was stimulated by the intensity with which they experienced the contrasts their urban-rural life afforded them. Heckel's painting of 1913, *Gläserner Tag*, is one of the best examples of this. It depicts the visionary transcendence of the pleasures of nature, experienced by a city-dweller of the twentieth century; it is a hymn to crystal-sculptured light and conveys the hallowed aspect of nature. The painting does not portray the freedom of natural oneness with nature but rather quite the opposite — the transcendental contrary thereof — which is the nostalgia for that oneness and a basically Romantic point of view. Nostalgia for their natural origins was experienced by city-dwellers directly, as a result of the loss of nature they experienced on an everyday basis. This was linked to a need for religious inspiration in order to obtain the strength to survive the urban experience, which comes to light very strongly in North German Expressionism. Religious motifs play a vital role in the painting and especially in the graphic arts of the Brücke artists.

The art of Emil Hansen, called "Nolde" after his birthplace in Schleswig-Holstein, comes close to the Brücke style. Nolde was encouraged by Schmidt-Rottluff to join the group for a while, but he soon withdrew although he remained on friendly terms with it. He loved the hazy, watery atmosphere of his birthplace and felt a need to return over and over again, so that this attraction came to influence his style. He can be stylistically distinguished from his Brücke friends as of 1910, since he no longer sought to capture the design within an energetically outlined color structure so as to consolidate his compositions. In his paintings, forceful streams of color merge into a heavily thickened, structured flow like the tongues of so many strongly colored glaciers slowly coming to a halt. Because the shapes are not linearly articulated, the effect of an illusion is also conveyed. Therefore, Nolde's painting means rather than defines and as such is comparable to the mysterious murmurs of a soothsayer. Nolde came to Berlin in 1902 but spent the following years living on the Danish island of Alsen. He settled down in Berlin for a longer period in 1909. He too felt fettered by city life which, exceptionally, inspired several paintings with urban motifs such as his *Paar am Weintisch* of 1911, which appears closest to Kirchner's work. But it was in Berlin that Nolde, in his mid-city studio on Tauentzienstrasse, began to work on his grandiose series of pictorial visions of the Life of Christ. The

60   Karl Schmidt-Rottluff: *Kämmendes Mädchen* (1919), oil on canvas, 90×76 cm. Berlin, Brücke-Museum
The pictorial strength of Schmidt-Rottluff's colors and imagery are reflected in the strongly contrasted modelling of surfaces and contours, which was the artist's personal mode of interpreting his experience with African sculpture.

61 Erich Heckel: *Männerkopf (Selbstbildnis)* (1919), woodcut in color, 46.1×32.7 cm. Berlin, Brücke-Museum
The Brücke artists were masters of wood engraving; the resistance of the material used encouraged them to purify shapes. "Gothic" elongation is a feature typical of Heckel's style.

62 Erich Heckel: *Gläserner Tag* ▷
(1913), oil on canvas, 120×96 cm. Munich, Neue Staatsgalerie (On loan from Mrs. M. Kruss)
This painting is the masterpiece of Heckel's Berlin period. His feeling for Nature seems to be metaphorically underscored by the crystalline structure of refracted light.

persuasiveness of those paintings is a product of the pressure of excessive sensitivity that drove the artist to create, and which still comes through to us today. The paintings are a reflection of North German Expressionism in its Protestant context. They can be distinguished from the religious conception of South German Expressionism such as the work of the Blaue Reiter Movement, because they strive to a lesser degree to transcend colors and shapes metaphysically. Rather they seek to convey poignantly the figure of Christ as the archetype of the evangelical gospel, that is, the humanitarian ideal of Christianity. The first paintings by Nolde, just after he had recuperated from a serious illness, were the *Abendmahl* and the *Pfingst-Bild* of 1909. The powerful feeling of faith transmitted by the fervent glow of the colors was not understood at the time of their creation. When exhibited at the Nolde Exhibition in Munich in 1912, they were criticized in a review in the *Münchner Post* as "a conscious perversion of esthetic norms and historical development... grotesque distortions... extreme esthetic nihilism".[1] Nolde had already submitted the *Pfingst-Bild* to the Art Exhibition of the Berliner Secession in 1910, but it was refused. To vent his spleen, Nolde violently lampooned the Secession and its president, Max Lieberman, by letter. Nolde's exclusion from the movement, which followed as a result, was one of the factors that provoked the formation of the Neue Sezession. Actually, it was just a minor factor, because the tensions that had been building up within the Berliner Secession, between artists of the older generation and those of the new one, openly came to a head in 1910.

Liebermann and the Impressionists, who had been artistic revolutionaries at the turn of the century, were no longer receptive to the goals of the younger artists. The selection committee for the 1910 exhibition rejected a great number of candidates, because the Secession's board of directors wanted to set an example. The committee attacked the young artists for their lack of technical proficiency and eliminated twenty-seven candidates, including Max Pechstein, Erich Heckel, Ernst Ludwig Kirchner, Otto Mueller and Karl Schmidt-Rottluff. The rejected artists joined forces to form the Neue Sezession, at the initiative of Pechstein and Georg Tappert.

Tappert is the Rubens of German Expressionism. Along with earlier landscape and still lifes of flowers, the main motifs of his paintings are naked women, whose sensuously sturdy corpulence and animal-like love of life are conveyed by the vigor of the artist's technique, the impulsiveness of his brush strokes and the luminous force of his colors. Georg Tappert's talent for communication (he was to be come a towering figure in the world of art education) predestined him to found the Neue Sezession group, which came into being, in a large measure, thanks to Tappert's persuasiveness. He gathered his rejected colleagues together at the Café des Westens and on April 22, 1910, they signed the group's foundation charter. The first art show of the Neue Sezession took place in the same year, at the Maximilian Macht Gallery. They used Max Pechstein's drawing of a naked bow-woman to illustrate the catalogue cover and posters. The Neue Sezession lasted as a group until 1913 and offered German Expressionist artists their first forum for exhibiting in Berlin.

Der Sturm

On the title pages of the first editions of the weekly, *Der Sturm*, which appeared in newspaper format in 1910, there are reproductions of distinctive, nervously graceful pen and ink drawings, spidery strokes of which twitch across the paper and immobilize people and events in psychographical "stills". Oskar Kokoshka's Indian ink drawings are portraits of prominent figures who had chosen to follow the new literary and artistic tendencies that ran counter to the officially recognized cultural norms. There is a portrait of Karl Kraus, the strict language censor — greatly celebrated in Vienna — who attracted a circle of admirers as a guest lecturer in Berlin. One also recognizes Paul Scheerbart, the utopic Berlin visionary, who prophesied glass architecture and described the peaceful creatures living on faraway planets, and Rudolf Blümner, who was a close friend of the poet,

63 Emil Nolde: *Am Weintisch*
(1911), oil on canvas, 88.5×73.5 cm.
Seebüll, Collection of the Nolde
Foundation
Nolde too was influenced by the
elegance of Berlin's street life. In
his rare café scenes, the figures are
bathed in pale, flowing light.

writer and stage director Herwarth Walden.
The portraits are accompanied by drawings
representing certain events, and the extraordinary poetic quality of the scenes is high-
lighted by the linear pattern of the pen strokes
that entangle the human figures. The drawings are entitled *Mörder, Hoffnung der Frauen,
Die Schlacht* or *Der Erstebeste darf der süssen
Lilith das Haar kämmen*. In a letter of recom-
mendation dated October 4, 1909, the architect Adolf Loos wrote from Vienna:

Dear Mr. Walden,

The painter Kokoschka wants to
set up an art show in Berlin. **I** guarantee it will be a tremendous success. Would there be room at Cassirer's? Is Meier-Gräfe coming to
Vienna soon to have a look at the

63

64   Emil Nolde: *Pfingsten* (1909),
oil on canvas, 87×107 cm. Berlin,
Staatliche Museen Preussischer
Kulturbesitz, Nationalgalerie
The beginning of North German
Expressionism. Nolde: "Then I
plunged into the mystical depths of
human and divine being. The
Whitsun painting was envisioned".

65   Georg Tappert: *Grüner
Rückenakt* (c. 1910), oil on canvas,
89×77 cm. New York, Leonard
Hutton Galleries
Outside of the Brücke artists,
Tappert was the most important
representative of the Expressionism
of Berlin. His paintings of nudes are
testimony to his vigorous
sensuousness.

matter? Are you coming to Vienna? Could you manage to stay a few days so that the collection could include your portrait? Please think it all over, about Cassirer (around fifteen half-length portraits), including K.K., Dehmel and myself. [2]

The portrait (1909) of Adolf Loos by Kokoschka currently belongs to the National-galerie in West Berlin. With Walden's help, the exhibition took place in Paul Cassirer's gallery that same year. Possibly, this encouraged Walden to follow through on the idea of opening his own art gallery. In any case, the spontaneous affinity between Walden and Kokoschka led the latter to settle down in Berlin, where he remained until the war broke out in 1914. In 1912, at his art gallery's first show, Walden exhibited Kokoschka's work. His paintings (the portraits as well as the allegorical pictures of hidden, mythically autobiographical, dream-flight scenarios, for instance, *Der irrende Ritter* and *Die Windsbraut*) differed from the Urban Expressionism of the Brücke artists right from the start, because they were the creations of an artist who had grown up in the city. Kokoschka's physiognomic Expressionism seems to unmask the soul of his subjects, using brush strokes as an instrument to probe under their skin and lay bare their nervous constitution. Such painting, a virulently executed art of psycho-neurological probes, is the product of a spiritual sensitivity that can only be explained by the particular cultural climate of Vienna during the first ten years of this century. At first glance, Kokoschka's paintings look frankly like counterparts to Freud's psychoanalysis and to the Viennese School. It should be noted that the analytical accuracy that comes to light in Kokoschka's work is not the result of an intellectually cal-

66 *Der Sturm* Vol. I, no. 32 (1910). Title page: lithograph of a pen-and-ink drawing by Oskar Kokoschka
Der Sturm appeared in newspaper format until 1919. From the start, the title page was decorated with Expressionist art work.

67 *Der Sturm* Vol. I, no. 20 (1910). Title page: lithograph of a drawing by Oskar Kokoschka
The title page is Kokoschka's illustration for the text of his Expressionist drama, *Mörder, Hoffnung der Frauen*, which appeared in this issue.

68   Oskar Kokoschka: *Herwarth Walden* (1910), oil on canvas, 100×68 cm. Stuttgart, Staatsgalerie
A painted psychograph, exhibited for the first time at the first exhibition in the Sturm Gallery in 1912. Walden founded the weekly *Der Sturm* in 1910 and the art gallery of the same name in 1912; both lasted until 1932.

culated revelation. It comes from the inspirational clear-sightedness that directs an artist's hand, without his being conscious of what he exposes of the driving forces and impulses under the surface. Kokoschka's 1910 portrait of Herwarth Walden, publisher of *Der Sturm*, represents the latter in profile only: an urban-intellectual figure lost in his thoughts and driven by nervous energy as he restlessly passes in front of the spectator – a phantom, a spectre, a phenomenon. The shaky lines of acceleration, which make the contours vibrate, describe the tempo of a movement that obeys the stimulus of a great inner turbulence. The profile of the intellectual dressed in an old wrinkled suit, stands out from a darkish-brown background. The light that illuminates him seems to emanate from him at the same time, producing a spiritual aura; dazzling strokes of lightning flash across the subject's body, like the electrical explosion of a Saint Elmo's fire. The artist not only portrays the outward likeness of Herwarth Walden but, with almost frightening insight, captures his very essence and character as well. Nell Walden, who had been his wife since 1912, describes her first encounter with Herwarth: "I was taken aback by his appearance. A blond musician's mane, a white face with blue, short-sighted, bespectacled eyes, very good musician's hands, slight of build; although ugly as such, he radiated an incredible vitality and intensity."[3] Kokoschka's portrait of Walden symbolically reproduces the urban intellectual's nervosity and turbulence, integrating them with the subject's mimic and physiognomic motor gestures, and captures the very substance of his character traits.

Although the circumstances differed, Walden can be considered comparable to Henry Kahnweiler as the most ingenious discoverer of talent and most energetic promoter of it in his times. His first wife, whom he married in 1901, was the poetess Else Lasker-Schüler. In the first annual volume of *Der Sturm*, she wrote an article about Kokoschka noting, among the descriptions: "All of Kokoschka's pictures irradiate light. Two hands of the Madonna reach down to the Child from the melancholy skies of Bethlehem. Many clouds and suns and worlds draw

Umfang acht Seiten   Einzelbezug 40 Pfennig

DER STURM

HALBMONATSSCHRIFT FÜR KULTUR UND DIE KÜNSTE

| Redaktion und Verlag
Berlin W 9 / Potsdamer Straße 134 a | Herausgeber und Schriftleiter
HERWARTH WALDEN | Ausstellungsräume
Berlin W 9 / Potsdamer Straße 134 a |

FÜNFTER JAHRGANG 1914   BERLIN-PARIS ERSTES JULIHEFT   NUMMER 7

Inhalt: August Stramm: Rudimentär / Guillaume Apollinaire: Le Ios du Douanier / Aage von Kohl: Der Weg durch die Nacht / H. W.: Ziele: Das Ziel der Klasse / Das Ziel der Pfingsten / Kurt Heynicke: Gedichte / Schmidt-Rottluff: Originalholzschnitt

Schmidt-Rottluff: **Originalholzschnitt**

near; blue merges with blue. Snow burns on his snow landscapes. It is as venerable as a jubilee tribute to the past: Dürer, Grünewald. Kokoschka's painting is the creation of a young priest: skies of his blue-brimming eyes, and lingering and haughty. He deals with people and objects alike and places them smilingly, like warm-hearted little figures, in [the palm of] his hand...." This text is a good example of the poetical atmosphere surrounding *Der Sturm* in 1910. The real origin of the word "Expressionism" is as debatable today as it was then. Walden did not invent the word, but it was he who made the term

69   *Der Sturm* Vol. V, no. 7 (1914). Title page: woodcut by Karl Schmidt-Rottluff
The extraordinary assertiveness of this title-page layout was obtained by combining the massive capitals in the title, *Der Sturm*, with an original Expressionist print.

70 Ludwig Meidner: *Revolution
(Barrikadenkampf)* (1913), oil on
canvas, 80×116 cm. Berlin,
Staatliche Museen Preussischer
Kulturbesitz, Nationalgalerie
An anticipatory vision of the
horrors of war and revolution. At
the bottom of the painting, a
self-portrait of the artist's frightened
head can be seen behind the
standard-bearer's back.

prevail by using it far beyond its meaning today, as an indiscriminate proclamation of all the trends of the 1910 stylistic revolution. The artists of the Expressionist vanguard found themselves united in the texts and pictures they contributed to *Der Sturm*, long before they were officially recognized as an avant-garde. To a great extent, it is due to Walden that the fine arts and literature met in Berlin, that the boundaries between artistic and literary Expressionism dissolved and that art became "literary", thus creating a basis for political commitment. Consequently, the first seeds were also sown for the concept of dissolving the boundaries that separated one field of art from another, allowing them to blend and fuse – a development that would be of great importance for the birth of the Dada movement.

In March, 1912, Walden opened the gallery Der Sturm. His first exhibition was entitled "Der Blaue Reiter: Oskar Kokoschka, Expressionisten". In April, 1912, the Italian Futurist art show caused a sensation in Berlin; handbills bearing the text of the Italian Futurist Manifesto were glued to poster pillars. Through the many art shows he subsequently set up, Walden gradually succeeded in assembling almost all of the new European art in Berlin. The city became the meeting place for artists of the European avant-garde.

The Erste Deutsche Herbstsalon was the high point of an impressive series of art exhibitions. It opened in September, 1913, and was the most important event of the year in the sphere of the visual arts. In retrospect, it can also be considered as a decisive event within the context of the history of twentieth-century art. It was a financially disastrous enterprise, torn apart by the newspapers: the show was not understood by the public at large and was considered scandalous. The exhibition became famous in the long run both because it was perpetuated by the commentaries of participants and their friends and because of the ensuing fame of many of the artists listed in the catalogue. It is classical proof that one should not come to any conclusions about the historical importance of an exhibition on the basis of the measure of its contemporary success.

The World Comes to an End

In 1912, Herwarth Walden's gallery, Der Sturm, exhibited the work of three artists who had recently joined forces. All three came from territories east of the River Elbe: Richard Janthur came from Zerbst in Saxony, Ludwig Meidner from Bernstadt in Silesia and Jakob Steinhardt from Zerkov in the district of Poznan. They called themselves *Die Pathetiker* ("the Pathetic Ones"), a title which was to become the battle cry, the core of Expressionist aspirations: pathos!

The sensation of pathos is the very essence of Expressionist style, conveyed in poetry by enhanced expressivity, which was obtained by condensing verbal imagery, by concentrating onomatopoeic words, by abridging, piecing and knitting together words, and by creating new ones: all of which was combined with the emotionally rhythmic compression of words and, finally, the break-up of syntax as well. The corresponding stylization in the fine arts translated the evocative quality of poets' word and sentence structure by increasing the luminosity and contrasts of colors so as to give dynamism to structural outlines. The extraordinarily intense sensorial forces, inherent in the creative impetus of Expressionism, tended to become accelerated under the influence of the encounter between Expressionism and urban life. The pathos of Urban Expressionism, an emotion provoked by that mutually influential exchange, reflected an accumulation of values that enhanced emotive elements and combined to generate a highly emotional aura: rhythm, dynamics, motoricity, agitation, tension, ecstasy.

Ludwig Meidner was the most outstanding artist of the Pathetiker club. He began to study art at the Academy in Breslau and came to Berlin in 1907, after studying in Paris. The short, shy and withdrawn artist assimilated urban life as if it were a demon born of man but no longer subservient to its creator, and whose nature was to devour men, like Moloch. Meidner's paintings depict landscapes in Berlin with houses and testify to the explosive effects of the mixture of all those emotionally intensifying values. His painting

71   Ludwig Meidner:
Schützengraben (1913), pen-and-ink
drawing, 46×60 cm. Berlin,
Berlinische Galerie
The trenches

Ich und die Stadt (1913), combines the two main motifs of his work: a self-portrait and the city. The painting is shattered by an explosion − streets bursting open and houses toppling over from the perpendicular in all directions, as if they were being blown away into the air. Expressive pathos also pervades the contents of the painting: the urban experience has triggered a vision of the end of the world. Meidner painted *Vision eines Schützengrabens* in 1911, *Die Abgebrannten* and *Brennendes Fabrikgebäude* in 1912. In the same year he produced the first of his *Apokalyptischen Landschaften*, and in 1913, he created what is probably his most famous picture: *Revolution*. The foreground of the painting is dominated by the figure of a wounded standard-bearer, with a red sash wrapped around his chest and shoulder and a white bandage on his head; his mouth is wrenched wide open by a scream. He is surrounded by battles on barricades, people shooting each other, bursting grenades spewing death and fire, and burning

houses collapsing. The composition is like a detonation of diagonals. The artist's self-portrait appears at the bottom edge of the painting − a head fearfully seeking cover. There is also a painting on the reverse with another *Apokalyptische Landschaft* depicting the city's condition at the end of war − the end of the world: a pale star pushes its way through the black smoke of conflagration in the sky and shines over the tombs on a battlefield.

Meidner's visions of the end of the world ominously foreshadow the trials of war and reflect a widespread mood among artists in Berlin on the eve of World War I, which they captured (figuratively) in painting as well as in the literature of that period. The contact and confrontation with the big city was transformed into an apprehensive nightmare, relished consciously and, at times even sensuously. The city is disclosed as a shamelessly superhuman and man-devouring creature. It is depicted mythically, and out of the myth,

71

which projected an oversized image of the city, emerges the dreaded allegorical vision of the end of the world, a ghastly picture that was to be direly confirmed all too soon.

Weltende is the title of a poem written by Jakob van Hoddis in 1911. It is the first in a collection of the newest poetry of that period, in an anthology called *Menscheitsdämmerung – Symphonie jüngster Dichtung*, published by Kurt Pinthus in 1920. [4] The poems included were, for the most part, written before or during the war. The first chapter of the collection is entitled "Sturz und Schrei" ("Crash and Cry"). The following ten poems make up the first part of the book: *Weltende* by Jakob van Hoddis, *Umbra Vitae* by Georg Heym, *Meine Zeit* by Wilhelm Klemm, *Verfall* by Johannes R. Becher, *Der Gott der Stadt* by Georg Heym, *Berlin* by Johannes R. Becher, *Städter* by Alfred Wolfenstein, *Die Stadt* by Jakob van Hoddis, *Bestienhaus* by Alfred Wolfenstein, *Dämmerung* by Alfred Lichtenstein. "End of the World", "*Umbra Vitae*", "My Times", "Decline", "City God", "Berlin", "City-Dwellers", "The City", "House of Beasts", "Twilight"... the mood of the period could hardly be more explicitly described. It was also in 1911 that Georg Heym translated his vision of war into powerful verbal images:

Aufgestanden ist er, welcher lange schlief,
aufgestanden unten aus Gewölben tief.
In der Dämmerung steht er, gross und unbekannt,
und den Mond zerdrückt er in der schwarzen Hand. ...

Einem Turm gleich tritt er aus die letzte Glut,
wo der Tag flieht, sind die Ströme schon voll Blut.
Zahllos sind die Leichen schon im Schilf gestreckt,
von des Todes starken Vögeln weiss bedeckt. ...

Eine grosse Stadt versank in gelbem Rauch,
warf sich lautlos in des Abgrunds Bauch.
Aber riesig über glühnden Trümmern steht,
der in wilde Himmel dreimal seine Fackel dreht.

("He who had slept so long stood up,
   stood up from the deep vault.
He stands in the dusk, large and unknown,
   and squeezes the moon in his black hand."
"Like a steeple he steps out of the last glow,
where day flees, the streams are already full of blood.

Countless are the corpses already stretched out in the reeds,
covered in white by the strong birds of Death."
"A big city sank in the yellow smoke,
noiselessly threw itself into the belly of the abyss.
But towers over the glowing ruins,
he who in the wild heaven turns his torch three times.")

Heym's poems matched Meidner's paintings and Alfred Kubin's print, *Der Krieg*, first published in 1903, could also have served as illustration.

Such words and paintings not only hide fear but also betray a certain fascination with,

72 Ernst Ludwig Kirchner: *Selbstbildnis als Soldat* (1915), oil on canvas 69.2×61 cm. Oberlin (Ohio), Allen Memorial Art Museum, Oberlin College (Charles F. Olney Fund 50.29)
The facial expression of the artist-soldier has been stiffened into a mask and his hand chopped off, signs of an inability to be creative. His being turned away from the female nude in the background may symbolize a fear of impotence.

73　Max Beckmann: *Selbstbildnis mit rotem Schal* (1917), oil on canvas 80×60 cm. Stuttgart, Staatsgalerie
The artist's face shows traces of the profound shock caused by his war experiences. Beckmann's Expressionist phase began with this painting, which testifies to his despairing questioning of himself.

a hidden desire for, downfall: a longing for death. They symbolize the contradictory nature of sensations and ideas that marked the art of Berlin during the period immediately preceding the war. Like the image of the city, war-imagery also became mythological. The danger contained in this development was that a belief in the inescapable and fateful necessity of war coming to pass was drawn like a veil across the concrete causes, obscuring an understanding of them. These causes were no secret to the critical intelligentsia, who acknowledged that the danger of war was the result of concrete social contradictions in the Empire, which finally came to light when it collapsed.

Franz Pfemfert was one of the most engaged representatives of that critical Berlin intelligentsia. He was the publisher of the weekly *Die Aktion*, the rival to *Der Sturm*. An aggressive intellectual and dyed-in-the-wool anarchist, he knew how to write highly polished texts. He was born in 1879 in Lötzen in East Prussia but grew up in Berlin and started his journalistic career as editor of the anarchistic newspaper, *Der Kampf*, published by Senna Hoy. *Die Aktion*'s basic anarchistic and trade-unionist tendencies became more and more conspicuous after 1918. Especially during the first years, Pfemfert (like Walden) promoted the unconventionally new and revolutionary style of young writers and artists, and in that respect the two men were similar. But in contrast to Walden, whose credo was "Revolution is not an art, but art is revolution", Pfemfert considered art, right from the start, as a tool to attain revolutionary political goals. As an anarchist Pfemfert was naturally also a rigorous pacifist; he was among the first to declare open battle, in no unclear terms, against the preparations and agitation for war in the leading German circles within the German Empire. During the war, he published a montage of texts entitled *Ich schneide die Zeit aus* ("Cut-Outs of the Times"); they were quotations from official glorification poetry and served to underscore the sarcasm of his attacks by their contrast to the reality of wartime events. Already in the 1912 volume of *Die Aktion* he wrote, in one of his very polished essays: "Europe's insanity seems incurable. What gives us the right to

babble about the progress of a civilization that puts its most wretched instincts on display? That is so criminal as to proclaim murder-on-command as a duty of 'national honor'? That glorifies fanatical ignorance as courage? What gives us the right to be proud of the culture of a generation on its knees before spectres of remote prehistoric times? Europe's insanity is incurable. What matter all the clichés of our platonic pacifist friends? Not a single bullet stays in the barrel because a few innocent dreamers are on the look-out for peace! Here and there peace prizes are distributed and peace conferences held, but there remains no time to get to the heart of the insanity with serious remedies." On June 28, 1914, the first shots rang out at Sarajevo; war was declared on Serbia by the Austro-Hungarian Monarchy on July 28; by the German Empire on Russia on August 1, and on France on August 3.

In the spring of 1915 Ernst Ludwig Kirchner was recruited into the field artillery in Halle. As he proved to be unfit for military duty, he was dismissed from the army in September "suffering from pulmonary disease and weakness". At that time he painted his *Selbstbildnis als Soldat*, in which he depicts himself with blind eyes and hands chopped off. The painting is staggering evidence of an identity crisis which, although already latent, was psychotically induced by the experience of being declared unfit for military service, an experience from which the artist was never to recover fully. In the same year, Kirchner produced some of his most important engravings: the woodcut cycle for Adelbert von Chamisso's *Peter Schlemihl*. That wondrous tale, from the pen of a German Romantic author, tells the story of a man who sold his shadow to the devil in exchange for seven-league boots that relentlessly drive him on, forever more. According to Gustav Schiefler, who was the first to publish Kirchner's cycle of engravings, it was "the story of a persecution maniac"; [5] Kirchner took the story as a paraphrase and used it to ponder about his own life. He reflected on the print *Begegnung Schlemihls mit dem Schatten*: "Schlemihl is sitting sadly in the fields, when his shadow suddenly comes over the sun-flooded land. He tries to put his feet in the shadow's footprints, under the delusion that he will become himself again. Analogous to the spiritual proceedings of someone discharged from the army". [6]

The end of the world, the twilight of mankind, which were the fundamental feelings in art at that period, materialized when individual confrontations with the reality of war and military service took place in the form of a loss of identity, a regression of sensibility. Kirchner was not the only example. Max Beckmann enrolled as a volunteer in the medical corps in 1914. During a visit in Ostende with the aged visionary painter Max Ensor, whom he greatly respected, Beckmann made the acquaintance of another medical volunteer, his Berlin colleague Erich Heckel. The latter was motivated by his war experience to produce one of his major works, his *Zeltbahnmadonna* (1916), which was unfortunately destroyed during World War II. (Long periods in the history of twentieth-century art also belong to the history of the destruction of art.) The soldier Beckmann suffered a nervous breakdown as a result of his war experience. He was discharged in the fall of 1915, and moved to Frankfurt-am-Main. His *Selbstbildnis mit rotem Schal* (1917) reveals the severely drawn traces of spiritual shock.

Volunteer George Grosz of Berlin was discharged as "unfit for military service" in May, 1915. He returned to Berlin, was drafted again in 1916, sent immediately to a mental clinic and again discharged, only to be redrafted on January 4, 1917, and sent to the military hospital of Guben on January 5, and to the mental hospital of Görden near Brandenburg at the end of February, 1917. He was finally definitively discharged from the armed forces at the end of April. He met volunteer Franz Jung in Berlin; the latter had deserted and been interned in an insane asylum for some time. The encounter between the two men was to play a role in the origins of Dada in Berlin. At the time Grosz was drawing nervously venomous scribble-sheets, depicting soldiers helplessly handed over to the horrors of the battlefields. In 1917, in a letter from Görden, he wrote to his brother-in-law, Otto Schmalhausen: "My nerves were torn to pieces before I saw the Front, the putrefying corpses and barbed wire this time; for the time being, I have been rendered

harmless — I have been interned awaiting a decision by the experts as to my military fitness. Nerves, every tiniest fibre, abhorrence, repugnance." In 1916, MG-gunner Otto Dix of Dresden, stationed at the western Front, became a fanatical war opponent: his paintings and etchings remain as testimony.

Postwar Expressionism and Dada

The religious kinship inherent in the pathos of Expressionism was decisively brought to the fore and strengthened by the shock that war and frontline experiences inflicted. This development was in part the result of the collision between individuals and the problem of the purpose of life. The existential design seemed to have lost its significance, because the injury inflicted had been accomplished by the individual's fellow man.

The existential damage done by man to his fellow man was represented by Christ in person. "Was not Christ revealed to you?" is the question appearing at the bottom of the woodcut illustrating the title page of Schmidt-Rottluff's Christ cycle. The strikingly designed head of the Man of Sorrows emerges from a clash of contrasts in black and white; His forehead is inscribed with the date 1918 like a scar, mirroring the Cain symbol of His torturers.

In 1917, in addition to his *Selbstbildnis mit rotem Schal*, Max Beckmann also produced his *Kreuzabnahme*. The stylistic fragmentation characteristic of Urban Expressionism, is transformed in this picture into fragility and gloom: the world is sick. Behind the *Kreuzabnahme* scene, the bulk of which displaces the picture's frame, a blood-red star blossoms in the sky.

The East Prussian Lovis Corinth, a contemporary and friend of Max Liebermann, and since 1900 past master of Berlin painters, was a vigorous Impressionist before 1911; through the intensification of his mode of painting, he progressively became more expressionistic. In 1922 he painted the expressively powerful *Der rote Christus*. Six years later, George Grosz was denounced for blasphemy, because of his lithograph (captioned "Shut your trap and soldier on"), a parody of the Crucifixion intended to be provoking, showing Christ wearing a gas mask.

This interpretation of the motif, conveying insolence, aggressivity, sarcasm and acrid irony, corresponded to the attitude of a new generation. It included those artists who were, on the average, ten years younger than those of the Brücke group; they had been called to war when just out of high school, and only at the war's end did they get around to themselves and to finding a personal, artistic mode of expression. It was a generation of men spiritually wounded by the war. The tone for their development was set by the trauma they had suffered, by the scar symbolizing the injury to their self-confidence, which remained conspicuous. That trauma was not only a starting point, it was also a driving force behind the originality of content and form they created to communicate their experience. These young artists also used Expressionist imagery, but soon transformed it. Pathos relinquished its claim to solemnity, and hence was no longer believable; only a parody of pathos remained. Mood-producing elements, which had originally played no role in Expressionism, now merged with stylistic motifs, which they transformed and finally dominated. These elements were inspired by the bitterness of war and its injurious sequels for personality: deception, sorrow, anger, aggressivity, ridicule, scorn, irony, sarcasm, loss of confidence, doubt, despair. The most distinctive aspect of Urban Expressionism − stylistic fragmentation − had progressively changed into fragility, as exemplified by Beckmann's *Kreuzabnahme*; then, at the end of the war, the forces latent in stylistic fragmentation were propulsed into action: into a rupture. This rupture was further intensified in Berlin's postwar art, by an intentionally clean break with past art, a cut-off. Rupture and cut, wound and scar were thus unmistakable esthetic symptoms of art in Berlin in the 1920's. It was a maimed art. Rupture and cut were not merely symbols of the identity crisis suffered by individual artists but came to be a new way of representing the external heterogeneity and contradictions of urban life.

Art in the Twenties was concerned with

the disparities of life in a big city and included not only work that originated in Berlin but also creations inspired by, or in reaction to, the latter. Max Beckmann's *Nacht*, for instance, one of the major creations of the era, was completed in March, 1919, when the artist was already living in Frankfurt. The deeply imbedded brutality of the impact of city life and wartime on the artist emerges from this depressing painting as a contradiction to all the moral values of mankind. Beckmann, a contemporary of Schmidt-Rottluff, found his way to graphic expressivity during

74 Karl Schmidt-Rottluff: *Ist euch nicht Kristus erschienen* (1918), woodcut, 50.1×39.1 cm. Berlin, Brücke-Museum
From the series *Neun Holzschnitte*, published by Kurt Wolff-Verlag, Munich: 1918.

75 Lovis Corinth: *Der rote Christus* (1922), oil on panel, 129×108 cm. Munich, Bayrische Staatsgemäldesammlungen
In his later work, Corinth, past master of German Impressionism, achieved an expressive spiritualization of form. The crucified Christ, bathing in red light, embodies the sum of humanity's suffering.

the war years, as the pressure one recognizes in his pictures (in the form of underscored oppression and gloom) attests. The black that emerges from the luminosity of the surrounding city night, to render the event taking place perceptible, is an impenetrable and invincible substance that bears down on all life in the picture. Beckmann's *Nacht* is the epitome of metaphysical pessimism. The black hole of a speaker of a phonograph gapes open to symbolize consummate despair, a picture of nothingness. The artist thereby sadly bade farewell to his belief in an unlost Paradise; his melancholy hides a deeply suppressed and boundless anger.

Another urban landscape typical of postwar Expressionism, *Der Tod des Dichters Walter Rheiner*, was painted in 1925 by Conrad Felixmüller, who was born in Dresden in 1893 and was the first to develop a style that

76   Max Beckmann: *Die Nacht* (1918-19), oil on canvas, 133×154 cm. Düsseldorf, Kunstsammlung Nordrhein-Westfalen
Three bandits have forced their way into the room. One man is being strangled; his wife bound. The cumbersome figures crowd each other painfully and are reminiscent of martyr scenes in paintings of the Middle Ages.

could deliberately be termed Proletarian Expressionism. He first came to Berlin with his paintings in a suitcase in 1914, and there he came into contact with the avant-garde. He became friends with Meidner and came to know Raoul Hausmann. In 1916, he exhibited his work at Walden's gallery. In 1919, he founded the culturally revolutionary group of artists, "Sezession 1919" in Dresden. Felixmüller favored motifs from the world of workers and of showmen, like his *Schaubudenboxer*. During and after the war, Felixmüller contributed woodcuts for the title pages of Franz Pfemfert's *Die Aktion*, illustrating the contents of main-feature stories. The combination of text and pictures was most effective. One of the title-page wood-engravings of *Die Aktion* in the fall of 1917 was entitled *Rettet Euch Menschen* ("Save Yourself, Mankind"). Six years later, his painting *Der Tod des*

Dichters Walter Rheiner exemplified the final phase of German Expressionism. In comparison with Meidner's earlier paintings, the composition had grown more complicated, more vehement and racier but also more calculated and stilted. This corresponded to a change in attitude, a playing out to their bitter end of the conflicts of urban life, conveying the chilling ecstasy of fierce disillusionment. Moloch opens his jaws and lays bare his vicious-toothed gullet; the big city gobbles up its children.

It was during the last years of the war that the young artists began to take issue and settle accounts with the very middle-class society to which they themselves belonged, but which had so profoundly abused their confidence by violating their ideals. George Grosz's *Widmung an Oskar Panizza* (begun in 1917 and finished in 1918) is also an urban landscape,

VERLAG · DIE AKTION · BERLIN-WILMERSDORF

HEFT 80 PFG.

77 Conrad Felixmüller: *Der Schaubudenboxer* (1921), oil on canvas, 95×110 cm. Berlin, Berlinische Galerie
Second-generation Expressionism: motifs from the world of the "little man", from fairgrounds and the workers' world, are depicted with the aggressive tones of social commitment.

78 *Die Aktion* Vol. VII, nos. 39-40 (1917). Title page: woodcut by Conrad Felixmüller: *Rettet Euch Menschen*
Felixmüller's graphic contributions to *Die Aktion* are the first examples of artistic comment, in Expressionist woodcut style, on current political themes.

but the world-weary pathos still visible in Meidner's prewar work is replaced by the bitterest sarcasm. A fleeting glance at the subject of the painting makes it appear as if an idiotic ogre had lifted up a city of building blocks and jumbled them all up – an earthquake, but one in which Reason quakes, a spiritual collapse. The composition has been carefully studied and organized with almost pedantic precision. This impression is confirmed by the fact that the author has painstakingly avoided using any verticals or horizontals; he uses only diagonals. The influence of Italian Futurism is unmistakable in the energy-laden diagonals that were a Futuristic compositional element. However, Grosz no longer uses them to convey dynamically motoristic movement, which was their original Futurist purpose; his diagonals appear broken in many places, like jolted bric-a-brac. A demoniac carnival march, bathed in bright red light, moves down the street; we ourselves are represented by the masks. Fallen mankind, in its insane victory, attends its own funeral. In order to convey the impression of total confusion, the picture is made up of a great many small and tiny particles. Composition is replaced by a new principle of visual organization – montage – which represents disparity, disintegration, disorganization and heterogeneity.

Montage instead of composition is a method that was also adopted by Otto Dix (a student at the Dresden Art Academy) in the paintings he made during the first years after returning from the war. He sought to cope with a reality that surpassed any nightmare and used his soul to depict the horror of his frontline experiences. Dix did not have to discover montage artificially, for the environ-

79   Conrad Felixmüller: *Tod des Dichters Walter Rheiner* (1925), oil on canvas, 180×115 cm. Berlin, private collection

The Expressionist poet Walter Rheiner of Dresden described his addiction to cocaine in short pieces of prose. Felixmüller's painting is an epilogue to his friend's suicide.

80   George Grosz: *Widmung an* ▷ *Oskar Panizza* (1917-18), oil on canvas, 140×110 cm. Stuttgart, Staatsgalerie

Among other works, Oskar Panizza, doctor and author, wrote *Das Liebeskonzil* (1895), a controversial satire on the Church. He was condemned for blasphemy and lese-majesty.

mental impressions treated in his paintings were in themselves a montage. The people he portrays are already made up of artificial pieces. The abrasive, counter-esthetic quality of his painting *Kartenspielende Kriegskrüppel* (1920) betrays the naked rage with which he thrusts the visible, day-to-day sequels of war into the faces of people who usually turn their heads away. Decomposition instead of composition: in order to construct his painting in terms of montage, the artist is obliged first to decompose the human figure, which is also the subject of his accusation. The painting is partially a collage. Dix integrated concrete tokens of everyday life – banknotes, playing cards from a Saxon-Altenburg deck of skat cards, as well as three pages of the *Dresdner neueste Nachrichten* at the top edge of the painting. As objects, these additions attract the eye and suggest the authentic reality of the whole painting.

Both paintings (by Grosz and by Dix) are encompassed within the scope of a movement difficult to grasp in terms of normal stylistic concepts, because it is the first one with a tendency to negate the traditional roots of the bourgeois conceptions of art – Dada.

In January 1917, Richard Huelsenbeck came to Berlin from Zurich to publicize the Dada movement. Once he had gotten to know artists in Berlin, he was able to write to Tristan Tzara in Zurich that Dada was already at work in Berlin.

Since the end of 1918, Berlin had been the capital of a young Republic seeking its unfamiliar way out of the ruins of Empire. Fights between Rightists and Leftists, street demonstrations and shoots-outs in the city combined to create a chaotic political scene. This atmosphere corresponded to the mentality of the Berlin Dadaists, who sought to participate in the nonsense – which they fully recognized as such – by making sarcastic comments and engaging in direct action. Dadaists were not Marxists fighting a class struggle, as they were considered at the time, but individualistic anarchists. Their artistic bantering incorporated the negation of their own middle-class habits. The behavior of the Berlin Dadaists exaggerated the attitude of the German petty bourgeoisie to such an extent that it became consciously self-defeating, which led the

Dadaists to create demonstrations absurdly reflecting the deliberate contradiction within themselves.

Two rival groups of friends made up the core of Dadaism in Berlin; they remained on friendly terms mainly due to the conciliatory and equananimous nature of Richard Huelsenbeck. Radically individualistic anarchists formed one wing of the group: the "Dadasoph" Raoul Hausmann, theoretician of contradiction and promoter of direct action, with his friend the *Oberdada* ("chief Dada") Johannes Baader (a former tomb architect), whose inborn burlesque lunacy was nourished by a combination of paranoid imagination and Prussian official style. The third member of this wing was Hausmann's friend Hannah Höch, who used gentle irony to convey Dadaism with a good conscience. The other wing consisted of the brothers Wieland Herzfelde and John Heartfield, and a friend with whom they formed a threesome, George Grosz. The latter was their main collaborator in the Dadaist rebellion and engaged in radical Leftist satire of a deeply cutting nature. The journals *Jedermann sein eigener Fussball* and *Die Pleite*, with Grosz's ferocious linear drawings, appeared successively with Malik-Verlag, the publishing house founded by Herzfelde. The journals were primarily directed against sentiments of militarism and law-and-order and against subservience to the armed forces, which characterized Germany's first Social Democratic government. And finally, scandals and prohibitions alternated with each other.

Two exhibitions were high points in the Dada movement, notably the Dada Exhibition at J.B. Neumann's Graphisches Kabinett in May, 1919, and the Erste Internationale Dadamesse, which opened on June 24, 1920, at Dr. Otto Burchart's and was a tremendous success with the press, with the public – and as a scandal. In order to challenge bourgeois taste, which was a proven Dadaist technique at this point, objects of sarcastic triviality were chosen as exhibit pieces and displayed in purposefully confused set-ups. Baader's Plasto-Dio-Dada-Drama, *Deutschlands Grösse und Untergang*, was a central piece of the exhibit, one of the first, large, assembled environments in the history of art. The

81 Otto Dix: *Kartenspielende Kriegskrüppel* (1920), oil on canvas, with montage of objects and parts of magazines, 110×87 cm. Constance, private collection An early example of montage in painting, with items from everyday life. The pieces of the montage are artificial adjunctions that underline the dramatic effect of the motif.

principle of montage using heterogeneous pieces and the alliance of unmatching elements was systematically advanced against the principle of composition, because the principle of Classical composition embodies the ideal picture of an intact world, while the principle of montage embodies the picture of the tangible contradictions within the world and most especially, within the urban world, with which we must cope today. The Dadaists did not need to conjure up this contradiction, since it was corroborated on a daily basis by new photographs in illustrated magazines. As a result, Berlin Dadaism made an original discovery that was its contribution to twentieth-century art: photomontage, actually a discovery jointly made by Raoul Hausmann and Hannah Höch. Hausmann's montages, for instance his *Kunstkritiker* (1919), appear at first glance to have been glued together during a sudden fit of rage, but upon closer inspection they reveal the cunning intelligence with which a replica of raging energy has been created. In contrast to Hausmann's energetic fundamentalism, Hannah Höch's montages are more restrained and milder examples of remote mockery. Nowadays Raoul Hausmann's "mechanical head", entitled *Der Geist unserer Zeit*, is considered the figurehead of the German Dada movement. The head is an application made up exclusively of miscellaneous objects he found. "Who needs a soul in times that keep going anyway mechanically?" was the question asked by Hausmann, and which, in his eyes, logically implied the absurd. Therefore, according to Hausmann, the artist should abstain from any individual originality in structuring existing banalities; he is merely an assembly-man for the prefabricated. This is the most important Dadaist thesis – the Dadaist testament. As a follow-up, George Grosz called himself a Dadaist assembly-man and used a rubber stamp to sign his paintings instead of his signature. The Dadaist attitude reflected a basic fear shared with other people living in a highly industrialized society: the fear that machines would ultimately triumph over man's spirit and feelings, would conquer human nature, would drain man's capacity to reason, and finally, would turn men into soulless robots.

DIE DEUTSCHE PEST

Rudolf Schlichter's watercolor of 1920, *Dachatelier*, is an impressive example of this thoroughly sensuous confrontation with the fear of the victory of machines. Disposed in a roof landscape rendered spell-binding by the glassy light, various models of human beings pose, in all stages of torpidity and pupation. The influence of Giorgio de Chirico's *pittura metafisica* can be felt here, but treated in an independent manner.

The suggestion of fright, which emanated from the motif of robot men, occurred in numerous pieces by George Grosz at the time. He combined his sharp and shrewd, watercolor and pen-and-ink drawings with photomontage. In one of his major pieces, Grosz depicted the blatant myth of a civilization born of fear, emerging from the motif of robot men: the procreation of new hybrid creatures, produced by wedding men to machines. Grosz's work, *Daum Marries...* (1920), is typical of his specific blend of pen-and-ink drawing, lettrist collage and mounted letters. These techniques also characterize the anti-militaristic and anti-capitalist satires he produced together with John Heartfield.

82   *Die Pleite*, Vol. I, no. 5 (1919) (Malik-Verlag: Berlin and Leipzig). Title-page drawing by George Grosz: *Die Deutsche Pest*
The newspapers for which Grosz worked—*Die Pleite, Der blutige Ernst* and *Der Gegner*—were constantly threatened with confiscation, and their publishers and collaborators risked arrest.

83   View of a room at the Erste   ▷
Internationale Dada Messe in Dr. Burchard's Art Salon, Berlin: 1920 (photo: Berlinische Galerie [Hanna Höch Estate])
This fair, which comprised 176 exhibits, was the most comprehensive exhibition of the Dada movement. (On the wall): photomontages meant to be provoking, with portraits of Hausmann, Grosz and Heartfield.

84   Johannes Baader: The   ▷
Plasto-Dio-Dada-Drama
Deutschlands Grösse und Untergang (1920), assemblage and montage (photo: Paris, Archives Nakov)
This construction, composed of Dada pamphlets, daily newspapers, spare parts for machines and trivial items such as a mousetrap, was exhibited at the Dada fair. The tailor's dummy in uniform with a stamp on its forehead is an allegory of the spirit of subservience.

85   Raoul Hausmann: *Der*   ▷▷
Kunstkritiker (1919), photomontage and collage, 31.5×25 cm. London, The Tate Gallery
Berlin's Dadaists invented photomontage. In this piece, Hausmann included newspaper clippings, money, stamps, his own visiting card, letters out of his phonetic poems and a rubber stamp from George Grosz.

83

84

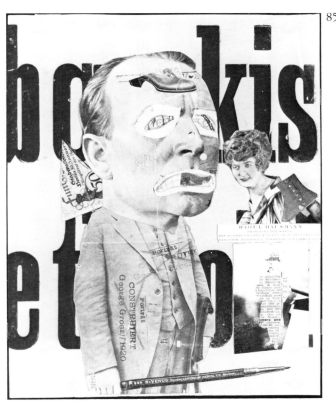

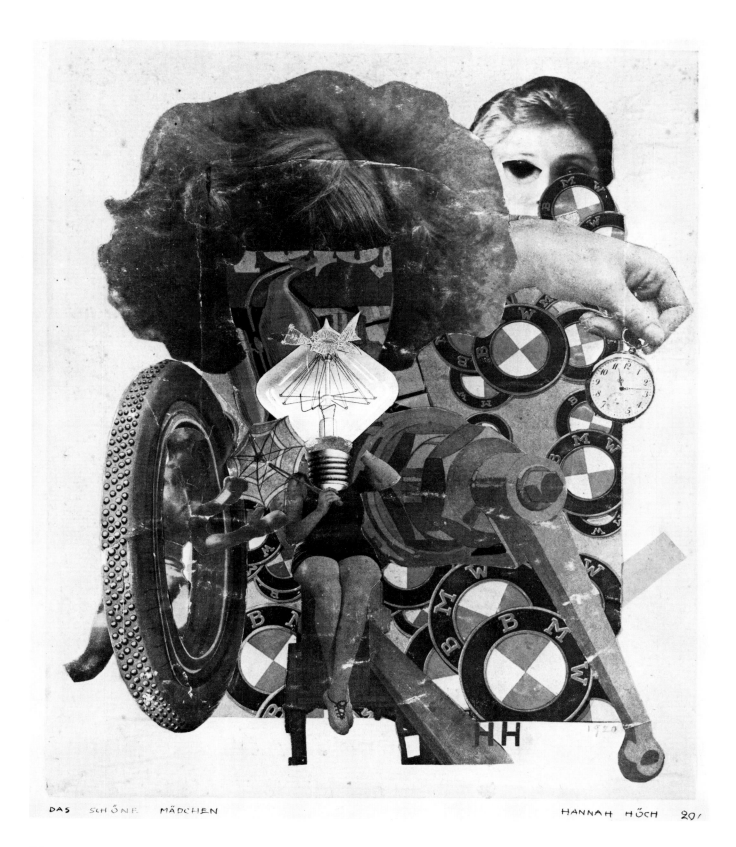

DAS SCHÖNE MÄDCHEN   HANNAH HÖCH 20.

86 Hannah Höch: *Das schöne Mädchen* (1920), montage composed of fragments of photos and ads, 35×29 cm. Private collection
Some of the artist's photomontages from her Dada period are paraphrases that subtly poke fun at the stereotyped image of women.

87 Kurt Schwitters: *Drucksache* (1919), rubber-stamp picture, 23×18 cm. Hanover, Kunstmuseum Hanover with the Sprengel Collection
The rubber stamp is an ironical and provocative substitute for handwritten signatures. Schwitters, the MERZ artist from Hanover, exhibited his rubber-stamp pictures, to which he added little matchstick figures, at the Sturm Gallery.

From Constructivism to Unity of Space-Motion-Time
The East European Avant-Garde

In October, 1920, two young Russians arrived in Berlin, the painters Ivan Puni and his wife Xenia. They took up lodgings at Kleiststrasse 43, in westside Berlin. Puni's friend, the Berlin Dadaist and Constructivist Hans Richter, remembers Xenia as "an extremely pretty, lively and altogether cheerful person, quite the opposite of Ivan, with his pointed nose, black hair and black eyes, whose sharp mouth rarely drew into a smile and who looked like a joy (or joyless) killer. And yet, he was one of the mildest and most lovable people I ever met."[7] The magnetism of both Russians soon made their studio the meeting point for a mixed circle of artists living in Berlin, none of whom had any money. Ivan Puni, an old friend and artistic comrade-in-arms of Kasimir Malevich, had signed the Suprematist Manifesto, together with Malevich and other artists, in Petrograd. In 1919, Puni taught at the Academy in Vitebsk, at Marc Chagall's invitation. But, upon returning to Petrograd that fall, he was obliged to acknowledge that the political situation had changed in the meantime. Because of his aristocratic roots, as well as the fact that he was suspected of sympathizing with the "Whites", Puni fled to Berlin via Finland. By doing so, he became one of the first of those emigrants, who had belonged to the intellectual pioneers of the Russian Revolution, to fall victim to its consequences. Caused by the mutual distrust among the various revolutionary groups, a collective neurosis, a symptom of the October Revolution's evolution from its expansive phase to one of bureaucratic centralization, began to manifest itself.

In February, 1921, Puni exhibited the work he had been able to bring along at Walden's gallery: Cubo-Futurist paintings, watercolors and drawings. They were all small; he had been obliged to leave the larger formats behind in the Soviet Union. Thanks to Puni's experience with the provocative modes of hanging paintings used at exhibitions in Petrograd, he was able to achieve an explosive and monumental overall effect at his exhibition, using a minimum of means, by presenting his work unconventionally: Puni covered the walls of Walden's gallery with dynamic, space-covering, diagonal compositions, made up of abstract human figures, big letters and abstract Constructivist symbols that he had cut out of sheets of packing paper and colored brightly. The exhibition gave the people of Berlin their first look at contemporary Russian art, which had developed on its own, along lines consistent with the Russian mentality. From gradual rejection of anecdotal, pictorial subjects, Russian art had moved to negation of the latter and to a radical Fundamentalism that reduced all pictorial elements to their basic forms.

Puni remained in Berlin for three years. It was there that he made speeches explaining his artistic concepts, published his book, *Die Malerei der Gegenwart*, participated in the exhibitions of the Novembergruppe and exhibited his painting, *Der Musiker*, at the Grosse Berliner Kunstausstellung; *Der Musiker* was the most important piece he painted during his years in Berlin. The painting is unique among Puni's creations, by the originality of his Chaplin-like mixture of interlocked cubical surfaces and realistically sculptural, painted bodies; it is a picture at the turning point of his style.

In 1924, he and Xenia moved to Paris permanently. It was the typical route for Russian emigre artists in the twentieth century. Puni was the precursor of the encounter between the East European avant-garde and the Berlin art scene, a confrontation that gathered enormous momentum over the following three years and subsequently flowed out of Berlin to make an impact on European art in general. The Russian, Hungarian and Polish artists who arrived in Berlin after the war's end came not only to propagate new artistic tendencies and to test reactions in the western and Central European art metropolis situated nearest to eastern Europe but also to use the experience and renown gained in Berlin to further their careers. Berlin served as a European "switching yard" for their ideas.

Jefim Golyschev arrived in Berlin from Odessa as early as 1919. He participated in the Berlin Dada movement and the exhibits of the Novembergruppe with his anarchistic,

88 Rudolf Schlichter: *Dachtatelier* ▷ (*c.* 1920), watercolors with pen-and-ink drawing, 45.8×63.8 cm. Berlin, Galerie Nierendorf
A triumph of mechanization: human beings in various stages of stiffening—the snob, the good little girl, the girl in disguise, the man with artificial limbs, the mannequin, the jointed doll, the anatomy model, etc.

89 George Grosz: *Daum marries…* (1920), watercolors with pencil and pen-and-ink drawing; montage composed of pieces of photographs and illustrations on watercolor paper, 42×30.2 cm. Berlin, Galerie Nierendorf
Sex and mechanics—a variation on the ancient theme of Death and the Maiden

90 Oskar Schlemmer: *Jagdschloss Grunewald* (1912), oil on canvas 40.8×32.5 cm. Berlin, Berlinische Galerie [on loan from private collection]
Schlemmer, who later became a master of the Bauhaus, already shows Constructivist tendencies in the shapes used in this German Cubist painting of his early Berlin period.

90

91

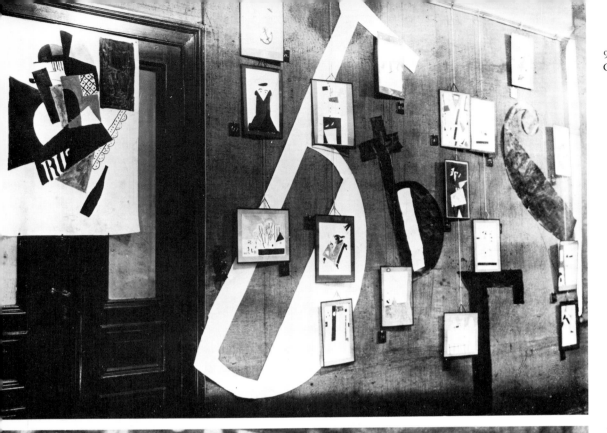

91   Ivan Puni: Exhibit at the Sturm
Gallery, Berlin: 1921

92   Ivan Puni's publicity in the
street, with Cubist costumes, for the
inauguration of his exhibition in
Berlin: 1921

93   Ivan Puni: *Der Musiker* (1921),   ▷
oil on canvas, 144×98 cm. Zurich,
Mr. and Mrs. Herman Berninger
Puni's major painting from his
Berlin period. The bulky forms of
the panels on the instrument
contrast with the sculptured curves
of the Chaplin-like figure. The
surface design translates the artist's
method of incorporating physical
relief.

"bruitistic" musical compositions and auto-mated drawings. A German version of Konstantin Umanski's book, *Neue Kunst in Russland 1914-1919*, came out in Potsdam in 1920. The same year, Laszlo Moholy-Nagy came to Berlin from Budapest via Vienna and stayed there until he was offered a job with the Weimar Bauhaus under Gropius. In 1921, Alexander Archipenko arrived in Berlin from Paris, where he founded an art school. Kandinsky came to Germany from the Soviet Union but did not care for Berlin; he only remained there a short time and designed a mural on packing paper for the Grosse Berliner Kunstausstellung. (Unfortu-nately the project was lost some time later.) On the occasion of an exhibition of their work in Walden's gallery in 1922, two Hun-garians, Lajos Kassák and Alexander Bortnik, came to Berlin for a visit and made numerous contacts. Marc Chagall stayed in Berlin for a few months and made his series of etchings entitled *Mein Leben* for the publisher Paul Cassirer. The sculptor Naum Gabo came to Berlin from Moscow and stayed until 1924.

The high point of the year, however, was the now legendary Russische Kunstausstellung which was inaugurated at the Van Diemen Gallery, and was the first official representation, promoted by the State, of

artistic trends in the Soviet Union. Although from today's standpoint one recognizes a lack of uniformity and certain difficulties mirrored in the choice of exhibition pieces, the exhibit itself may be considered of great historical importance. The commissioner in charge of the exhibition, who accompanied it to Berlin, was Eliezer (El) Lissitzky. He had a gift for communication, which enabled him to ally the competence of an artist with that of an organizer and pedagogue. Within a very short time, he made many friends and contacts, and obtained numerous art commissions. He remained in Germany until 1923, when symptoms of tuberculosis obliged him to leave for a stay at a sanatorium in Locarno. But before leaving, Lissitzky displayed his *Prounenraum*, the first large Constructivist environment, at the Grosse Berliner Kunstausstellung of 1923. The Hungarians Lajos d'Ebneth and Laszlo Peri, as well as the Pole Henryk Berlewi were among the artists who came to Berlin between 1921 and 1922. All three were attracted by Walden's reputation and exhibited their work at his Sturm Gallery.

One of Herwarth Walden's major achievements was that, in the eyes of the young East European artists, his art shows had sparked a keen interest in Berlin as a showcase; furthermore, the attentive Berlin public was somewhat prepared to accept new artists, for ever since he had founded the Sturm Gallery, and even during the war years, Walden had sought to familiarize the public with the new art from the East European countries. It began when he instinctively included examples of that art in the Erste deutsche Herbstsalon, (1913), which was followed by numerous one-man shows. Walden was particularly devoted to two artists: the sculptor Alexander Archipenko, whose work he exhibited separately in 1913, 1914 and 1918; and Marc Chagall, whose work he exhibited at one-man shows in 1914, 1917 and 1918. Both have Walden to thank for the beginnings of their worldwide renown.

Nonetheless, Berlin did not represent the ultimate goal of emigre artists from East Europe; it was an important intermediate stopover for them, but the mecca of their artistic aspirations had always been, and still remained, Paris. The reasons were inextricably connected with the history of European culture. Two Moscow businessmen, Sergei Shchukin and Ivan Morozov, had been collecting French art, from Impressionist to contemporary works, since the beginning of the century. They also brought back the most recent art from Paris, such as pre-Cubist and early Cubist pieces by Picasso, whom Morozov had met in Paris in 1905. Both collections were a sensation and served as a source of inspiration for young Russian artists whose style changed fundamentally in the twentieth century. That is why so many took the road to Paris themselves whenever possible.

It is also the reason why, at the end of World War I, Berlin, which was serving as a sort of overflow basin for the Russian Revolution, prospered at the crossroad of a two-way traffic of interest for Russian artists — for those coming West from the East and for those who had already been in Paris for years (for instance Archipenko) and who felt the effervescence of all that was going on artistically in Berlin. In his Memoirs, Nicolas Nabokov writes: "After the war, Berlin had become a sort of caravansery, where everybody met on their way to Moscow or to the Occident." Also, "I didn't come to Paris directly from Moscow. I was in Berlin for a few months before; in the feverish atmosphere of inflation and difficult beginnings of the Weimar Republic, I met again many of my friends from Vitebsk, Leningrad and Moscow."[8] In 1922 or 1923, the author Viktor Shklovskii described his stay in Berlin: "Racketeers saunter along the streets in coarse coats, as well as Russian professors, by twos, with their hands behind their backs clasping their umbrellas. There are many streetcars, but it's hardly worth using them to ride through the city, because the city looks the same everywhere. Palaces made out of the business of prefabricated palaces. Every monument — a service. We don't go anywhere; we live in crowds in the middle of the Germans like a sea between its coasts. There are no winters. Sometimes it snows, sometimes it thaws.... Helena Ferrari lives in a house across the street from Ivan Puni on Kleiststrasse, ...the *U-Bahn* ["Underground"] flies upwards out of the earth between these two famous houses and howls its way up to the upper track." Eberhard Steneberg commented: "Shklovskii is going to the *Gleisdreieck* ['track triangle']. No one had ever used that expression to describe Berlin the way Shklovskii used it, as a metaphor for Berlin. Out of curiosity, I once got off there in 1940; the bleakness was truly frightening".[9] It is even more so today.

For a Russian living in Berlin in 1920 "the city looks the same everywhere". What he would miss was a discernible centerpoint that stood out, an old city, a crowning point, a Kremlin like Moscow or an Île de la Cité like Paris. Berlin had nothing of the kind. It had no skyline. That is what characterized Berlin as a stage-setting. This lack of any sort of identifying mark was its distinction; it was what inspired artists living there to introduce montage into their work. To the Russians who came there, it made the city appear to be naught but a huge waiting room.

The ring formed around Berlin by the *S-Bahn* ("fast train") network has two strategically important transfer stations: Westkreuz and Ostkreuz respectively, which are the cardinal points of a turntable. It very aptly defines Berlin, the communication point between East and West: moving to Berlin, the Russian artists had also brought along the principle of montage, but their principle had originated in an altogether different spirit than that of the artists of Berlin. In Berlin, both trends encountered each other, crossed, interpenetrated and provided fresh impetus. The stylistic labels "Constructivism", "Functionalism" and "Concretism" are only approximate designations of the result of that encounter. It was actually a matter of reducing graphic representation to its fundamental elements and of the ensuing efforts to use those elements in a manner that previous limits had hindered. Upon arriving in Germany, Russian artists found artistic considerations similar to their own, especially within the context of the Weimar (later Dessau) Bauhaus, and in Berlin and Hanover too.

It was El Lissitzky who played the major role in initiating contacts. From Berlin, he set up connections with Weimar and Hanover. In 1922, he made a speech on Constructivism in Düsseldorf. In Berlin, he published the Constructivist magazine *Wjechtsch-Gegenstand-Objekt*, together with Ilia Ehrenburg. There Lissitzky worked on projects for new typography and symbolic imagery, and in that city as well, he published his *Geschichte zweier Quadrate*, a Constructivist comic-strip that explains how Functionalism can serve as an easy-to-understand means of reproducing socialist subject-matter.

All the above confirms Lissitzky's great talent as an organizer and educator. However, his most important contribution to the new style's success was his *Prounenraum*, which he displayed at the Grosse Berliner Kunstausstellung in 1923 at the Lehrter Train Station. That first Constructivist environment should be taken as a picture-in-the-round. The pictorial elements are liberated from the boundaries defined by a two-dimensional surface and can occupy real space. The spectator does not face the picture; he is surrounded by it, he is in the picture. Consequently, since he cannot take in the entire picture at one time, but has to follow it around the room, which takes a few moments, a time element is obviously incorporated into the original spatial context.

El Lissitzky's *Prounenraum* is the outcome of his *Proun* paintings and gouaches, in which the pictorial elements used to give cohesion to the design's structure already seem to hang freely in mid-air, suspended in the perspective of an intangible, and therefore infinitely empty, simulation of pictorial space: they obey no defined cardinal point, and as a result, have no gravitational or static problems. "Proun" is an artistic term invented by El Lissitzky and is an abbrevation of *Pro Unovis*, which can be translated as "in favor of founding new forms in art". A speech made by Professor Hermann Minkovski, a Lithuanian-Russian, at the University of Göttingen in 1908, is quoted by Eberhard Steneberg: "The spatial and temporal concepts about which I should like to speak to you have their roots in experimental physics. That is their strength. Their trend is radical. From now on, space as such and time as such should melt away into the shadows, and only a sort of combination of both should remain sovereign".[10] These thoughts accurately foreshadowed the intentions of the Russian artists. In the era of the theory of relativity, they were searching for modes of expression appropriate to a non-Euclidean art, cancelling the boundaries formed by space and time, in order for those elements to function jointly in a new energetic model of the world. Thus the boundaries between space and time in the fine arts were dropped as well.

It took a great deal of courage to attempt to create works of art as dynamic and energetic models in keeping with the concepts mentioned above, which corresponded to ideas and conceptions forged by strictly Russian points of view and beliefs. Painting left the two-dimensional surface to become relief; painting and sculpture merged, giving rise to a new artistic category. Moreover, it was a specific trait of Russian avant-garde art to relate directly to the materials used. The partially controversial exchange of ideas between Malevich, Tatlin and Puni on this question, produced the following point of view: they were not pursuing "scientific" materialism as preached by Marxism but, in the words of Puni, "a painter has nothing to do with matter but with the embodiment of ideas". The term "embodiment" is the important word here: materials are considered as the incarnation of ideas. The materials used in a painting form the concrete and tangible "skin" of the idea portrayed. Metal is the embodiment of metal, wood of wood, color of color; and, in addition, a letter of the alphabet is an embodiment of that letter, rendered autonomous by its sensuous concreteness. The idea behind a pictorial image is revealed by the materials used to compose it, which appeal directly to the senses. Embodied by an image, an idea can be grasped both visually and tactilely. A painting is a palpable, concrete and living idea.

The palpability of the materials turn the painting into a relief, and a relief into space, not merely illusory space but into "genuine" space. This is what distinguishes the thinking of the Russians from that of the French Cubists, both with regard to artistic goals and to the results. In contrast to the elegance of the French work, the Russian "material" paintings, reliefs and counter-reliefs, seem rigged together and appear rough-looking and almost primitive. However, this is just what gives the impelling force to their thor-

oughly energetic impact. On the other hand, this rough-hewn quality made the Berlin public feel responsive to them. "Art is dead — long live Tatlin's machine art" is the inscription on the poster with which Grosz and Heartfield were photographed at the Berliner Dada-Messe of 1920.

A development took place for the Berlin painters in terms of perspective. The two

97 Henryk Berlewi: *Flaschenstilleben* (1922), body colors on pasteboard, 55×37 cm. Berlin, Staatliche Museen Preussischer Kulturbesitz, Nationalgalerie Berlewi: "The production principles of machines should thus be... the basis for contemporary painting. With the help of mechanization... of modes of painting, a whole new structural system is established."

98   Kasimir Malevich: *Gelb Orange Grün* (after 1914), oil on canvas, 71×64 cm. Amsterdam, Stedelijk Museum
Suprematism—the fundamental triumph of form over content. Basic elements are combined, without being linked to the picture frame, as if suspended in an imaginary universe.

99   Erich Buchholz: *Neue Tafel Nr. 14* (1923), wooden relief, 51×36 cm. Stuttgart, Staatsgalerie
Buchholz's reliefs are icons of faith in Pythagorean mathematics, which reveal universal reason according to the "secret" laws of artistic perception.

artists who did the most to spread the East European style in Berlin in 1922 und 1923 were the Russian El Lissitzky and the Hungarian Laszlo Moholy-Nagy. They already represented the synoptic phase of the development; both were ingenious pedagogues and therefore eminent mediators. Moholy-Nagy, especially, produced a synthesis based on his practical artistic experience and the tenets of his artistic theory. The theory he set forth proclaimed: from painting to relief to space to movement to space-in-motion to unity of space-motion-time. He used models of that functional unity in his Constructivist paintings; they are represented in a state of rest that is the product of eccentrically suspended kinetic signs – rotative symbols and guiding vectors – that oscillate in an equilibrated fashion. Moholy-Nagy's theory of a dynamic Constructivist power system led him to build the first functioning kinetic work of art in the history of art: his *Licht-Raum-Modulator*, which he began in 1922. The subsequent, logical outcome of his intellectual development can be inferred from the titles of his two books, which appeared in the Bauhaus series: *Malerei, Photographie, Film* (1925) and *Von Material zu Architektur* (1929).

Henryk Berlewi was the Polish artist whose work with *Mechano-Faktur* ("geometrical paintings") brought to light the aspect of mechanical structuralization that enables emotionally expressive values to be stereotyped and standardized. He proclaimed his theory by publishing a Manifesto in the weekly *Der Sturm* in 1924.

The patriarch of the East European avant-garde was Kasimir Malevich, who did not arrive in Berlin until 1927. His trip was under an ill-omen. A special exhibit of his work was set up at the Grosse Berliner Kunstausstellung at the Lehrter Train Station at the end of March, 1927. His Suprematist theory was like the primeval First Word of Creation: it provoked the genesis of the Russian avant-garde. Suprematism meant domination over the white Nothingness, according to Malevich. His work has a shock-producing effect that hides intense piety, but it is a piety that leads to a vision of emptiness, comparable to the vision of the German Romantic author

Jean Paul in his novel *Siebenkäs*: "*Rede des toten Christus vor dem leeren Weltgebäude*" ("Words by a dead Christ before the empty edifice of the world").

Outwardly, Malevich's theory of Suprematism seemed to express an atheistic metaphysical outlook, but in fact he was imbued with a fervent faith in fulfilled Nothingness, a mystical achievement of his imagination. On April 7, 1927, Malevich left Berlin to visit the Dessau Bauhaus; he returned the next day without having met anybody, since everyone had gone off on vacation the day before. On May 27, while he was living in the house of the sculptor Alexander von Riesen in Berlin, Malevich received a letter that convinced him to return to Leningrad immediately. He left a voluminous package behind at the Von Riesen house, with instructions that, should he not be heard from in the meantime, it could be opened in twenty-five years' time, and the contents dealt with as seemed best. He entrusted the architect Hugo Häring with the care of the paintings he left behind in Berlin. Malevich never came back. INCHUK, his art institute in Leningrad, was closed down in 1929, and his theory of Suprematism was dismissed as an objectionable artistic trend. Malevich died in 1935. At the end of World War II, the paintings he had left behind in Berlin became the property of the Stedelijk Museum in Amsterdam. Alexander von Riesen's house was destroyed by grenades during the siege of Berlin in 1945, but in 1953, while it was being demolished as a ruin, construction workers found Malevich's package undamaged in a corner of the cellar. It contained numerous manuscripts by the artist on his theory of Suprematism; these documents now also belong to the Stedelijk Museum in Amsterdam.

Among the manuscripts there was a draft of ideas for a film on Suprematism, which Malevich had planned to make with Hans Richter; however, it never came to that. Richter narrates: "But the most important matter linking me to Malevich was to express in motion his ideology of Suprematism as continuity. He had seen my abstract films and thought we could, or should, work together to realize that dream. There is no question but that we often met to work on the project. The

100, 101   Hans Richter: Two
designs for scenery from a ten-part
series for the abstract film *Präludium*
(1919), pencil on paper,
c. 100×58 cm. Berlin, Staatliche
Museen Preussischer Kulturbesitz,
Nationalgalerie

strange part about it is that, although I have
a good memory for minute details out of my
far past, I cannot remember at all working on
the film with Malevich".[11] That unaccom-
plished experiment is additional evidence of
the road that the painting of the East European avant-garde would have taken had it
been granted occasion to continue to develop
without interruption – the road to motion
pictures, movies. Malevich had found the
right collaborator in the person of Berlin's
Hans Richter, who was already working in
that direction. Stimulated by the handling of
counterpoint in Ferrucio Busoni's music, he
had been studying jointly with the Swede
Viking Eggeling (since 1918) the Constructivist form for abstract films. Eggeling moved
to Berlin in 1921, and that same year Richter's first abstract film, produced in collaboration with Eggeling, was ready to be
presented.

The ideas and work of another Berlin
artist, Erich Buchholz, a painter and creator
of utopic architecture, were confirmed by his
encounter with East European artists. Buchholz was born in Bromberg in 1891. By birth
he was himself East European and therefore
felt an inner kinship with the work of his colleagues. In a fashion similar to Malevich, he
came to Constructivism after having experienced nullity, nothingness: he was totally
shattered by the war at the front. Buchholz's
last realistic painting was created in 1919. It
is a large, unfinished Crucifixion, with no visible cross. The body of Christ is attached to
an imaginary triangle in tumbling space.
Once again, a dead Christ stands before the
empty edifice of the world – the painting is a
product of despair. Buchholz described its
creative development as his own "re-birth
through martyrdom". From that point on, he
began to concentrate on Constructivist form.

101

102 Jacoba van Heemskerck:
Landschaft, Bild I, (*c.* 1914), oil on
canvas, 80×100 cm. Berlin,
Berlinische Galerie
Sailboats, harbors and sea coasts are
the pictorial motifs of the Dutch
artist Jacoba van Heemskerck, a
member of the Sturm movement.

His paintings (woodcuts and painted wooden reliefs, done mainly in black, red and gold) are like icons of cosmic universal sensitivity. His forms, despite the rationalism of their pythagorean mathematical calculation, are very sensitive and reflect a religious nostalgia for a sustaining universal cause in which to believe. Buchholz termed the era of artistic and ideological upheaval, which he consciously experienced at the beginning of the 1920's, "the big caesura".

Fusion of Styles: The "Novembergruppe"

The German Revolution started when the sailors of Kiel revolted in November, 1918. In Germany, the term "November" became synonymous with revolution, and several new associations claiming to be in the spirit of the times, prefixed that term to their name, including the Novembergruppe. The initiative in forming the group was taken by the painters Max Pechstein, Georg Tappert, César Klein and Moriz Melzer. The sculptor Rudolf Belling and the architect Erich Mendelsohn, among others, participated in the meeting on December 3, 1918, that set up the group and named it. These men, with the other four, formed the core of the association. They were joined quickly by other artists who had survived the war – Expressionists, artists from the Sturm group, Berlin Dadaists – and, soon thereafter, by members of the Bauhaus. The idea had caught on because it held out the hope for a new community of cultural activities. Thus, Berlin's Novembergruppe was the first postwar collective movement of German artists, especially of the younger ones.

The motto on the exhibition catalogue of 1919 reads: "The Novembergruppe is a union of radical artists – radical in their use of new means of expression". The beginning of their circular of November 13, 1918, states: "The future of art and the seriousness of present times forces us, intellectual revolutionaries, (Expressionists, Cubists, Futurists), to unite and to collaborate closely with each other. Its closing lines continue: "as initial evidence of our agreement, we are planning a joint exhibition, which will take place in the larger cities of Germany and later of Europe". The rather lofty beginning of the text was an ideological allusion, whereas the conclusion was of a more practical nature. Luckily, the focus remained mainly pragmatic, and thus the Novembergruppe was able to flourish for more than a decade, until it was dissolved by the Nazis. The group left behind numerous documents concerning its cultural activities: minutes of meetings, catalogues, invitations to exhibitions, speeches, poetry readings, musical evenings and carnival balls. However, in her book on the Novembergruppe, [12] Helga Kliemann points out rightly that the group represented an incohesive ideological and stylistic whole. Disagreements on policy, members who left or feuded boisterously among themselves encouraged the internal contradictions. This was due, in the first place, to the fact that the founding artists, notwithstanding the pathetic distortions shaping their allegiance to revolutionary goals, had never understood Revolution in political terms (despite their pretensions), but merely in politico-cultural terms, in individualistic utopic terms, i.e., in accordance with their bourgeois origins and each in his own way. As a result, naturally, it was impossible to achieve harmony.

The far-reaching attraction of the Novembergruppe was rather that it was eminently suited to act as a lobby and means of achieving the concrete goals of artists. Thus, after a revolutionary beginning, the group remained an association for exhibitions, content to put up with compromises as a surrogate for harmony. The result of those compromises was variegated, which is an achievement in itself. It is a result that has been significantly reflected in the fine arts in Europe and in the United States since the mid-Twenties. In his memoirs, the poet Carl Zuckmayer describes life in Berlin at the time: "Berlin had scrubbed and repainted its facades. The nibbled down and crumbling aspect of many houses during the postwar years had disappeared. Everything looked new – almost too new, as if [it had] just [been] bought ready-made, but smart and spruced-up. 'Wer wird denn weinen' was still being sung but was completed by other popular tunes imported from

103   Ernst Fritsch: *Der Wächter*
(1921), oil on canvas, 100×88.5 cm.
Berlin, Berlinische Galerie
The watchman at night is the
epitome of human solitude. The
houses in the nocturnal city
resemble stage sets.

104   Walter Kampmann: *Der
Feldherr* (1922), oil on canvas, with
painted frame, 64×74 cm. Private
collection
A painting typical of the
Novembergruppe: the general's
head appears split and fragmented,
as though the energetically
intersecting lines were pulling it
asunder.

DER FELDHERR

105   César Klein: *Mann mit Pfeife*   ▷
(1920), oil on canvas, 115×90 cm.
Berlin, Berlinische Galerie
Klein, a co-founder of the
Novembergruppe, was a member of
its board of directors for many years
and the group's last chairman, in
office until 1931.

the United States, like 'Oh, yes, I have no bananas'. The exterior traits of the city – commerce, restaurants, street life – seemed less confused, less profiteering, and less adventurous. There was a new 'Kurfürstendamm society', whose parties were swankier and more exclusive than those of the good old 'sharks' of 1920, and who, therefore, resorted to an even more blatantly exaggerated and snobbish cynicism.... War and postwar were forgotten. They lived life and feared nothing".[13] Zuckmayer portrays the middle-class and petty-bourgeois establishment in the capital of the first German Republic, and continues: "Over and above all, Berlin was experiencing an intellectual, artistic, cultural and social boom, which, within little time, attracted the most distinguished and important personalities from all the other European capitals to that city".[14]

This boom was especially evident in literature, the theater and films. But by 1923, the fine arts had already gone beyond the high point of stylistic creativity, represented by Urban Expressionism, Dada and Constructivism. A period of consolidation followed, which lasted until the end of the 1920's. The technique of montage, the inventive contribution of the fine arts to the portrayal of our civilization, was being adapted to other artistic media. An example in narrative literature is Alfred Döblin's novel *Berlin Alexanderplatz*; examples in dramaturgy are the plays and staging of Bertolt Brecht; Erwin Piscator's decors are examples of such stage design, and there is a profusion of examples in the realm of film – our century's addition to the classical artistic media, a new field of expression, characterized by cutting and montage.

The distinguishing feature of the fine arts at this time was their medley of styles; the trend began in the early 1920's and increasingly gained new adherents, especially among the younger artists. The many stylistic discoveries from the preceding years – Expressionism, Cubism, Futurism, abstract art – which had been conscientiously separated according to the respective modes of interpretation at the time of their discovery, were now thrown into one pot, which served as a reservoir for stylistic syncretism. As a logical consequence, the original motifs were de-ideologized, but the mixture gave birth to an altogether particular style.

European artistic syncretism of the 1920's was a bastard art, which is probably the reason why it has not yet been correctly described, nor named, except in the field of design, where the label Art Deco has been adopted in the meantime. In the fine arts as well as in design, we are dealing with a mode of expression which – even in the eyes of laymen, in fact, especially in their eyes – brings to mind a cultural image of the "roaring, golden, horrible Twenties". Art historians resort to compound words like Cubo-Expressionism or Cubo-Futurism. Artists of the Twenties had their own, affectionately derisive term for this art: *Zackezismus*, literally "zigzagism", derived from the many *Zacken* ("zigzags") in pictorial composition.

The Novembergruppe was not only an association of Expressionists, Dadaists, Constructivists and abstract artists; it also attracted artists who wanted to fuse Cubist, Expressionist and Futurist elements into a new whole. It was their work that lent the exhibitions their specific characteristics, although even this style did not originate with the Novembergruppe. Herwarth Walden, who defined the concept of Expressionism in an extremely wide sense, considered such works of fusion as the principal representatives of the Expressionist trend. This is understandable if one considers the effect of the energetic high tension, on the verge of release, which was drastically brought to the fore in such artistic production.

Jacoba van Heemskerck (an artist on the staff of *Der Sturm*, for whom Walden set up at least seven one-woman shows) produced the prototypes in Berlin of this genre. By connecting monochrome planes of color with hard contour lines in her paintings of ships and sea coasts, she stylized those motifs into greatly simplified and effective, latticed structures that resemble stained glass windows. Her style, tersely and energetically punctuated, is comparable to the choreographic annotations on partitions for expressive German dances in the Mary Wigman line.

Despite the progressive "rediscovery" of European stylistic syncretism by art historians during the Twenties, it is still not appre-

106 Issai Kulvianski: *Meine Eltern*
(1925), oil on canvas, 150×125 cm.
Berlin, Berlinische Galerie
As he leaves services at the
synagogue, the artist's father
solicitously takes the arm of his
waiting wife; Kulvianski's father's
furniture factory can be seen in the
background.

ciated as a coherent phenomenon, which is certainly the reason why the names of the artists who represent it are less well known than those of their contemporary colleagues, whose stylistic origins can be more clearly defined. Since recognition of this trend will no doubt materialize someday, we present the work of several members of the November-gruppe, in an attempt to represent this style in all its variations, for the originality of a mixed style – as much to its advantage as to its disadvantage – is the wide range of its "keyboard".

Ernst Fritsch's earlier paintings epitomize the quintessence of Expressionism, by the relationships they establish among luminous colors (including gold) and Cubist forms that alternate with loosely defined planes of color.

107   Moriz Melzer: *Segnung* (1917),
oil on canvas with painted lamellae,
136×103 cm. Berlin, Staatliche
Museen Preussischer Kulturbesitz,
Nationalgalerie
Melzer's Cubo-Expressionist
painting was inspired by
Archipenko's counter-reliefs. The
lamellae give the painting a
changeable aspect that foreshadows
Op-Art effects.

His pictures represent a synthesis of the styles of Chagall, the Brücke and the Blaue Reiter movements.

Issai Kulvianski, a Lithuanian who belonged to the Novembergruppe's committee for hanging exhibits for a time, painted in a style on the knife edge between outgoing Expressionism and the beginnings of New Realism. His style shows the imprint of his Jewish origins, which explains his artistic kinship with Chagall and Jankel Adler. Almost every artist named in this context represents a special group on the extensive stylistic "keyboard".

César Klein's *Mann mit Pfeife* is a classical example of the fusion of Expressionist and Cubist imagery. The amalgamation is no longer either Expressionist or Cubist but, like an alloy, has new qualities of its own. This is true of Walter Kampmann's painting, *Der Feldherr*, too; it carries the specific imprint of Berlin in the European stylistic synthesis. His forms collide heavily in space; angular unswerving, straight stretches intersect taut vibration lines, and the quartered pictorial surface depicts a choreography of aggressivity. The painting is composed in tones of gold-red and black-blue and makes free use of Cubist forms to attain a prismatic fragmentation of the composition that carries over to the painted frame. This prismatic style, which strives to synthesize the figurative with the abstract, is an outstanding feature of the Berlin Novembergruppe's painting. Moriz Melzer continued the development in a splintered expressive direction that resulted in his lamellar pictures, which foreshadow the visual manipulation that would only reappear in the Op-art of the 1960's.

Arthur Segal gave the prismatic style a systematic imprint with the light-space-lattice paintings of his Berlin period. Combined with calculations for the compositions based on Pythagorean numerical figurations, the German-Pole, Stanislav Kubicki, painted in a dynamic Cubo-Expressionist style, which revealed its metaphysical, intellectual background in progressively clearer fashion later. Kubicki belonged to the select circle of artists around Franz Pfemfert's *Die Aktion*. Together with the other artists of that circle, he founded the Berlin group, Die Progres-

sive, whose most important members soon moved to Cologne. Otto Freundlich, whose importance has been increasingly recognized recently, also belonged to that group. The Cubo-Expressionist style of his early Berlin period, exemplified by his painting *Die Mutter*, also reveals a metaphysical inclination in its carefully structured colors, based on a radial design, and almost esoterically calculated values.

Cubist imagery was initially conceived on a theoretical level in France, but it was the particularity of German art to have translated it metaphysically and transcendentally into a prismatic structuralization of color. The clearest expression of the transcendental variant of prismatic Cubo-Expressionism can be found in the paintings of the German-American Lionel Feininger. Feininger, a Bauhaus master, was also a member of the Novembergruppe. He created the famous woodcut *Die Kathedrale des Sozialismus* as a signet for the Work Council for Art. Max Dungert's painting *Turm* resembles Feininger's work in the way it builds up radiating, interpenetrating, light zones of color, but it is far closer to abstract art than Feininger ever was.

In another vein, this synthesis of figuration and abstraction led to such paintings as Thomas Ring's *Aggression*. The door-size painting depicts a masquerade, magically hovering between festiveness and fear, glee and burlesque. The composition includes decorative elements too; in both its strong points and weaknesses this painting corresponds wholly to widespread conceptions of the style of art in the 1920's.

After the Nazis came to power, they prohibited Ernst Fritsch from working or exhibiting. Issai Kulvianski was pursued by the Gestapo and emigrated to Palestine, via Italy, in 1933; most of the works from his Berlin period were lost. César Klein retired to the country, since he no longer felt secure in the hostile atmosphere of Berlin. This was also true of Walter Kampmann. Max Dungert, who tried to keep his head above water in Berlin by running a private art school and who was thus able to help some of his colleagues, was shot under martial law by the soldiers of the Russian occupation troops, who mistook him for a wanted Nazi.

108 Arthur Segal: *Helgoland*
(1923), oil on canvas, with painted
frame, 101×130 cm. Berlin,
Berlinische Galerie
Segal's faceted style of painting is the
result of systemizing the
Cubo-Expressionist mode of
composition. Natural light seems to
be disrupted by a prism into the
square structures.

109 Nikolaus Braun: *Strassenszene*
(1921), oil on fiberboard,
74×103 cm. Berlin, Berlinische
Galerie
The Hungarian Nikolaus Braun, a
pupil of the Rumanian Arthur Segal,
adopted the latter's structuralized
surface design, but transformed it
into a means of conveying the many
facets of street life in Berlin.

110 Otto Freundlich: *Die Mutter* ▷
(1921), oil on canvas, 120×100 cm.
Berlin, Berlinische Galerie
Freundlich: "The interdependence
of forms in nature is not sublime;
the sublimeness is rather its somatic
manifestation beyond the physical,
which permeates the ENTIRE
universe. We acknowledge another
nature in nature, which permeates
the ENTIRE universe."

111 Stanislav Kubicki: *Der Eintretende* (1919), oil on pasteboard, 95×45 cm., Neustadt an der Weinstrasse, Private collection
The German Pole Kubicki was a co-founder of Bunt, a group of Expressionists in Poznan, and the first to exhibit their work in Berlin. He founded Die Progressiven group with Freundlich, Hausmann and others.

112 Max Dungert: *Turm* (1922), ▷ oil on canvas 180×90 cm. Berlin, Berlinische Galerie
Berlin artists succeeded in giving cubic forms a transcendental sense, which corresponded to Central and East European mentalities but would have seemed paradoxical to the French.

113 Thomas Ring: *Aggression* ▷▷ (1928), oil on canvas, Berlin, Berlinische Galerie
Ring, a friend of Walden's, was a painter, poet and cabaret artist who worked with Piscator's theater, wrote for the Workers' Theater and also published learned books on astrology.

Stanislav Kubicki emigrated in 1934; he joined the Polish Resistance when the war broke out and was captured and executed by the Gestapo in Poland. Otto Freundlich, a German artist of Jewish origin, moved to Paris in 1928. He was interned by the French in 1939, because he was German by birth and thus considered a foreign enemy. He managed to flee to the Pyrenees, but the Germans arrested him in Saint-Martin-de-Fenouillet and deported him to Poland. His traces were lost there, but presumably he was killed at the Maidanek concentration camp. Arthur Segal, Rumanian by birth, emigrated to Majorca in 1933; from there he went to London, where he opened a private art school; today his work is better known in England than in Germany.

Such was destiny of those artists who belonged to a generation that had just begun to acquire renown in the 1920's: their chances were nipped in the bud, which may explain why so many of them have been forgotten to date.

Urban Realism

As early as 1922, Paul Westheim, an author living in Berlin who wrote on art, entitled an essay he published in his own magazine, *Das Kunstblatt*, with the question "New Naturalism?". A few years later, he published the results of his survey "Is Expressionism Dead?" and set off a violent debate. Undeniably, the meaningful, disruptive versatility of styles during the Twenties gave rise to an Urban Realism, characterized essentially by the clarity of its glassy rigidity, comparable to the crystallization of all previous motion in painting into frozen energy. This tendency continued to make inroads on art and, by the end of the decade, stood in the foreground of the art scene.

At the end of the Twenties, two aspects of Realism stand out above the others; a glazed stillness and a clear-as-glass distinctness or definition that reproduces every detail minutely. The emphasis on stillness provided a means of conveying the idyllic — one of the tendencies of the moment — while the over-exaggeration of unsightly details, nigh to caricaturization, was more in keeping with the tendency of giving socially critical portrayals of various milieus. Realism in the Twenties oscillated between the two poles, i.e., the inner peace of the idyllic and the aggressivity of social criticism. Often a mixture of both traits is evident in these works of art.

Art in Berlin could already rely on a distinctly Realist tradition that can be traced back, without interruption, to the beginning of the nineteenth century. The Realist Adolf von Menzel was the most important of the nineteenth-century artists in Berlin. When he died in 1905, many artists of the next generation in Berlin carried on the Realist trend in art in their fashion. Since its foundation, the Berliner Secession had included a Realist wing. Max Liebermann's North German "silver-lined, rain-clouded" Impressionism presents a certain decidedly realistic strain also.

The work of some of the Realists of the socially critical wing of Realism who had already made a name for themselves by the beginning of the twentieth century, was very influential into the 1920's. Käthe Kollwitz, the wife of a family doctor in the poorer section of north Berlin, sympathized with the want and poverty of workers' families. Her pity stimulated her to produce accusatory single prints and print cycles. She had already acquired renown by the end of the nineteenth century through her cycle of etchings, *Ein Weber Aufstand*, completed in 1898; they were followed by the *Bauernkrieg* series of 1908. The plight of the people remained her theme in the postwar years, when she lent her creative strength to workers' self-help organizations in the form of publicity posters, distinguished by their graphic black-and-whiteness and monumental conciseness. The captions read: "Free the Prisoners", "Hunger", "Help Russia", "War on War", "Bread".

Hans Baluscheck was a contemporary of hers. Labelled, at the beginning of the twentieth century, by Emperor William II and his courtiers, a "gutter artist" (like Kollwitz), Baluscheck's scrupulously observed milieu portrayals reported on life in the workers' quarters, at the factory doors and in garden allotments from the beginning of the century to the early 1930's.

114   Oskar Fischer: *Blitzmaschine* (1922), oil on canvas, 80×66 cm. Private collection
The Sturm artist Fischer has been forgotten today. The *Blitzmaschine* is his only preserved work known to us; it is a poetical metaphor on machines in a Cubo-Expressionist style, with a slight hint of Dadaism.

Such realism in painting, already backed by somewhat of a tradition in the postwar years, encountered new stimuli in the Dada trend of the 1920's. The particular features that gave Realism, in Berlin of the Twenties, such an explosive effect can be traced to that contact. It developed into a mixture of sloppiness and precision, of challenging opinions and unfriendly aloofness that was purposefully insulting, proletarian affectation and snobbishness, leather jackets and tuxedos – impudence, pep, sensitivity and sentimentality. A sentimental pathos had been aroused but was expressed through clenched teeth: "*Ach Brüder, lasst euch uns zur Warnung sein/Und bittet Gott, er möge uns verzeihn*" ("Oh brothers, let us be a warning unto you/and pray God that he forgive us") [*Dreigroschenoper*].

Industriebauern by Georg Scholz and *Grauer Tag* by George Grosz are two paintings that illustrate the transition from Dada to Urban Realism. Scholz participated in the Dada movement in Berlin from Karlsruhe. *Industriebauern* is a vicious satire that relies on two mutually intensifying stylistic means to achieve its vehemently sarcastic effect: the Dadaist method of introducing new elements into painting with collage and photomontage, and the overly distinct "photographic" portrayal that gives a detailed image of people and objects captured statically in space.

It was natural for the Urban Realists of the Twenties to assimilate photography into their work. This did not mean that they copied photos, but rather that by painting, they could accentuate the new vision of reality that

115 Georg Schrimpf: *Bildnis Maria Uhden* (1918), oil on canvas, 65×48 cm. Private collection
Schrimpf was married to the artist Maria Uhden. This portrait marks the beginnings of Magic Realism: enormous inquiring eyes, a calm pose, graphically depicted silence—a human still life.

116 Hans Baluschek: *Bahnhofshalle* (1929), pastel, 99×70 cm. Berlin, Berlinische Galerie
Berlin in the Twenties: a view of the railroad station.

116

117 Käthe Kollwitz: *Deutsche Heimarbeit* (1925), lithograph, 34.3×42.7 cm. Berlin, Berlinische Galerie
The print was created as a poster for the Deutsche Heimarbeit Exhibition in Berlin-Alt-Moabit, an exhibit sponsored by the Society for Social Reform.

had inadvertently crept into everyday consciousness through photography. As a result, commonplace truths became recognizable in these rather spectral, exotic forms.

Photography was the first of the technological visual media to make home delivery of a secondhand reality to serve as a stereotyped surrogate for the original and, via film and television, it has radically changed our habits as spectators by disastrous manipulation.

Photography depicts a slice of reality "canned" in a picture. The can's contents incline to be posed and banal. Being photographed encourages stiffness; stiffness creates distance, and distance makes all that is familiar appear alien. Stiffness or rigidity, however, is exactly what Urban Realism took from photography as a source of inspiration in order to portray the remoteness of all that is near, and the unfamiliarity of the intimate.

Urban Realism of the Twenties paints man's alienation from his fellow man and from his environment. George Grosz's *Grauer Tag* is an example of that alienation: land-register officials and war cripples pass each other by in the city, unfeelingly and unsolicitously. They are separated by a wall. The doll motif, the robots and the soulless machines that appear in the Dadaist watercolors of Grosz and Schlichter gradually began to acquire Realistic traits.

Urban Realism in Berlin, the painting of alienation, reached its high point in 1929, when Otto Dix completed his triptych *Grossstadt* – an *ex-negativo* tribute to Berlin. The scenes and figures are pointedly exaggerated; the colors shine in sumptuously colorful tones of pearly iridescence. The hieratic-

sacral shape of the triptych serves a a ritualistic basis for depicting a celebration of Man, staged to satisfy the individual in society. A Black Mass, a vulgar Mass, takes place: an ego Mass of savage Philistines amidst the counterfeit pomp of glitter and glamor, a festive display of absolute insipidity.

Alienation is self-alienating and, at the same time, estranges us from others. This can be seen in portraits done in Berlin at the end of the Twenties. The portraits painted by Christian Schad are masterful examples of this genre. Brilliantly executed on a technical level, they portray the epitome of glazed inner rigidity. Schad, a former Dada dandy, transferred his dandyism from Dadaism to Realism. The contrast between simulated insensitivity and sensuous involvement gives the

118 Georg Scholz: *Industriebauern* (1920), oil and collage on panel, 98×70 cm. Wuppertal-Elberfeld, Von der Heydt-Museum
Realism criticizing the times, using montage

119 George Grosz: *Grauer Tag* (1921), oil on canvas, 115×80 cm. Berlin, Staatliche Museen Preussischer Kulturbesitz, Nationalgalerie
Grosz: "My art, in any case, should serve as rifle and sword; I would consider my drawing pens as useless as blades of straw if they did not participate in the fight for freedom".

120   Hannah Höch: *Roma* (1925),
oil on canvas, 90×106 cm. Berlin,
Berlinische Galerie
The transition from Dada to
Realism: Hannah Höch translates
her experience with photomontage
into painting. Tourism in
Rome—Asta Nielsen's long arm
banishes Mussolini from the picture.

119

impression of wallowing in contradiction, of a perceptible anesthetizing of sensitivity, caused by increased awareness, an ether intoxication, a position on the borderline of calculated schizophrenia. This impression corresponds exactly to the feelings, aggressions, affinities and fears that resulted from the spectator attitude of urban intellectuals in the last years of the Weimar Republic.

An explicit example of a portrait of alienated mankind is Otto Dix's portrait of the journalist Sylvia von Harden, depicted with short hair like a man, a monocle, a mini-dress and wrinkled silk stockings, sitting at a little marble table in the Romanische Café; another example is Rudolf Schlichter's portrait of the leather-jacketed playwright Bertolt Brecht, who brought the principle of cutting and montage to the stage and incorporated the technique of alienation into his plays as an appropriate expression for estrangement.

Jeanne Mammen's *Revuegirls* was created around 1929 or 1930. It is a painting full of charming *tristesse*. The individuality of the faces of both girls is cancelled by the uniformity of their music-hall costumes. Dance troupes that were beginning to march in step.

The glazed distinctness of these paintings of frozen sentiments is also visible in the portrayal of landscapes, for instance, the bleak houses amid rubble in Franz Lenk's *Hinterhäusern* or the street scenes by Gustav Wunderwald – portrayals of Berlin, seen through the eyes of the 'little man'. Wunderwald was described by Paul Westheim, as the "Berlin Utrillo", in Westheim's first review for the *Das Kunstblatt*. Today Berlin looks like it was depicted in those paintings: Berlin being demolished; Berlin being built and rebuilt – Berlin as a stage set. It is certainly no coincidence that German film – the UFA-film – started out on its road to success from Berlin. For stage sets, above all for films, are clearly the architectural expression of our century's urban society. Dwelling quarters have replaced homes in that society, and the inhabitants of those areas are as interchangeable as the dwellings themselves: a characteristic of urban society is multiple changes of residence.

Exodus

In autumn 1924, a man forty-one years old arrived in Berlin from Vienna, carrying a

123 Otto Dix: *Bildnis der Journalisten Sylvia von Harden* (1926), oil on canvas, 121×89 cm. Paris, Centre national d'art et de culture Georges Pompidou
Verity as exaggerated realism; appealing "ugliness" results from an overemphasis on the individual's mimical and physiognomic traits.

124 Rudolf Schlichter: *Bildnis Bert Brecht* (*c.* 1926-27), oil on canvas, 75.5×46 cm. Munich, Städtische Galerie im Lenbachhaus
Brecht came to Berlin in 1925, where he frequented the Schlichter restaurant that belonged to the artist's brother. The most important physiognomic detail in this portrait is Brecht's leather jacket, making him look like a proletarian.

125 Rudolf Schlichter:
Verstümmelte Proletarierfrau (*c.* 1924),
pencil, 63.2×47.9 cm. Berlin,
Berlinische Galerie
Schlichter, like his contemporary
Grosz, was a brilliant draftsman
given to social criticism; ferocious
anger guided his pencil.

126 Jeanne Mammen: *Revuegirls*
(*c.* 1929), oil on pasteboard,
64×47 cm. Berlin, Berlinische
Galerie
Kurt Tucholsky about Jeanne
Mammen: "Her figures are
clean-cut, and spring forth from the
paper [complete] with skin and
hair."

127 Franz Lenk: *Berliner Hinterhäuser* (1929), oil on canvas, 64×110 cm. Berlin, Berlinische Galerie
Berlin in the Twenties—view of a condemned house

128 Karl Hubbuch:
Jannowitzbrücke (1926), etching,
23×30.5 cm. Berlin, Berlinische
Galerie
The picture serves as social
testimony; the crayon records the
details.

129 Gustav Wunderwald:
Berlin—Travemünder Strasse (1927),
oil on canvas, 61×85 cm. Berlin,
Berlinische Galerie
Berlin in the Twenties—a view of a
factory

127

portfolio with around a thousand portrait drawings. As he himself later remembered, within a week, he had sold "oddly enough, nineteen to each one" of the editorial staffs of *Tage-Buch*, *Literarische Welt* and *Querschnitt* respectively. The man was Dolbin, whose real name was Benedikt Fred Pollack; his most outstanding physical feature was an enormous nose, which he was prone to exaggerate affectionately in his self-portraits. Pollack's successful sales experience encouraged him to settle down permanently in Berlin in 1925. From then on he could be seen everywhere that anything was happening. He soon became one of the best-known press artists of the Twenties and acquired the nickname of "the headhunter". He created thousands of sketches, portraying almost all of the celebrities in Berlin during the critical years of the late Twenties and early Thirties: composers, dancers, authors, painters, actors, producers, film stars, boxers, wrestlers, diplomats and industrial leaders.

In his Preface to a catalogue, Will Schaber notes: "In November, 1933, the 'non-Aryan' Dolbin was suspended from the Nazified Reich's German press association. In March, 1934, he received a communication forbidding him to publish more than four drawings a month. In February, 1935, the Reich's Fine Arts Department forbade him to continue to exercise his 'professional activity' as a 'commercial artist'. But Dolbin had not waited for matters to get to that point; he was already in the midst of preparing to emigrate. In late autumn 1935, in his fifty-second year, he and his third wife, the former Berlin actress Ellen Herz, and her daughter landed in New York." [15]

Many of those he had drawn met with the same fate: Bertolt Brecht, Marlene Dietrich, Lion Feuchtwanger, Valeska Gert, George Grosz, Alfred Kerr, Fritz Kortner, Fritz Lang, Lotta Lenya, Max Reinhardt, Arnold Schönberg, Kurt Weill, Franz Werfel — all were forced to emigrate, and their names stand for countless more. The representatives of culture in Germany were thrown out of the country or killed in concentration camps. In a variation on the classical saying by Friedrich Nietzsche, it was an rejection of German intellect in favor of German stupidity.

130 Dolbin: *Fritz Lang* (*c.* 1929-30), pencil, 28.5×22.5 cm. Berlin, Berlinische Galerie
Fritz Lang (b. Vienna, 1890; d. Beverly Hills, 1968), a film director whose work includes *Dr. Mabuse, der Spieler* (1922), *Die Nibelungen* (1924) and *Metropolis* (1926), emigrated to the United States during the Third Reich.

131 Dolbin: *Joachim Ringelnatz im* ▷ *Matrosenanzug* (*c.* 1928), pencil, 28.5×22.5 cm. Berlin, Berlinische Galerie
Ringelnatz [Hans Bötticher] (b. 1889, Wurzen; d. Berlin, 1934), a lyricist and cabaret artist who wrote poems in the spirit of street ballads.

132 Dolbin: *Mary Wigman* ▷ (*c.* 1929-30), pencil, 28.5×22 cm. Berlin, Berlinische Galerie
Mary Wigman (b. 1886, Hanover; d. Berlin, 1975), a dancer. Her first performance in 1919 set the tone for a new rhythmical and expressive style of dance.

Those Germans who followed the piper entangled themselves inextricably in their blameworthy doom, and were then unable to free themselves from its shackles.

"Even today, perhaps more so than ever, we are making a mistake in historical awareness by considering January 30, 1933, as the exact date on which the Nazi era began. This date indicates a turning point in German history. But just like a turning point in the life's work of an artist, which can hardly be explained without considering external and internal reasons, the historical date 1933 did not come out of the clear blue sky. Every person still in possession of his mind and spirit could see and understand the symptoms of the change long before it came to pass. Moreover, it should also be noted here that the whole world did not come to an end on January 2, 1930; the perversions of the National Socialist leaders and their hirelings were translated into action and incorporated into everyday life step by step." [16]

Instead of adding to all the inadequate interpretations of events and their back-

Mary Wigman
Todesruf

ground, we prefer to set forth another passage from Carl Zuckmayer's memoirs:

The disconsolate crowds had long since run out of 'Berlin jokes', sandwich fillers and coal, and had hardly any strength left to complain or cause a row because some agency was closing early, due to overwork, or because rumor had it that potato prices were again on the rise while they were standing in line waiting for their starvation wages.

Throughout Germany, as well as in Berlin, they were standing in front of the employment offices, the pay registers, the consumer co-ops, the factories that could only employ single shifts, the shafts and pits of closed mines. More than six million of them were standing around that way in Germany during the years 1931 to 1933 – the unemployed, condemned to inactivity and to waiting, and progressively, condemned to hopelessness, dissatisfaction

Veleska Gert   Valeska Gert   „Koloratursängerin"

133 Dolbin: *Valeska Gert*
(*c.* 1930), pencil, 28.6×22.3 cm.
Berlin, Berlinische Galerie
Valeska Gert [Gertrude Samosch]
(b. 1892, Berlin; d. Kampen on the
island of Sylt, 1978), a dancer who
invented the Expressionist
"grotesque" dance. After emigrating
to the United States, she opened the
Beggar's Bar in New York.

with everything – with the world in which they lived, with the State that laboriously managed to keep them barely alive, with themselves, and with their patience.

... The 'little people', who had had a relatively easy life during the Imperial era, had had no part in the 'boom' and felt bitter against anyone 'from above', against the 'big shots' in the ruling parties, who represented Democracy, as well as against the financial circles that still lived in wealth and luxury and lulled their secret fears by hoping for a 'new wave of prosperity'. It was out of these middle-class people, who refused to let themselves be 'proletarianized', and who would have considered it a disgrace to be a 'Red Socialist', that the

'Brown Shirts' emerged, the National Socialists who called themselves a German workers' party, a German folk movement, and who attracted an enormous number of members and followers. Not even Father Hindenburg, who, in the spring of 1932 had won re-election against Hitler as Reich's President with a considerable majority, was in a position to inspire the masses with real confidence – and rightly so, for the noble old man, who for years had retained his democratic Chancellor Brüning and refused to have that 'Bohemian corporal' (as he called Hitler) in the government, had himself become, unconsciously, a pawn in the hands of diverging economic and political interests.

134 Karl Hofer: *Arbeitslose* (1932),
oil on canvas, 167×172 cm.
Cologne, Baukunst-Galerie (Hofer
Bequest)

Heavy industry and the *Reichslandbund*, an organization protecting the agrarian interests of big landowners, mainly in East Germany, were enemies, and it was through the gap between these two hardened fronts that Hitler was able to slip into power, like an eel. [17]

Zuckmayer, who wrote his memoirs after the war ended, had emigrated in 1938 from Austria to Switzerland, and thence to the United States.

The misery of social developments is depicted in the best examples of Berlin art. Carl Hofer's painting *Arbeitslose* (1932) is like an impressive, anticipatory illustration of Zuckmayer's commentary. In 1934 Hofer, who had been a professor until then, was suspended and forbidden to work or to exhibit. He was expelled from the Prussian Academy of Art in 1938. Afterwards, Hofer, who had painted mainly landscapes of the Tessin, serene maidens and harlequins, created gloomy visions of his impressions of the times. He entitled his paintings *Schwarzmondnacht, Fliegeralarm, Ruinenlandschaft, Totentanz.*

Werner Heldt was thirty at the time; his charcoal drawing of 1935 is a melancholy satire portraying a parade of nonentities: rows of empty flags and empty slogans before rows of houses with rows of empty windows. Felix Nussbaum's *Selbstbildnis mit Judenstern* speaks dramatically for itself, especially since all accusations seem to be suppressed behind the objectively restrained form of graphic representation.

Rudolf Schlichter's painting, *Blinde Macht,* is an allegory of iron-clad insanity. The

135 Werner Heldt: *Aufmarsch der Nullen (Meeting)* (c. 1935), charcoal drawing, 46.5×63 cm. Berlin, Berlinische Galerie

136 Felix Nussbaum: *Selbstbildnis mit Judenpass* (1943), oil on canvas, 54×47 cm. Osnabrück, Kulturgeschichtliches Museum ▷

137 Rudolf Schlichter: *Blinde Macht* (1937), oil on canvas, 177×100 cm. Berlin, Berlinische Galerie
The Nazis forbade Schlichter to exhibit. His work, like that of many other artists named in this book, was removed from German museums.

138 John Heartfield: *Wie im Mittelalter—So im Dritten Reich* (May 31, 1934), photomontage for the *Arbeiter Illustrierte Zeitung*, Prague, (photo: courtesy of Mrs. Gertrud Heartfield)
From its Dadaist beginnings Heartfield developed his style to a mastery of photomontage that took National Socialism as its target. He fled to Prague in 1933, lost his German citizenship in 1934 and fled to Paris in 1935.

painting takes up a vision already captured in a drawing by Alfred Kubin shortly after the beginning of the century. While the oppressively titanic fury of war in Kubin's drawings still contains a trace of belief in war's sublimity, the product of Schlichter's mighty imagination is nothing but horrifying and disgusting. The painting is not significant because it is a masterpiece, for it is not one. It is not even especially well painted, nor was it supposed to be especially well painted. Its importance lies in the fact that it reveals the climate of the times during which it was created. The painting is parched and tough; the colors are blistered and smutty, as if they had been scorched. Schlichter had become well-known in the Twenties for the energetic and audacious opposition contained in his drawings. In this painting, he incorporated the only feelings — helpless rage and fierce despair — that remained in his heart.

Painting in Berlin during the first thirty years of this century was no innocent bouquet of flowers. Among the flowers depicted in all hues were some containing potent poison — that is what makes them so fascinating. Art is an indicator. It does not directly reproduce reality but is a reflection of the common reality experienced by people living at the time of its creation. This is what gives the diagnostic value to urban art; it is the imprint of our own civilization. Schlichter's painting was not created during World War II but before it, in 1937. Ten years earlier, Paul Reich, an outsider among psychoanalysts, had written: "If culture is a sublimation and not a collective neurosis, all the rest should evolve by itself".

Only what is worth knowing about Herwarth Walden's later destiny remains to be mentioned. In 1932, he moved to Moscow, where he was followed by his last secretary, Ellen Bork; they married in Moscow. It was his fourth mariage. As of 1937, he published essays in the *Das Wort*, a magazine for emigrants published by Bertolt Brecht, Lion Feuchtwanger, and Willi Bredel. In an essay of 1938, entitled "Vulgar Expressionism", he defended German Expressionism against Fascist slander. He was arrested in Moscow by the Russian State Police on March 13 of that year. He died of starvation, on October 31, 1938, imprisoned at Saratov on the Volga. This chapter on the fine arts is dedicated to his memory.

English Titles of the Works Illustrated in the Following Chapter

III SCULPTURE

Joachim Heusinger von Waldegg

Preface

After having acquired worldwide recognition during the nineteenth century, the significance of sculpture in Berlin had dwindled, by the turn of the twentieth century, to an average regional level. The lavish work representative of the William II era had averted attention from new scopes of activity for a long time. The progressive artistic strains that emerged during the first third of our century transcended confining categories, and it hardly seems relevant to consider them in terms of the individual realms of art. Yet rhythm, tempo and responsiveness to change are more difficult to detect in sculpture than in its "sister" arts. Revolutionary deviations proved to be less enduringly influential and relatively short-lived, as is shown by the carvings created by the Expressionists of Der Sturm and by Berlin's Novembergruppe after 1918. Finally, the resistance the materials involved offered to the sculptor and his inherent dependence on the painstaking techniques of his craft were also important factors retarding the assimilation of innovations in sculpture, a genre in which tradition and progress carry on a continuous dialogue.

In Berlin, realistic figurative sculpture was in the majority; it was based on the traditional Classicism of Berlin, a style that inspired many sculptors and continues to do so even nowadays. Therefore, it comes as no surprise that a retrospective show (in 1978) of sculpture in Berlin over the last two hundred years[1] represented the figurative tradition exclusively, with special emphasis on the substantive and moral aspects in the representation of human beings: "on archetype and imitation". It might be worthwhile to trace parallels and constants up to present times in work based on similar traditions, but it is much more significant, as is obvious after just a glance at the various ways similar motifs have been handled, to consider the shifts in accent and the changes in interpretation.

Political and social changes had an influence on the substance of academic figurative sculpture, leading to the redefinition and new formulations of traditional themes. An anti-Classical "Primitivism" also emerged temporarily, in opposition to academic traditions; it was exemplified by the "mechanical" dynamics of some of Rudolf Belling's figures, the wooden sculptures by Ernst Barlach and the Brücke artists, or the architecture of a head made of structural elements without bulk in the work of Hans Uhlmann.

An invigorating element of tension was provided by the few experiment-minded, progressive artists who stood out at the time among the sculptors steeped in traditions. For a while Franz Metzner and Ernesto de Fiori, Wilhelm Lehmbruck and Alexander Archipenko, Laszlo Moholy-Nagy and Rudolf Belling worked side by side in Berlin. They are impressive proof of the varied modes of expression and tolerant working climate in a city so greatly shaped by the art trade. Ernst Barlach complained at times that the Berlin public was "taken in by Secessionist kitsch" yet, at the same time, he felt very indebted to his art dealer, Bruno Cassirer: "If Cassirer hadn't discovered me," he remarked, the year after his trip to Russia, "I would probably have turned into something like a *Simplicissimus* illustrator."[2] Thanks to enterprising art dealers, especially during the early Twenties, Berlin developed into a center for the distribution of new artistic ideas, also in the realm of sculpture, as evidenced by Moholy-Nagy's experiments with light, Naum Gabo's constructions of transparent materials or Alexander Calder's wire sculptures, which attracted so much attention at an exhibition of 1929 at J.B. Neumann and Nierendorf's art gallery in Berlin. Berlin welcomed experiments with long unheard-of enthusiasm, thus encouraging an influx of talent from all parts of Germany and Eastern Europe.

During the Twenties, sculpture spilled over into the neighboring disciplines of architecture, design, theater and film. Architecture, furniture and interior design became flexible and functional, as exemplified by the light, transparent appearance of tubular steel furniture, which replaced cubic, bulky types of furniture. Very quickly, it became obvious that the distance between sculpture and the turn-of-the-century trends, including the pathos that ear-marked monument style, had widened. Alfred Flechtheim's art and society journal, *Der Querschnitt*, used a neo-objective, snotty tone to parody, with perceptive understatement, the sculptures commissioned at

139 Ernst Barlach: *Der Berserker* (1910), bronze, H. 55.5 cm. Hamburg, Ernst Barlach Haus Tension generated by directional contrasts, symmetry and asymmetry, active and passive masses. Intensified movement as the expression of ecstatic emotion. Cubically massive, tautened form.

the beginning of the century by William I for the Siegesallee. At best, the sparse attempts by established sculptors to pay tribute to the young Republic (for example, portraits of the Reich's president, Friedrich Ebert, in 1925 and 1927 respectively, by Georg Kolbe and Rudolf Belling) testified to the artists' courageous sincerity.[3] Only the representatives of the National Socialist regime were again to revert to the abandoned requisites of historically spectacular representation, with the avowed intention of awakening appropriately patriotic devotion.

The Secession Movement: Tradition and Avant-Garde

A fleeting glance at the catalogue of the twentieth exhibition by Berlin's Secession group in 1910 is enough to ascertain that, among the pieces listed, very few went beyond the framework of a moderately reformed Classical tradition — in fact, only Ernst Barlach's "Gothically" expressive wooden figure, *Der Berserker*. The same year, at the Parisian Salon d'Automne, Wilhelm Lehmbruck exhibited his *Grosse Stehende*, defined by Julius Meier-Graefe in terms of "antique tranquillity".[4] Henceforth, sculpture in Berlin was shaped by the tension between Expressionism and the renewal of Classical traditions. To reduce the debate to the influence of two sculptors only — Rodin and Maillol — would be an inadmissible oversimplification. Almost all the sculptors of Berlin's Secession movement were temporarily influenced by the reforms of the turn of the century, including the movement's two most famous members: Lehmbruck and Barlach.

The mainly decorative functions of *Jugendstil* ("Art Nouveau") sculpture were too restrictive for those artists seeking new forms of expression. Barlach's anti-Classical esthetics ran counter to the goals of the majority of the Secession's members. "Truly, beauty and charm are not our force, nor strength," he wrote in 1895, from Paris, to his friend Friedrich Düsel, "rather the contrary — ugliness, demoniac passion, the grotesque quality of size and, above all, humor, with its host of original shapes." Käthe Kollwitz spoke in

140   Karl Schmidt-Rottluff: *Arbeiter mit Ballonmütze* (*c.* 1920), wood, 66 cm. Berlin, Brücke-Museum
A theme from the postwar era, handled without the acute verity of contemporary Realist painting (e.g. Dix, Grosz); refined treatment of the surfaces in contrast to the roughly hewn sculpture of the Brücke group.

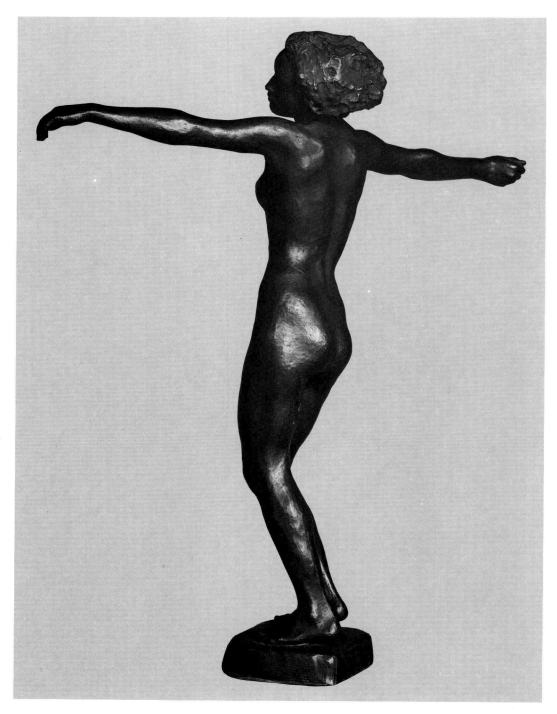

141 Georg Kolbe: *Tänzerin* (1911-12), bronze, H. 154 cm. Berlin, Staatliche Museen Preussischer Kulturbesitz, Nationalgalerie
Gracefully spirited; flowing body motion captured in weightless gestures. Inspired by the ideal of physical liberation in *Jugendstil* ("Art Nouveau").

similar terms about the emaciated figures of Berlin's proletarians, which were her speciality; she explained that it was the "feeling" that these figures were "beautiful" which inspired her in the first place. [5]

The material at sculptors' disposal was redefined; manual work with wood, as practiced by Barlach and the Brücke artists Heckel, Pechstein and Schmitt-Rottluff, supplied new stimulation and emphatically con-

142 Bernhard Hoetger: *Sent M'Ahesa* (1917), gilt bronze, H. 38 cm. Graphisches Kabinett Wolfgang Werner KG, Bremen An ingenious combination of elements from diverse stylistic trends, including Art Nouveau and Expressionism: stylized contours and a preference for exotic— "Egyptian"—features.

to the catalogue of the 1912 exhibition Ausdrucksplastik at the Mannheim Kunsthalle, "but the number of sculptors who consciously oppose the conventional and cultivate new feats is growing." Kolbe's appraisal was corroborated by the fact that young sculptors no longer accepted State commissions and orders for representational work. The naked single figure, rippling with dance movements, is central to Kolbe's work, no doubt reflecting the influence of the reformers' ideal of liberating the body, which he sought to define on a higher level: he carried through a variation on the figure of the dancer Nijinsky for the Heinrich Heine monument in Frankfurt-am-Main. The terms chosen by the art critics to describe Kolbe's work around 1910 – simplicity, strict forms, statically balanced construction – could be applied to Maillol's bronze figures as well. Maillol's influence progressively supplanted Rodin's although the latter had still been honored at the exhibitions of the German Secession group at the turn of the century. Kolbe achieved a skillful synthesis, fusing together all the elements of varied models, which, no doubt, was the basis of his long-lasting success.

During the first decades of the twentieth century, sculptors had reached an impasse between academic requirements and the goals of reform; a thorough reconsideration of traditions was necessary to overcome the resulting stagnation. Wilhelm Lehmbruck, a product of this situation, first managed to extirpate himself by a detour via the methods of coping with form of the Parisian avantgarde (Brancusi, Maillol, Archipenko), resulting in his expressively elongated and symbolic single figures (*Die Kniende, Der Gestürzte, Der Trauende*). Reflecting alternating French and German influences, his development was symptomatic of that of sculpture in Berlin at the turn of the century. This alternation emphasized the tension between the regional tendencies of the Classical tradition, on the one hand, and international, emphatically anti-Classical, experimental tendencies on the other. In 1911, all the Brücke artists participated as a group, in the inauguration of the Neue Sezession at the Maximilian Macht Gallery in Berlin.

trasted with the tradition-bound work of those who used such pliable and plastic materials as plaster and clay. Under the pen name L. de Marsalle, Kirchner wrote about his work: "It is very significant that, right from the start, Kirchner rejected as unartistic the work modes of current sculptors, who use clay models and plaster castings to lead to the actual material of their work, and created his figures directly out of the material...." [6]

Directness and naturalness as "expressions of life today" were also catchwords for contemporaries of the Expressionists such as Hermann Haller and Georg Kolbe, whose development began to show signs of separating from the academics. "For the official world honors the academic tradition, the enemy of free art," Kolbe wrote in a preface

Expressionism

In his preface to the catalogue of the 1912 exhibition in Mannheim, *Ausdrucksplastik*, Fritz Wichert acknowledged that the most important element in the revival of German sculpture was the rediscovery of "inspiration", which would occur in proportion to the sculptors' capacity to free themselves of "the influence of certain laws and formulas". The process of liberating the most recent sculpture from conventional models was a sticky one for, in the wake of Impressionism, "painting-like values" had penetrated everywhere, including into Berlin's Secession movement. Sculpture as a separate catagory of art, with its own structural elements, had difficulty in defining itself. Although the public was hardly aware of what was going on, the argument between traditionalists and avant-gardists deepened among the Expressionists. As late as the Twenties, E.L. Kirchner could still assert that he was the "only sculptor of our times, whose forms are not oriented towards Antiquity. He [Kirchner] creates his figures directly from everyday experience, as he does in his paintings."[7]

This reference to Kirchner's painting was a helpful comment on the sculpture emerging among the Brücke artists, who came closest to creating "Expressionist sculpture". Their contemporaries did not consider the new expressive art as a specific, coherent style but rather as a sum of manifold tendencies, primarily destined as a counter-reaction to the previous "Impressionism" of Rodin. In 1916, Kasimir Edschmid noted that "when Hoetger turned his back on Rodin, the new times turned their back on the old".[8] Lehmbruck's, *Die Kniende* (1911), exhibited at the Secession exhibition in Berlin in 1912, marks a change of style from his *Grosse Stehende* of the previous year and inaugurates a new phase in his work. It replaces the sensuous fullness and roundness, modelled on Maillol, by gracefully elongated forms and "unclassical proportions". Traces of the Parisian avant-garde style (Brancusi, Modigliani, Archipenko) were linked with those of the artistic styles of the 1900's, such as Georg Minne's adolescent figures, which made an enormous impact on

143   Umberto Boccioni:
Spiralförmige Ausdehnung von Muskeln in Bewegung (1913), plaster, probably destroyed (illustration from the catalogue of the 1. Deutscher Herbstsalon Herwarth Walden, Berlin, 1913)
Dynamic penetration of forms achieved by bunching the planes of the figure into fields of force; the body's volume is allowed to continue into space: "environmental sculpture" (-Boccioni)

the Expressionist generation of sculptors. Minne's influence became explicitly manifest in the exaggeratedly slim, closely cohering figures of adolescents by the Secessionist Ernesto de Fiori (*Stehender Jüngling*) or in the work of Ernst Wenck (*Träumender Knabe*) and the wooden sculptures by Haller (*Stehendes Mädchen*), all of which were created in 1911. These works also contain the basic elements that shaped the symbolic gestures of German sculpture during the Twenties and Thirties. However, expressive (that is to say Expressionist) features can also be distinguished in the work of such artists as Barlach, Hoetger, Lehmbruck and, for a time, Otto Freundlich, Rudolf Belling, Herbert Garbe and Emy Roeder. They were connected less by common stylistic denominators than by their basically anti-academic attitudes and by the internationalism of their artistic conceptions. The rejection of nineteenth-century Naturalism and of the idealization of the human figure implied a return to the wellsprings of creativity.

144   Alexander Archipenko: ▷
Boxkampf (1914), bronze, 59×45 cm. New York, Solomon R. Guggenheim Museum
Dynamic interlacing of cubistically simplified, positive and negative volumes: voids become important structural elements.

145   Otto Gutfreund: *Industrie*   ▷▷
(pendant to *Handel*) (1923) painted wood, H. 76 cm. Prague, Nationalgalerie
In contrast to the earlier preference for Cubist forms and literary figures, as of 1920 genre-type group scenes from the working world or of life in society appear in a sober "New Objective" form.

Archipenko, Barlach and the Brücke artists were even more radical than Kolbe, Haller and Kogan in their conception of the battle against incrusted academic structures. They sought their inspiration in Russia, Africa and the South Seas. In comparison to Kolbe's *Die Tänzerin*, the thematically similar wooden sculptures by the Brücke artists reveal a deeper commitment to emotional and natural values. While Kolbe's figures incarnated the "psychological man" of the Realist generation of 1900, Kirchner's compressed and expressive "hieroglyphics" were based on the "existential man": [9] the Jugendstil ideal of "living the good life" was replaced by Expressionist "frenzy", [10] which was satisfied by the tensions of extremes of contrasts in feelings. The understanding of Primitivism in art was also characterized by the polarity of opposites, being considered anything from Arcadian to demoniac. In retrospect, although the Primitivism of the Brücke artists appears as a continuation of a long tradition of anti-academism — a response to being fed up with civilization and routine work — the innovative integration of a human "attitude and style" [11] is the particular achievement of those artists. And, last but not least, Kirchner's designs for furniture and housing proved that Primitivism was more than an art — it was a life-style as well.

Herwarth Walden's weekly, *Der Sturm*, and especially the art gallery of the same name that he founded shortly thereafter, were a reservoir for the manifold tendencies in prewar art, which we have grouped together in this chapter as "Expressionism" but which appeared chaotically diversified to contemporary observers and were impossible to label at the time. After Walden's Erster Deutscher Herbstsalon in 1913, at the latest, the Berlin art scene was divided into a conservative and a progressive faction. Karl Scheffler, a partisan of Berlin's Secession movement as well as a supporter of Lehmbruck and the man who "discovered" Barlach, sharply criticized the exhibition in an article for the *Vossische Zeitung*, thus making himself a target of Walden's derision. "Sturm" became the battle cry for the most diversified, radical proclamations in the fields of politics, the fine arts and poetry.

The 366 works at the Herbstsalon were a sampling of the latest international art trends – especially Futurism. Sculpture was represented by the the work of, among others, Archipenko (*Recherche plastique de 1913*), Otto Gutfreund and Umberto Boccioni (*Spiralformige Ausdehnung von Muskeln in Bewegung*). The titles of the exhibits testify to the artists' preference for modern themes, for dynamic continuity in forms, for rejecting of "traditional elegance" and marble and bronze as materials, and for opening mass to space. Boccioni had ranted against the "Grecian professorial clique" in Berlin and Munich, in his manifesto of 1912 "The Futurist Plastic Arts"; his demand for a new orientation in sculpture

146 Wilhelm Lehmbruck: sketch for *Der Gestürzte*, charcoal, 26.7×42.7 cm. Lehmbruck Estate

147 Wilhelm Lehmbruck: *Der Gestürzte* (1915-16), bronze, 78×83×239 cm. Berlin, Staatliche Museen Preussischer Kulturbesitz, Nationalgalerie
Elongation of the body as an expression of psychic tensions; interiorization of the pathos of suffering, a state between revolt and resignation. The voids within the structure underscore its expressivity.

148 Fritz Klimsch: war memorial for Prenzlau (1921-23), bronze. Prenzlau

culminated in the concept of "environmental sculpture": "Let's tear the figure open and integrate environment".[12] In a preface to the Archipenko exhibition, which took place at Walden's gallery in 1913, the same year as the Herbstsalon, Guillaume Apollinaire considered the sculptor's relationship to tradition, acknowledging that the artist's lack of dependence on models led to the discovery of reality, thus widening the concept of reality in abstract art. "Archipenko constructs reality and his work is getting closer and closer to 'pure sculpture'."

The many ideas concerning form – the inclusion of negative volumes and the use of montage – developed before World War I by Archipenko and his comrades, did not immediately take root among the younger sculptors. For instance, according to his claim, Rudolf Belling "missed" the Archipenko exhibition at Walden's gallery and only got to know the artist's work much later, from illustrations. Yet, it is more significant that young sculptors in Berlin subjected the arsenal of new forms to the ideological dictates of a radicalism that emphatically contrasted with the compromises of conventional sculpture. The strength of their activism and of their utopic reformism, which was manifested in their striving for a "transvaluation of all values" in Friedrich Nietzsche's terms, was based, above all, on their trials and experiences in World War I. For Lehmbruck, Barlach, Kollwitz, Freundlich and Belling – to name but a few – World War I was a key experience and the basis of their intransigent pacifism.

The crucial state of affaires can be recognized in concentrated form in Lehmbruck's *Der Gestürzte* (1916), a work that represents an existential symbol beyond the realm of traditional monument sculpture. Lehmbruck thus paved the way for a series of monuments that depict the sorrow, mourning and despair of the hero rather than his heroism or desire for revenge. Barlach's *Der Rächer* still represented the heroic mood of the years before the war; Lehmbruck's *Der Gestürzte* marks the beginning of the new line of development, leading to Barlach's monument to war victims for the Magdeburg cathedral and to Kollwitz's kneeling parents for the military cemetery in Eessen (Flanders). This small

group of monument sculptors appears all the more significant when contrasted with the great increase, at the beginning of the Twenties, in the number of monument sculptors who glorified the ideas of war or of revenge, despite the temporary pacifist mood of the first postwar years. At that time, Adolf Behne and Bruno Taut, of the Working Council for Artists, were encouraging substitutes for war monuments, but these either never got past the planning stage or could not be built in the face of the obstructions of a reactionary public, as was the case with Belling's project for a memorial to the students of Berlin University killed during war, which was to bear the caption "What for?".

Lehmbruck's *Der Gestürzte* can be distinguished from the "heroic" war monuments at first glance. For comparative purposes, one could consider Fritz Klimsch's war monument for the city of Prenzlau, which depicts a naked youth rising out of flames with a drawn sword. The contrast is as obvious in the formulation of the figure as in its attributes. Lehmbruck depicts a broken man, who, while collapsing, seems to make a last effort, expressed especially in the tensed and arched line of the figure's back. The piece is a symbolic re-interpretation of a theme that had long been overlooked, although it was quite widespread during World War I: that of Saint Sebastian on his knees, pierced by arrows. It is a motif that can be found in paintings and prints by Otto Dix, Willy Jaeckel, Willi Geiger and Christian Schad; and in wood carving in Karl Albiker's *Saint Sebastian* (1920-26).

However, notwithstanding possible thematic connections, the substance of *Der Gestürzte* is a direct outgrowth of sculptural formulations. Repeated allusions have been made to the figure's spatial penetration, the way the bent limbs carry the stretched torso almost architecturally. Yet the figure's relationship to space is not confined to the architectural implications. Space itself plays an important role; it defines the vacuum surrounding the figure and thus makes it appear marooned in space. *Der Gestürzte*: an Expressionist existential figure, caught between striving and reality. "... The chaos and horror of an existence between heaven and earth,

such as ours; the drama of idealistic striving, inserted like a thumbscrew in the vulgarity of reality...." [13]

Most of the late Expressionist sculptors had nothing more to offer in response to Lehmbruck's tragic dimesions rooted in existentialism than a superficially enhanced consciousness. The condensed and streamlined imagery of Belling, Herbert Garbe and Milly Steger corresponded to an extremist way of life. "Intensity" was the catchword for revolutionary ecstasy and liberated visions. The structural principles of Archipenko's sculpture were used by his colleagues when they corresponded to their ideological purposes. The work of some artists of the Novembergruppe circle is clearly a continuation of Archipenko's concepts and a re-interpretation of his constructive forms into magic symbols (Ewald Mataré) or theatrically

expressive gestures (Herbert Garbe, Georg Leschnitzer, Rudolf Belling). This led temporarily to bold experiments with abstract-rhythmical shapes such as *Lebendiges Eisen* (1916) by the Sturm sculptor William Wauer or *Verzückung* (1919) by a member of the Novembergruppe, Oswald Herzog; Herbert Garbe's *Schlaf* (1919) or Rudolf Belling's *Dreiklang* (1919): experiments in forms that elaborated concretely motivated elements of motion into an absolute form of expression. But these were exceptions in the œuvre of these artists, and obviously they themselves were oblivious to the implications, as the elegance of the rest of their "spatial sculptures" proves. In the post-Cubist sculpture of the time, the extent of this tendency to penetrate space is illustrated by the work of several academically oriented sculptors: Milly Steger or Karl Albiker. The latter's wooden sculp-

149 Rudolf Belling: *Geste Freiheit* (1920-21), assemblage, manually covered with wire, fabric and plaster, H. *c.* 150 cm. Destroyed
The revolutionary mood of the postwar period also influenced the fine arts: formal audacity and experimental endeavors, crystalline splintering of forms, and gestures that penetrate space.

150 Oswald Herzog: *Verzückung* (1919), painted wood, H. 53.5 cm. Mannheim, Städtische Kunsthalle
The fitted parts pass through different phases ("aggregate states") of their spatial development in rhythmic succession and symbolize processes of growth and transformation. Exhibited at the Art Exhibition of 1919 in Berlin, in the Novembergruppe section.

146

151 William Wauer: *Flucht* (1916),
Indian ink, 21.6×27.2 cm.
Mannheim, Städtische Kunsthalle

152 Herbert Garbe: *Schlaf* (1919),
wood, H. 45 cm. Hanover,
Kunstmuseum with the Sprengel
Collection
Elementary simplification of the
body. Rhythmically intertwined
gestures representing the
existentialism of the original
Expressionist source of inspiration,
close to symbolic dance.

ture, *Saint Sebastian* (1920-26, today at the Albertinum in Dresden) created a sensation at the time – in a fashion similar to Belling's *Dreiklang* – by incorporating empty space into the structure as an important element. Both, Belling and Albiker, almost simultaneously, favored an interpenetration of body and space at this point; thus they linked up with Rodin, whose *Cathedral* (the folded hands) combined modern spatial feeling with the development of energetic corporeality. The sculptures created by Belling, Herzog and Freundlich around 1920 show traces of "space-bursting energy" in condensed and stretched-out forms. Yet the theoreticians of sculpture demanded that the normal achievements of Modernism be applied to themes in tune with the times.

Sculptural experiments in Berlin during the early Twenties were for the most part concerned with "applied" Modernism. [14] This was most true of the work of Belling, whose eclecticism could be compared to that of Hoetger during the prewar years. Belling's early groups were persistently characterized by resolute rhetoric (e.g., the gestures of *Die Verwundete* and of the erotic *Das Kampf* are almost interchangeable), whereas his late Expressionist work of the postwar years (incarnations of recognizable phenomena, including attempts at abstraction [*Dreiklang*]) was transformed into rational constructions with an emphasis on the mechanical and fashionably "objective" (*sachlich*) forms, which reflected the technological values produced by economic and social life during the so-called stabilization period under the Weimar Republic, after 1923 or 1924.

A comparison of Schmitt-Rottluff's *Arbeiter mit Ballonmütze* (1920) with Belling's *Skulptur 23* brings to the fore the impact of postwar experiences on Expressionism and, at the same time, characterizes the movement's capacity to evolve. Earlier Expressionist work makes its impression with the monumental aspect of its figures, with its audacity and (stimulated by African sculpture) with its meaningfully simplified forms that underscore a commitment to the times. The date of creation is an indication of how the theme of a war cripple was handled: the planes of the thighs and the open hand held

◁ 153   Milly Steger: *Jephthas Tochter* (*c.* 1919), plaster model for bronze, H. (with base) of original bronze 161 cm. (The bronze, formerly in the Museum Folkwang, Essen, was destroyed.)

154   Raoul Hausmann: ▷
Mechanischer Kopf (1921), wooden and metal components, H. 32.5 cm. Paris, Musée national d'Art Moderne
Dadaist persiflage of the "spirit of the times", made of the rubbish of civilization glued to a dumb, doll-like head—a hairdresser's model for wigs.

155   Rudolf Belling: *Skulptur 23*   ▷▷
(1923), bronze, partially silver-plated, 48×19.7×21.5 cm. New York, The Museum of Modern Art (A. Conger Goodyear Fund)
Technical shapes of smooth perfection form a robot-like, architectural head of magico-primitive expressivity; its mimetic insinuations show traces of the fashionable (Art Deco).

forward convey a helpless distancing of the figure from its surroundings; nonetheless, it retains its human dignity. Schmitt-Rottluff's wooden sculptures integrate African concepts of form into a personalized imagery; Belling's *Skulptur 23*, on the contrary, conveys a magic alienation by combining the techniques of constructing strictly geometrical forms with those used for primitive heads, and thus it comes close to the perfection of anonymously technical forms – the magic of Primitivism captured by fashionable abstraction.

Constructivism

Like the political situation, the situation in the arts in Berlin around 1918 and 1919 could not have been more contradictory and full of tension. The character of the times was not only shaped by late Expressionism and by the anti-Expressionism of the Dada movement but also by a wealth of -isms. In 1921, Paul Westheim could already point to several trends that co-existed with Expressionism: Suprematism, Tatlinism, Compressionism, Cubo-Futurism, Neo-Classicism and Neo-Primitivism. [15] In retrospect, this chaotic, manifold and partly overlapping abundance of stylistic tendencies forms a relatively coherent picture, characterized by a common striving to be radical. Political events – the October revolution, the November disturbances, military occupation and inflation – created appropriately fertile grounds for utopic proclamations and programs of the most varied tendencies. The proponents of these tendencies were drawn together by their avowed intention to become involved with life and to surmount the traditionally marginal position of the arts by using them to make a direct impact on the masses.

The members of the Novembergruppe, a reservoir of progressive artistic trends (see their circular of December 15, 1918), considered themselves "intellectual revolutionaries". They intended to go beyond the confining limitations of professional goals and to become involved in politics with the help of the fine arts; they wanted to reform city planning and art education and have a voice in the reorganization of museums. In a circular they drew up when the group was founded, they stated that "the future of art and the seriousness of present times forces us, intellectual revolutionaries (Expressionists, Cubists, Futurists) to unite and to collaborate closely with each other". Whether the desired brotherhood with the masses was not achieved due to a lack of ideological cohesion or to the marked individualism of the group's members, its failure caused several of the group's politically committed members to withdraw from it in 1921.

Among post-war groupings of artists, some of which were quite short-lived, the Dadaists were noted for their outstanding aggressivity, especially because of their conscious rejection of conventional concepts of art and artists. The later work of some artists such as Jean Arp and Kurt Schwitters has its roots in this context. Connections with Constructivism, montage and technology, paradoxically enough, made this "anti-art" movement extremely stimulating for the arts. The Dada Messe in Berlin in June, 1920, featured a sign saying: "Art is dead. Long live TATLIN's machine art". The roughly 175 exhibits included Hausmann's photomontage *Tatlinsche Pläne* and a *Tatlinsche mech [anische] Konstruktion* by Grosz. The precision and anonymity of engineering designs supplanted Expressionist gestures; the ideal of an impersonal collectivity replaced the former bourgeois ideal of individualism. In the photomontage "Tatlin at Home", the forehead is replaced by a machine. Hausmann's *Mechanischer Kopf* of 1921 (subtitled: "The Spirit of Our Times"), though purportedly satirical (Hausmann: "The only capacities of an everyday person were those that hit him on the head by coincidence, on the outside; the mind was empty". [16]) was clearly intended to be a radically technical accomplishment. Shortly thereafter, Constructivist ideas made inroads on tradition-bound sculpture. Function, used as a stylistic means, implied redefining original purposes and was symptomic of the harmonization of opposing trends that was taking place with the development of the Weimar Republic. Programmatically, Belling's *Skulptur 23* seems just as strangely robot-like as Hausmann's *Geist unserer Zeit*, although more homogeneously structured

156 Hans Arp: *Relief* (1916-18), ▷
painted wood, 42×60×11 cm.
Berlin, Staatliche Museen
Preussischer Kulturbesitz,
Nationalgalerie
Arp's lively forms evolve in a realm between human and plant life. The rough-hewn forms and dilettantism of the montage are not hidden but rather underlined in provoking fashion.

into a virtual "mechanical man", and it is equally indicative of the development that concretized Constructivist ideas towards the mid Twenties. Belling's predilection for perfection of form paved the way for linking sculpture with design (for a while Belling designed mannequins for store-window publicity). For a time, the abstract charm of shapes clashed strongly with more concrete intellectual content. Belling's sculpture advertizing tires at the Avus racing track is like an idol with applied emblems. A similar combination can be noticed in Mies van der Rohe's monument to the murdered leaders of the 1919 revolution, Karl Liebknecht and Rosa Luxemburg, commissioned by the German Communist Party and unveiled in Berlin in 1926: a "formalistically" structured brick construction with the star of David and a flagpole, typical of architectural sculpture (cf. Pl. 11).

The motto of the new sculptors was *Architektonik des Plastischen* ("architectonic elements in sculpture"), taken from the title of the book by Paul Westheim that appeared in 1923 and featured the "Cubist" sculpture of Archipenko, Jacques Lipchitz, Constantin Brancusi and Rudolf Belling from the standpoint of *Architekturwollens* ("architectural strivings"). Even conservative figurative sculptors — Scharff, Kolbe, Steger, Garbe — paid tribute to Cubism: stricter compositions and sharper contour lines were generously labelled "Cubist" at the time. That this designation did not apply only to stylistic features was indicated by the titles of some of the figures: *Soldat* by Fiori (1918) and *Adam* by Kolbe (1920).

The principles of the new "spatial sculpture" had not spread very far, however. Yet, as the late Expressionist wave began to ebb, *Der Sturm* and *Das Kunstblatt* gradually began to feature articles on Constructivist art. The Erste Russische Kunstausstellung, organized by El Lissitzky in 1922, at Van Diemen's gallery in Berlin, was the high point of the movement. The Russian "experimental artists" and the Hungarian Constructivists Laszlo Moholy-Nagy, Lajos Kassák and Laszlo Peri exhibited at the Sturm Gallery; Alfred Kémeny defined the basic Constructivist principles in *Das Kunstblatt* in 1924: ele-

mentarism, relativism, economy — principles that ran parallel to methods of industrial production. Objective and structural factors replaced descriptive and subjective psychological ones; machine-produced materials replaced bronze and marble, and modern technical procedures replaced the crafts of modelling and carving. Space as a component became a central factor of potential energy in structural creations without bulk. Thus in a manifesto on kinetic sculpture, [17] Moholy-Nagy and Kémeny encouraged "activating space through a dynamic constructive system of energy".

Gabo and Pevsner were mainly concerned with the phenomena of transparency and with opening up volume. Moholy-Nagy went a step further, developing "a new spatial feeling" by integrating artificial light and electromotive power. In his *Lichtrequisit*, a mobile construction of metal and glass created between 1922 and 1930, the sculptor's material was transformed into a transparent "energy carrier" for a light-space synthesis. Under the spotlights, the static sculptural forms were transformed into moving images, whose appearance was designed to change constantly as the elements combined. The influence of such experiments in combining light and space can be seen in the sculptural discoveries and work with transparent materials of the Sturm artist Erich Buchholz and of Walter Kampmann, a member of the Novembergruppe; the resulting constructions can be classed somewhere between a picture and a spatial construction, for instance, *Porträt meiner Frau* or *Das Nichts und ich* (1923), which consists of a freely swinging ball in front of an empty canvas. Obviously, there is more involved here than overcoming the confining boundaries within the arts; these artists sought a new way of looking at things. Moholy-Nagy noted: "Technology, machine, Socialism... Constructivism is pure matter. It is not confined to picture-frame and pedestal. It expands into industry and architecture, into objects and relationships. Constructivism is the socialism of vision." [18] Constructivism was intended as an all-embracing structural principle, influencing architecture, design, tubular and unit furniture, and publicity.

157 Kurt Schwitters: *MERZ Kijkduin* (1923), painted wooden relief, 74.3×42.5 cm. London, Marlborough Fine Art, Ltd. Poetic pictures, in which painting and miscellaneous objects were combined, evolved from the Dadaist anti-art of Schwitters. Exhibited at the MERZ Exhibition, held at the Sturm Gallery in Berlin, 1925-26.

158 Wassily Luckhardt and Rudolf Belling: *Reifenreklame* (1920), H. 600-800 cm. Berlin, Avus auto-racing track
A racy ("crystalline") Expressionist shape combined with the descriptive efficiency of an ad: a combination typical of the times—half idol and half standardized trademark.

159 Naum Gabo: *Säule* (1923), ▷ plastic, wood and metal, H. 104 cm. New York, Solomon R. Guggenheim Museum
New, industrially manufactured materials in a montage that reflects the increased use, in the arts, of modern technological procedures. The poetic effect of the construction is achieved by the transparency and apparent weightlessness of the materials.

154

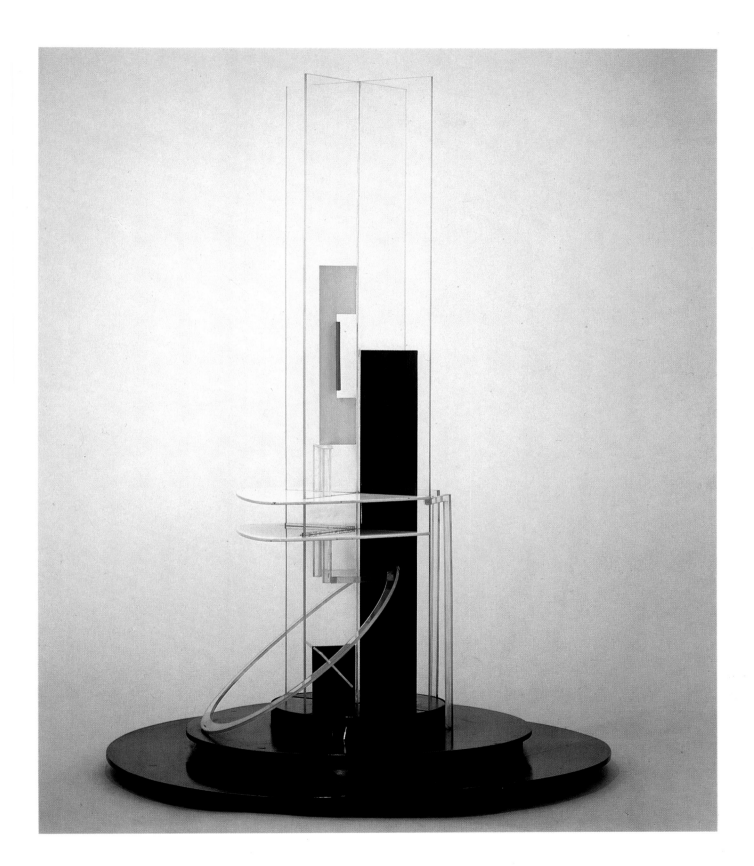

160 Laszlo Moholy-Nagy:
Licht-Raum-Modulator (1922-30),
metal, glass and wood, H. 151 cm.
Cambridge, MA., Harvard
University: Busch-Reisinger
Museum
Motion and light as basic
components of a mobile sculpture:
the transformation of material
forms into the immaterial play of
light.

162 Walter Kampmann: *Porträt* ▷
meiner Frau (1928), various
materials. Missing
Constructivist and Expressionist
styles combined in a manner proper
to this artist.

163 Erich Buchholz: (left) ▷ ▷
Glasplastik (1921-22), (right)
Metallstäbe, Metallplatte-Plastik
(1921-22), plastic and plaster;
illustration from Michel Seuphor,
Die Plastik unseres Jahrhunderts,
Cologne, 1959
Inspired by East European
Constructivists: transparent
materials used to explore perceptible
connections

156

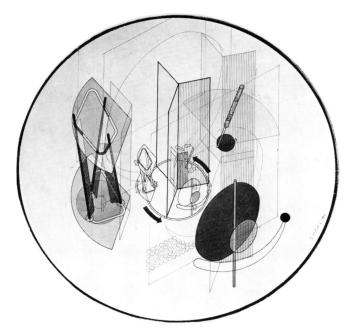

161 Laszlo Moholy-Nagy: *Die Mechanik des Lichtrequisits* (1922-30), watercolors and India ink. Berlin, Bauhaus-Archiv

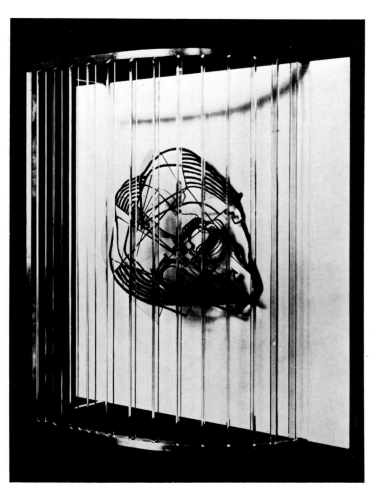

164 Philipp Harth: *Schreitender Tiger* (1929), pen and pencil; sketch for the sculpture *Der Tiger*, with lined squares for the transfer Accentuation of generally "Classical" contours and palpable surface values, in connection with a planned realization in bronze

New Objectivity and Utilitarian Logic

The beginnings of the Weimar Republic's so-called stabilization phase, based mainly on economic factors, marked a regression in the experimental Constructivist tendencies that had, until then, represented the revolutionary motor of postwar artistic strivings. A *neue Sachlichkeit* (new objectivity and realism) began to emerge in painting and photography and, to a lesser extent, in sculpture–more an approach to reality than a coherent style. [19] The tendency was the result of an "objectified" attitude that could be identified in fashion, new housing and publicity as well. The term caught on when it was used as the title of an exhibition presented by Gustav Hartlaub at the Mannheim Kunsthalle in 1925. Schlemmer made the following entry in his diary in April, 1920: "If today's arts love the machine, technology and organization, if they aspire to precision and reject anything vague and dreamy, this implies an instinctive repudiation of chaos and a longing to find the form appropriate to our times." [20] Shortly thereafter, Hartlaub wrote more pragmatically, in a preface to the Mannheim catalogue, that artists "in the midst of a catastrophe, remember what is closest [at hand], most reliable and lasting: truth and craftsmanship". Such unlimited faith in tangible values corresponded to a factual culture with a preference for functional methods of production.

As of about 1923 or 1924, all aspects of the fine arts were characterized by sobriety and by the commonplace: forms became smoother, more finished, and technically objectified. Such features were especially noticeable in the work of those artists who had shown Expressionist verve in their earlier periods (Rudolf Belling, Philipp Harth, Herbert Garbe and Ewald Mataré of the Novembergruppe) and who then shifted over to impersonal forms that erased all traces of the work process, forms that had to be simple and precise, to focus on objects and be free of sentimentality. Hence the wooden sculptures by Mataré (mostly representing animals), exhibited at a first one-man show at J.B. Neumann's Gallery in 1923, were characterized by a smooth, supple surface and totally soothing contours. Mataré sought to avoid the Expressionist "mistake" of refusing to copy nature; he clearly acknowledged nature as a "teacher", to be "freely followed" if one wanted to depict essentials. [21]

The change in stylistic approach implied a change in favorite themes: cosmic ecstasy and

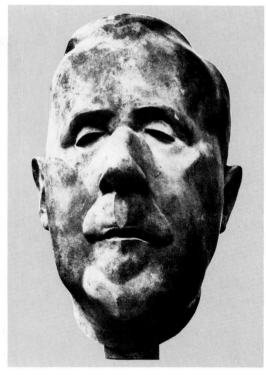

165 Renée Sintenis: *Self-Portrait* (1923), cement, H. 28 cm. Cologne, Wallraf-Richartz-Museum

166 Edwin Scharff: *Heinrich Mann* (1920), bronze, H. 33 cm. Hamburg, Kunsthalle

revolutionary posturing were abandoned in favor of cold appraisals of social facts and descriptions of the simple life and peaceful existence such as that found in Mataré's animal sculptures. Thus, for instance, Eugene Hoffmann, who had begun with painted, figurative wooden sculptures, in the style of the Brücke artists, by the mid Twenties preferred objective portraits (portrait of Otto Dix) or full-length portraits of "types": employees, the petty bourgeois or athletes. Fritz Maskos created naturalistically painted portraits, and Otto Gutfreund depicted soberly objectivized figures from the worker's world. At this point, the magazine *Deutsche Kunst und Dekoration* remarked on the "new receptivity to sculptural portraits". [22] There was little leeway for sculptural portraits under Expressionism, because of that trend's emphasis on idealization. Thus it is hardly surprising that there was a great increase in high-quality portraiture in the later Twenties, for the limitations imposed by the subject-matter, which left little room for artistic variations in treatment, corresponded to the emerging "objectivity" of the times. The tension between the artists and what they sought to represent often produced an exchange of energy that encouraged psychologically striking character studies. Figurative and portrait styles were not obliged to synchronize their evolution, and the stylistic means used in portraiture were hardly suited to the abstract demonstration of formalist progress. [23] Thus Georg Kolbe's portrait of the Impressionist painter Max Slevogt (1926) appears to follow the optical impression very spontaneously. Kolbe knew how to ingeniously combine a roughened surface that "vibrates" with light, like Rodin's, with a face structured in clear, basic forms that are unaffected by the dishevelled head of hair and the beard. Kolbe was an extraordinarily successful portraitist. However, the fact that his portrait of Friedrich Ebert (1925) for the Reichstag was rejected – the expert was the sculptor Hugo Lederer – is indicative of the Classical criteria that were applied when evaluating officially commissioned portraits. In comparison, Scharff's bust of Hindenburg (1927) shows a certain pictorial approach but is more formally stylized.

The portraits of the poet Gottfried Benn by Gustav H. Wolff and of the author Heinrich Mann by Edwin Scharff prove that portraying the desired resemblance, i.e., objectivity in the reproduction of a form and the psychological essence of the subject did not have to be mutually exclusive. New Objectivity sharpened the vision of what was typical of the times in a portrait, as illustrated by a feeling for the erotic aura of a face that the sculptress Renée Sintenis demonstrates in her self-portrait and in her portrait heads of Ludwig Klages and André Gide, and by Ernesto de Fiori's flair for the striking features that characterized the era's stars, found in his portraits of Benjamino Gigli, Jack Dempsey and Marlene Dietrich. His blasé and mundane facial expressions – on, for instance, *Die Engländerin* – can be understood as the expression of a specifically contemporary, corporeal feeling. "He also thought of the soul," H. von Wedderkop wrote in 1925 about *Die Engländerin* (a naked, strutting woman in highheels, described in 1925 in Alfred Flechtheim's art magazine, *Der Querschnitt*, published in Berlin), "for the facial expression implies a latent, highly attractive cynicism, a theoretical perversion, a restrained but boundless vulgarity, which could, according to stylistic possibilities or requirements, span the entire scope of *sans-gêne*." De Fiori's *Die Engländerin* embodied the fashionably glamorous "Miss" typical of those years, whose social alienation is very poignantly captured in this work.

In opposition to this are the earnestness, ethical commitment and convictions propounded in several artists' self-portraits around 1930 – Blumenthal's, Kolbe's, Scheibe's, Karsch's – which, in a large measure, owed their singular expressivity to the prevailing background of growing rightist political pressure. Käthe Kollwitz's self-portrait with explicitly clear features, an important factor in her graphic work as well, is representative of the suffering of the times that characterized her motifs, e.g., *Turm der Mutter, Trauerndes Elternpaar*. The strivings to individualize and typify the contours of sculpture corresponded to the aims of portrait art around 1930. Often, simple forms were com-

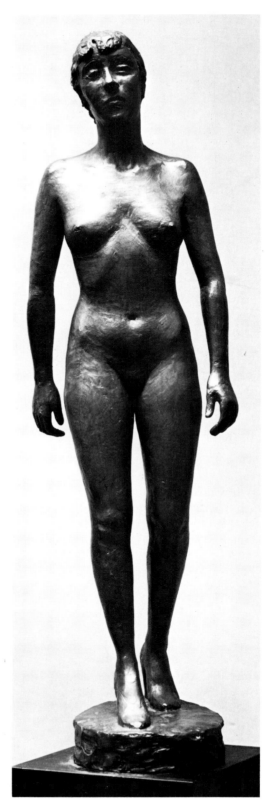

167 Ernesto de Fiori: *Engländerin* (1924), bronze, H. 21 cm. Mannheim, Städtische Kunsthalle
Fiori was one of the portraitists most in demand by prominent figures in Berlin. In this statuette, he portrays an emancipated woman of the big city.

168 Käthe Kollwitz: *Turm der Mütter* (1937-38), bronze, H. 38 cm. Düsseldorf, Kunstmuseum der Stadt Düsseldorf
The artist's expressive Realism is rooted in her capacity for empathy, which developed from her solidarity with those against whom society discriminated and from her combative engagement in their favor.

169 Marcel Breuer and Walter Gropius: bedroom for Erwin Piscator (1927)
"New Objectivity" in furnishings and the logic of Functionalism: the bedroom becomes a transformable, multi-purpose room with sport equipment; this interior reflects a thoroughly organized life style.

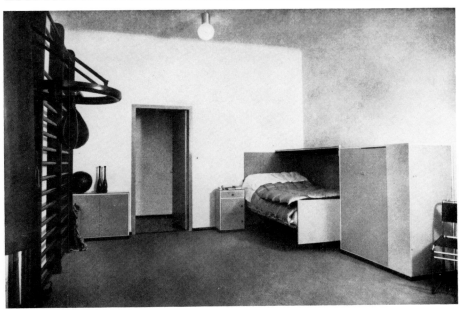

bined with naturalistic details. Gerhard Marcks (portrait of the painter Alfred Partikel), Joachim Karsch, Fritz Koelle and Christoph Voll underscored the expressive topicality of their portraits by reproducing visible reality, including period clothes. In their desire to streamline and simplify, the archaizing portraits by Edwin Scharff, Hans Mettel and Gustav Seitz totally neglected the mimicry personalizing an expression, without showing indifference to their subjects. Moreover, by relying exclusively on the expliciteness of form and material, Ludwig Kasper's *Mädchenkopf* comes far closer to the austerity of the still undeveloped possibilities of purely sculptural means.

By the late Twenties, sports and all connected activities were virtually transformed into a myth, providing sculptural themes for such artists as Kolbe, Sintenis, De Fiori and, for a time, Dietz Edzard and Blumenthal. The sporty attitude as an example of a practical life style could also be seen in furnishings. In 1927, the stage director Erwin Piscator had Walter Gropius and Marcel Breuer design his bedroom as a gymnastics hall, with a punching bag, Indian clubs and wall bars, etc. The sober interior looked like the realization of one of Georg Grosz's postwar visions, which he entitled "The New Man".

The Turning Point: Between Resistance and Adaptation

The new conservative attitude in the wake of New Objectivity also affected sculpture negatively, by greatly restricting experimental endeavors in the postwar years; it also helped pave the way for a renewal of Classical traditions in sculpture, although this line of development had never, in fact, been completely interrupted in Germany. The work of the older generation of sculptors — Georg Kolbe, Josef Thorak, Arno Breker, Fritz Klimsch, Richard Scheibe — was particularly influenced by this trend, yet with nuances. An increasing number of artists began to criticize the New Objectivity (*neue Sachlichkeit*); Kémeny and Eisler had already dismissed it as "short-sighted Realism" and Brecht, who at first had embraced the movement, later considered it altogether reactionary.

The German art historian Ulrich Christoffel praised Kolbe's synthesis of "nature and intellect", a combination of the "vivacity of Rodin and the lucid, objective form of Hildebrand". And it is a fact that his *Tänzerin* suited such diverse architectural expressions of the Neoclassical trend as the brick construction exhibited by Wilhelm Kreis at the Glass Palace in Munich in 1927 (a utilitarian construction of descriptive architecture) or the transparent glass architecture of Mies van der Rohe at the World Exhibition held in Barcelona in 1929. The reasons for such versatility

can be attributed mainly to the decorative and rhythmic elements of Kolbe's sculpture, to its unique tectonic aspect, to the severely subdued and thus restrainedly pathetic "corporeal imagery". His Rathenau fountain, [24] in Rehberge's public park (later destroyed by war) illustrates another source of Kolbe's successful combination of abstraction and substantiation. The fountain resembled a stylized torch with its shaft encircled by a spiral, a formula for representing the principle "Upwards". The abstraction conveyed something threatening, imposed by the alienating sleekness of the form. Nevertheless, in this historical context, it is obvious that the artist's

consciousness of mass and form could serve as a rampart against contemporary ideological indoctrination with nationalist, collectivist and racist concepts. At this point, noticeable changes occurred in Kolbe's figures: the sporty figure was characterized by slim proportions, the torso usually less developed than the limbs, and the head, the expressive focal point, was often quite large in proportion to the rest of the body.

A growing number of monuments testified to the new pathos: *Beethoven-Denkmal* (1930), *Der Ruf der Erde* (1932), *Segnung*. The discreet figures of Edwin Scharff, H.G. Wolff and Gerhard Marcks, based on sobriety and craftsmanship, contrast favorably with Kolbe's at times somewhat pining, sentimental ones, with Breker's coldly brutal and monumentally exaggerated, triflingly sweet ones, and with Klimsch's fashionable illustrations of the National Socialist type of woman. The underlying pathos of the former "ecstatic sculptors" – Belling, Garbe, Steger – who now preferred stone as a sculptural material, to the wood they had used previously, was a reply to the anonymous tectonics of Scharff's pupils: Hermann, Blumenthal, Hans Mettel, Gustav Seitz. Yet it was not the themes and motifs but the approach that differentiated the younger generation of sculptors from the official ones. The simplification of shapes into basic forms – spheres and cones – and the renunciation of an artistic "handwriting" brought them into contradiction with the "picturesque" personalization of Kolbe's work, just as his eloquence contrasted with the taciturnity and naiveté of the facial expressions on the work of the younger artists, as the titles themselves revealed (e.g., *Adam* by Blumenthal or *Heidnischer Mann* by Mettel). Despite the severity of their forms, neither Blumenthal nor Ludwig Kasper wanted to create anonymous robots; they knew how to avoid mechanical or rigid effects in their figures by giving them precise movements. It was more a question of an updating of their personal experience of our common Greek heritage which, in keeping with contemporary tendencies of interiorization, drove them to look for the timeless aspects of everyday life. Kasper's *Knaben mit erhobenen Armen* became a powerful sublima-

tion; Karsch connected the portrayal of commonplace gestures (e.g., *Lesendes Paar*, a paraphrase of Barlach's *Lesende Mönche*) with pious expressions and attitudes of "listening to the cosmos". If, at this point, emphasis is increasingly put on mythical aspects in a context of growing Primitivism, these myths are a far cry from those of the National Socialist ideology described by Adolf Hitler in his speech at the inauguration of the Haus der Deutschen Kunst in 1937.

Gerhard Marck's Hellenism was manifestly different from the blasé, arrogant, Neo-Grecian trend of the National Socialists and from Breker's muscle-men. Marcks attempted to link up with traditions specific to Berlin in his couples and realistic small sculptures – *Ragazzo*, *Hemdauszieher*, *Arbeitsloser* – and wanted to combine Greek ideals with modern vitality. But he too was admittedly influenced by the "spirit of the times", as can be seen in his description of an archaic Greek figure: "A severe construction. The legs are opened, one a bit in front of the other, like open scissors' blades.... Back and legs are like a pair of arrows, bound at the top, then separated, rhythmically punctured into shoulders, buttocks, thighs, calves and heels. Planes push against planes; mountains against cavities, with lucid, virile discipline". [25] Interest in the "objectivity" (*Sachlichkeit*) of the more recent, archaic stylization in French sculpture was understandably lively at the time. In 1937 in Berlin, under the patronage of Ambassador André François-Poncet, there was a large exhibition of contemporary French art, in which the sculptures of Aristide Maillol, Marcel-Antoine Gimond and François Pompon were prominently displayed.

Naturalist features now became more pronounced in Marcks's work. As the critic Will Grohmann noted in 1938: "If, for a time, Marcks's work resembled Lehmbruck's, today [it is] penetrated by the Gothic and Renaissance spirits. (Riemenschneider)". [26] The allusion to Riemenschneider is no surprise: even Blumenthal who turned his figures into stiff frameworks of limbs (thereby underscoring the modern, interrogatory expression of his fragile, Lehmbruck-like figures) tended, at this point, to focus on the mythical aspects of everyday life, just as

◁ 170 Hermann Blumenthal: *Grosser Kniender* (1929-30), bronze, H. 103 cm. Berlin, Staatliche Museen Preussischer Kulturbesitz, Nationalgalerie
In this symbolically enhanced youth, in line with the works of Bernhard Hoetger and Wilhelm Lehmbruck, Blumenthal is trying to convey the unassuming persuasiveness of everyday appearances.

◁ 171 Ludwig Kasper: *Sitzende* (1936), stucco, 95×58×44 cm. Mannheim, Städtliche Kunsthalle
The sensuousness of Maillol's corporeal imagery translated into a severely systemized, architectonically ordered structure

172　Gerhard Marcks: *Kleine Schwestern* (1934), bronze, H. 70 cm. Frankfurt-am-Main, Städtische Galerie im Städelschen Kunstinstitut
Revival of antique models in a modern sober interpretation of the human figure, a continuation of the Classical sculptural tradition of Berlin.

173 Max Beckmann: *Mann im
Dunkel* (1934), bronze, H. 56 cm.
Bremen, Kunsthalle
Like the paintings of this period,
Max Beckmann's sculpture
represents the somber mood of the
times in cryptic symbolic figures in
the style of antiquity. Figure and
space are interrelated.

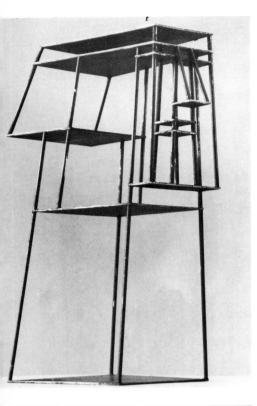

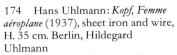
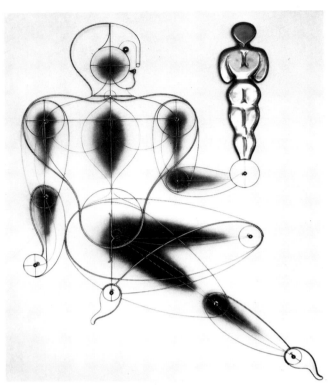

174 Hans Uhlmann: *Kopf, Femme aéroplane* (1937), sheet iron and wire, H. 35 cm. Berlin, Hildegard Uhlmann
A continuation of Constructivist methods of montage: a transparent construction of lines and planes, forming the plot—like units of construction—basic shapes and expressive originality.

175 Oskar Schlemmer: *"Homo" mit weiblicher Rückenfigur* (1930-31), replica from 1968, wall sculpture on wire, (board) 309.5×257 cm., (sculpture) 295.5×234 cm. Stuttgart, Staatsgalerie
Schlemmer strives to synthesize an idealistic image of man, having composure and dignity, with the modern, technically accurate esthetic.

176 Otto Freundlich: *Auffahrt (Ascension)* (1929), bronze, 225×107 cm. Cologne, Museum Ludwig
A rejection of traditional sculptural constructions of harmony and balance in favor of a gradual unfolding of forms unlike real effigies—another development of the dynamic, Cubist aspects of motion in prewar sculpture.

177 Alexander Calder: *Porträt Dr. Hans Cürlis* (1929), steel wire, 32×18.5 cm. Berlin, Dr. Hans Cürlis
The continuity of the lines produces an impression of strength and motion: an example of sculpture as a symbol in space—lightheartedness and subtle humor.

178 Karl Hartung: *Weiblicher Torso* ▷ (*c.* 1939), brass, H. 24 cm. Cologne, Museum Ludwig
The female body as an organic synthesis of form: Arp and Brancusi inspired the ambiguously variable sculptural forcefulness.

Joachim Karsch sought timeless elements in the trivial. Both found themselves in the company of other international artists; for at the same time in Italy Arturo Martini and Marino Marini were experimenting, trying to discover up-to-date means of producing sculptural portraits of well-known people; like the Berlin artists, they were stimulated by Greek archaism and Etruscan sculpture. However, the archaic elements in German sculpture were often updated by existential traits: for instance, Blumenthal's doubting young man or Max Beckmann's mythical, secretive figures that move through space and time as if in a trance. At the beginning of the Thirties, Kasper, Marcks and Blumenthal formed a promising group of sculptors. For a while, they worked together in an atelier building on Klosterstrasse, which became an artists' refuge during the Nazi period, and where Käthe Kollwitz was also taken in. [27] Although the development of that generation of sculptors was hindered by the unlucky circumstances of the period, they did manage to

make themselves heard. Berlin's Buchholz Gallery became a retreat during those dark years; there, they occasionally contrived to put on one-man or collective shows, e.g., the exhibition of 1939 on the The Antique Spirit in Recent Times. Art critics like Will Grohmann and Werner Haftmann and art historians like C.G. Heise, Alfred Hentzen and Christian Adolf Isermeyer strongly promoted their work.

While in Berlin sculptors loyal to the regime obtained commissions for colossal monuments – Joseph Wackerle's *Rosseführer* for the Reich's Sport Field (1936) and Brecker's allegorical muscle-men in *Partei* and *Wehrmacht* for the courtyard of the new Reich's Chancellory (1938), for example – Blumenthal and Kasper exerted most of their influence behind the scenes. The extent to which archaic concepts of figures continued to hold sway over young sculptors in Berlin is demonstrated by the fact that these concepts also served as a basis for very different attempts, like that of Uhlmann's Constructivism. His transparent metal constructions are closely related to international Constructivism and comparable to the work of Oskar Schlemmer, Willy Baumeister and Otto Freundlich, although those artists were oriented towards Paris rather than towards Rome and Greece, as were the Berlin Neoclassical and archaic artists. Uhlmann's constructions of heads, open to space, spread the ideas of Gabo and Pevsner.

Alexander Calder, who exhibited at J.-B. Neumann's gallery in 1929, should be mentioned here as well. The Constructivist context of the postwar years is clearly visible in his wire sculptures: "The conveyor belt rationalization, man's conquest of the air... have been naively decontaminated, humanized, have become art. Calder regenerates certain aspects of the sculptural experimentations of the Russian Constructivists. But the Constructivism of Calder is not mechanized... it is playful." [28] This was obvious in the portrait of the Berlin critic, Hans Cürlis, who had made a short film on wire figures Calder exhibited at J.B. Neumann's gallery: the individually defined shapes of the faces are combined with a gay, playful mood. A comparison between Calder's constructions, on the

179 Arno Breker: *Die Wehrmacht* (pendant to *Die Partei*) (1939), bronze. Originally erected in the court of honor of the new Reich's Chancellery. Destroyed
The empty pathos of National Socialist propaganda-art

one hand, and Belling's sculptural work that is closely related to 1930's Art Deco, on the other, makes Uhlmann's development appear particularly consistent and logical, but the comparison also explains why he did not enjoy wide acclaim.

During the domination of the National Socialists, Karl Hartung also had to work secretly; he followed another aspect of the Twenties: organic abstraction. Hartung received a long-lasting stimulus from Jean Arp and Constantin Brancusi during a stay in Paris in 1929. Contrary to Belling, who emigrated and accepted a position as professor at the Art Academy in Istanbul, Hartung and Uhlmann stayed in Germany and worked in seclusion, continuing to develop their oeuvre. They became two of the most important German sculptors of the post World War II period.

IV FILM IN BERLIN

Ulrich Gregor

A description of film in Berlin until 1933 perforce covers the "German" film industry as a whole, for, in contrast to the development of production centers in Munich and Hamburg for regional films after 1945, the history of film production in Germany until 1933 was, with very few exceptions, always identical to that of film production in Berlin.

This was already the case in 1895 (even before the projections of the Lumière brothers in Paris!), when the Skladanovsky brothers first showed films at the Wintergarten, Berlin's vaudeville theater. This predominance of Berlin in the German film industry was characteristic of both the advent of film in Germany and of the major era of German film production during the Weimar Republic. All the most important production companies had their headquarters in Berlin. The multiple sources of inspiration afforded by that cultural metropolis, as well as the influence of related artistic spheres, shaped the stylistically varied trends of German film during the Twenties. As of the mid Twenties, foreign films, especially from Russia, provided an additional source of inspiration, but they too were distributed by the film metropolis Berlin, by import and distribution companies, film theaters and, last but not least, by the film press. The major film magazines, although they were trade publications, maintained high standards in their reviews and publicity; the most important were published in Berlin under the titles *Lichtbildbühne* and *Filmkurier*.

German film was able to set the tone worldwide during the Twenties and early Thirties only because film production and film-goers both were firmly rooted in Berlin, a European metropolis and a city that, at the time, was a strong pole of attraction for foreign film directors and film stars as well. Although in 1926, at the instigation of the Reichswehr, the film censorship board censored *Battleship Potemkin*, on the whole, nonetheless, the policy it followed was more liberal than that of its foreign counterparts (in France, the same film was not officially allowed to be shown until 1945). In the Twenties, Berlin was a center for the exchange of ideas in film and an incomparable seat of creative experimentation.

The "Archaic" Period

The years from the discovery of film making in 1895 until about 1918 can be described as the "archaic" period of film production in Germany or Berlin. Around the turn of the century and for the next few years, films were shown mainly at circuses and fairs, where short strips sufficed: documentaries, burlesque skits and melodramas, mostly of French, Italian or American origin. Native German films were not produced prior to 1910, except for strips by the discoverer of films and film pioneer, Oscar Messter, who was the first film producer to settle on Berlin's Friedrichstrasse. The German "market" was controlled in the main by two French companies; Pathé and Gaumont. By around 1910, however, the number of established movie houses had already notably increased: according to statistics, Old Berlin already harbored 139 "cinematographic theaters" at that time.

The first film magazines appeared: *Kinematograph* in Düsseldorf in 1907, *Erste Internationale Film-Zeitung* and *Lichtbildbühne* in Berlin in 1908. The expression *"Kientopp"* ("movies") became popular. Certain improvements, on the dramaturgical level, were made in the (still short) films, which resulted in the first sensationalist and romanticized dramas. A summary of 1913 describes one of the films as follows: "Violetta's lips curl into a bewitching smile, and her brightly flashing eyes reveal that the Privy Councillor has found the key to her heart".

After 1910, interest in films among writers, artists and intellectuals also increased. Two trends can be distinguished. The first was that of the "movie reformers":

teachers, educators and representatives of church associations attacked films on grounds of their "immorality" and showered the public with a flood of lampoons and polemic pamphlets warning of the dangers inherent in the new medium. As early as 1907, a commission was charged by the Association of the Friends of National Schools and Educational Institutions in Hamburg with considering the question: "How can we protect our children from the harmful influences of the theater of living photography?". These reformers, who made no secret of their reactionary and orthodox views, were encouraged for a time by the many theater directors who attributed the decrease in their box-office receipts to the competition of the movies. The "movie reformers" continued their negative publicity until 1919 but could not

180 Film atelier in Neubabelsberg: *c.* 1912
The cameraman, Guido Seeber, a special-effects expert, used a movable screen to have this picture made; it shows him six times in various jobs.

181 Paul Wegener and Lyda Salmonova in *Der Student von Prag* (by Stellan Rye: 1913) One of the first German "author films", the central theme of which was an identity crisis.

put a stop to, nor deflect the triumphant progress of films. At the most, they contributed to the emergence of a temporary alternative to the "plebian" mass spectacles for fair-style films; these alternative films, by analogy with French *films d'art*, sought to elevate the artistic standards of films. Using material from history, literature and the legitimate theater, these films were intended to appeal to the "educated classes" but soon proved to have the wrong approach for subsequent cinematographic developments.

Unlike the movie reformers with their pathetic proclamations, writers took an early interest in the new cinematographic medium, acknowledging its inherent possibilities. Thus, in 1909, Alfred Döblin wrote an essay on "The Theater of the Little People": "From now on they [the little people] throng to the movies, which have emerged in the northern, southern, eastern and western sections of the city, in smoky backrooms, stalls, unused shops, in large halls, spacious theaters. The best of them offer enjoyable photographic techniques, marvelous realism, optical illusions, as well as little comedies, novels by Manzoni: very delicate. My but this technique

has possibilities, almost ripe for art .... *Panem et circenses* has been fulfilled: pleasure [is] as necessary as bread; a bullfight [is] a popular necessity." [1]

In a lecture in 1912 at the inauguration of a movie theater in Berlin, Egon Friedell attacked the pseudo-ideals of enemies of movies: "This brings us to the main objection commonly made to movies: that they lack words and, therefore, can only portray crude and primitive things. But it is my belief that words no longer enjoy such absolute hegemony nowadays.... Words are gradually losing their reputation. Something like a regression of the spoken word is taking place.... It is just like Homer's Zeus: he moves his eyelids and all Olympus shakes. So too is modern man: a twitch of his eyelashes, a lowering of his eyelids, and the whole world moves." [2]

The year 1913 marks a certain caesura in the process of recognition of the new medium by educated circles, as well as in the development of more discriminating German and Berlin films. It was in that year that Kurt Pinthus's *Kinobuch* was published and that the so-called "author-films" were born. When Pinthus, a Leipzig theater critic, published a "well-intentioned and carefully thought out" review of the Italian superfilm *Quo Vadis*, he was criticized for having "degraded" his publication. He discussed the problem with some writer friends, criticizing the "false ambitions of recent silent films, which strive to imitate static, stage-bound theater dramas or word-bound novels, instead of using the infinite possibilities available in film technology of moving pictures". [3] He prevailed upon his friends, including Max Brod, Albert Ehrenstein, Walter Hasenclever, Else Lasker-Schüler, Heinrich Lautensack, Ludwig Rubiner and Franz Blei, to write original drafts for films, so-called "movie plays", which were compiled in the above-mentioned *Kinobuch* and published in 1913. As Pinthus points out in his preface to the 1963 reprint of his book, it was certainly an exceptional event in film history of the period from 1910 to 1920 "that in the year 1913, contrary to 'renowned' authors, more than a dozen younger authors [dared to] write plays in the *Kinobuch* consciously destined for movies and for its new, purely visual technique, for films of the future, as a challenge, without consideration for their literary reputations nor [a view to] cinematographic exploitation". [4]

In 1913 as well, several films that belong to the earliest milestones of German film history came out. They incarnated themes and styles that were to become the trademarks of German films during the period from 1919 to 1925, generally classified as "Expressionist"; thus, before World War I, they already foreshadowed film trends of the Weimar era. These later themes, already formulated in the earlier "author-films", include split personality, spiritual withdrawal, fantasy and fabulous happenings in a world of fables and fairy tales.

The actor Paul Wegener, a member of Reinhardt's troupe (like Lubitsch and Murnau), was one of the first to develop German films in this direction. According to a description by Siegfried Kracauer, Wegener's "Mongolian face... told of the strange visions that haunted him... a sinister actor calling up the demoniac forces of human nature". [5] Together with the author Hanns Heinz Ewers, Wegener wrote the scenario for the film *Der Student von Prag* ("The Student of

Prague", 1913), in which he played the leading role under a Danish director, Stellan Rye. The film's plot concerns an identity crisis: a magician buys a student's reflection and lets it commit a murder; the student is accused of the crime and driven to commit suicide. Although the film does not yet have the nightmarish forcefulness of later films by Murnau or Lang, and even appears relatively crude in comparison to the afore-mentioned (it was filmed almost entirely in real settings), it does show traces of the efforts made in the realm of pictorial composition and its plot is well-conceived. Consequently, it may be considered as a sort of primitive model of the early Twenties for Weimar-era films. Other films that relate to *Der Student von Prag*, either thematically or formally, include *Der Andere* ("The Other", 1913) by Max Mack, based on a theater play by Paul Lindau, describing a case of split personality (of the Dr. Jekyll and Mr. Hyde type) that created a sensation, because it was the first movie role of the famous stage actor Albert Bassermann. The film itself is less interesting, from a cinematographic point of view, than *Der Student von*

182 *Der Golem, wie er in die Welt kam* (by Paul Wegener and Carl Boese: 1920)
Film sets by Hans Poelzig: architects and set designers also contributed to the esthetics of Expressionist films.

Prag. They also include Max Reinhardt's fanciful pantomime, *Venetianische Nacht* ("Venetian Night"), in which Cupid plays his tricks on a group of students (also 1913); Alfred Wegener's second film, *Der Golem* (1915), which he directed himself together with Henrik Galeen, and the six episodes of the *Homunculus* thriller series (1916), directed by Otto Rippert. The last two films deal with artificial "men" who finally slip away from their creator's control and become rebels, monsters or dictators.

Unfortunately, the first *Golem* film and most of the *Homunculus* episodes (except one) have been lost. In her book *Dämonische Leinwand*, Lotte Eisner points out that the tendency of Expressionist German silent films to make use of chiaroscuro, fantasy and magic derives from such early films as *Homunculus* and *Der Student von Prag*, i.e., from influences that preceded Reinhardt's staging of Reinhard Sorge's *Der Bettler* (1917), an Expressionist drama with marked chiaroscuro, which probably had a strong impact on film.

In 1920, Paul Wegener and Carl Boese refilmed the *Golem* material and entitled their film *Der Golem, wie er in die Welt kam* ("How Golem Entered the World"). Hans Poelzig designed the film sets and Rochus Gliese was responsible for the costumes in this film, which already shows distinct traces of Expressionism and may indeed be considered one of the major Expressionist films. In his book *Expressionismus und Film*, Rudolf Kurtz wrote: "Poelzig's Golem city is not at all like a medieval settlement, but has all [the characteristics] of a Gothic dream". [6]

Moreover, the period from 1910 to 1918 was significant to the history of German film, because during that time, the foundations of film's commercial and industrial framework were laid. In 1911, the Deutsche Bioscop Corporation built the first factory made of glass in Neubabelsberg near Berlin; it was the first element in what was to become the film city of Babelsberg. Since the war impeded the importation of foreign films from 1914 to 1918, the sales prospects for native German films were strengthened. A *Bild- und Filmamt* ("Picture and Film Office") was created in 1918 by the War Ministry, in order to make use of films for propaganda purposes as well. And, in the same year, three major film concerns – Nordisk, which was originally Danish, the Messter group and the Union group – financed to a large extent by the Reich's government, merged to form Universum Film AG, abbreviated as UFA: an organization that was to play an important, if not always constructive, role in the development of the German film industry. Many of the artistically significant films of the Twenties, including those by Murnau and Lang (as of 1924), were UFA productions. On the other hand, during the late Twenties and early Thirties, the UFA lent support to the reactionary trends in German films and, in Hitler's Germany, as of 1933, the UFA soon became the unique, dominating State film corporation that absorbed all the others. The powerful economic hold of the UFA, which merged with the Hugenberg group in 1928, was based on its combination of means of production and distribution and on its ownership of movie theaters.

Expressionist Film

The climate in Germany during the first postwar years was unusually favorable to the development of films, due to the economic conditions of the times. The devaluation of the mark gave producers an exceptional chance to export their films abroad (the proceeds of a German film shown in Switzerland were enough to cover production costs), while making the German market uninteresting for foreign films. German film production reached a high point in 1922: 474 long-feature films were produced that year, a figure that has never been matched since. Most of these films were, of course, commercial consumer wares, often of the "manners" and "sex education" type that was the specialty of, for example, the director Richard Oswald; the production of such films benefited from the fact that there was no film censorship at all in Germany for several years after 1918. Another specialty, notably of the UFA, was that of historical or period superfilms, based not only on Italian historical films but on ideas from Reinhardt's staging as well.

183   Pola Negri in *Madame Dubarry*
(by Ernst Lubitsch: 1919)
A theatrical crowd scene, handled
by Lubitsch along the lines of his
teacher, Max Reinhardt.

184   Pola Negri in *Die Bergkatze*
(by Ernst Lubitsch: 1921)
The later historical and period films
by Lubitsch are filled with humor,
fantasy and surprises; the decors
have become dramaturgical
elements.

Ernst Lubitsch was the most talented director of the historical film; he began his career as an actor under Reinhardt and made a name for himself during the war with his intelligent comedies. In his historical films *Madame Dubarry* (1919), *Anna Boleyn* (1921), *Das Weib des Pharao* (1922) – Lubitsch made relatively little use of dramatic pageantry, spectacular effects or scenic extravagances, although the crowd scenes in his films contain thoroughly impressive, theatrically stylized passages. The human weaknesses and caricatures of representatives of authority central to his film plots, lend themselves far more to humor, irony and ambiguity. Even in those of his films which do not fall into the period category such as *Die Puppe* ("The Doll", 1919) and *Die Bergkatze* ("The Mountain Cat", 1921), there are traces not only of the fanciful, stylized settings that he favored but also of parody and comedy as well. Lubitsch never became a total convert to the use of magic that characterized so many German films at the time; he was more likely to snap his fingers ironically at the trend. Lubitsch left Germany in 1922 for the United States, where he successfully continued his career.

Das Cabinet des Dr. Caligari ("Dr. Caligari's Office") by Robert Wiene (filmed in 1919 and premiered in 1920) stands head and shoulders above the rest of the films from postwar Germany as an exemplary Expressionist work. Carl Mayer and Hans Janowitz wrote the scenario for this resoundingly successful film, which narrates the weird, mysterious story of a showman and his medium, Caesar (Cesare). Caesar, whose actions

185 Conrad Veidt in *Das Cabinet des Dr. Caligari* (by Robert Wiene: 1919-20)
The masterpiece of cinematographic Expressionism. Painted decors (by Hermann Warm, Walter Reimann and Walter Röhrig) created a nightmarish world.

depend on the showman, is accused of a murder (which the medium had predicted) and of an attempted murder. The showman turns out to be no other than Dr. Caligari, director of an insane asylum. The whole story is further relativized, since it is narrated by the inmates of the asylum Dr. Caligari directs.

There are several versions of the film's genesis. Some say that the story within the story (i.e., the fact that the narrators of the film are themselves insane) took the edge off the original scenario, which the authors Mayer and Janowitz had intended as an attack on the overwhelming power of State authority. According to this version, Erich Pommer, director of Decla-Bioscop, the production company, and the film's director, Wiene, insisted on this dramaturgical context, at Fritz Lang's instigation (he was to have directed the film originally) and against the will of both authors of the scenario. But in the meantime, other participants in the film have contradicted this version; it is also debatable whether the story within the story takes the horror out of the central plot or, on the contrary, accentuates it. In any case, the film can be considered exceptional for its decors, which, contrary to conventional film methods of the time, were painted directly on flat canvas, by three painters — Hermann Warm, Walter Reimann and Walter Röhrig (who were closely associated with the Sturm movement). Consequently, the decors themselves became symbolic, a first in film development — they act as metaphors for moods.

Rudolf Kurtz, the best interpreter of Expressionist films, described *Caligari* as a film where the plot "takes place entirely within the dark depths of the soul"; and he stated that the performance by the two main interpreters, Conrad Veidt and Werner Krauss, "forcefully conveys a metaphysical conception". Of the film sets, he had this to say: "The decorative effects of Expressionism have been most successfully achieved. The architecture seems to emerge from a creative conception. Light is painted; mysterious ornaments underline the mood, like applications of extraneous elements on paintings; streets twist and turn, seem to run into each other. The monotony, narrowmindedness

and decay of the small town are unerringly captured. The trees are fantastic struggling mazes, leafless and spectral, that tear the image into pieces in a freezing manner. Like so many alien elements, little projecting constructions crowd together; oblique-angled staircases groan when used, supernatural forces inhabit the doors, which are nothing but empty, yawning openings." [7]

"You must become Caligari" was the slogan thought up by the production firm to launch the film *Das Cabinet des Dr. Caligari*; it

186 Werner Krauss in *Das Wachsfigurenkabinett* (by Paul Leni: 1924)
A film in several episodes in exotic localities, using fantastic decors and performed by eccentric actors.

187 Ruth Weyher in *Schatten* (by Arthur Robison: 1923)
A nocturnal hallucination: dreams turn into reality for guests at a party.

Das Cabinet des Dr. Caligari set an example that was followed subsequently, during the early Twenties, by a series of films that likewise sought to use Expressionist decorative elements, but which do not come through quite on the same artistic level. The one exception, which can be classified as an Expressionist masterpiece on a par with *Caligari*, is Karl Heinz Martin's *Von Morgens bis Mitternacht* ("From Morn to Midnight"), based on the play by Georg Kaiser. This film, like *Caligari*, was shot exclusively in painted decors; Ernst Deutsch plays the main role. In the rest of the films, the fantastic-Expressionist elements often appear disconnected, in juxtaposition with naturalistic components, and degenerate into something of an exterior decoration. Consequently, one can say that the number of truly "Expressionist" films is quite restricted in the history of German film. To be sure, "echoes" of Expressionism appear in many other films, including those by Fritz Lang or by Murnau.

The following films are Expressionist in the strict sense of the term: *Raskolnikow* (1923), also by Robert Wiene; *Das Wachsfigurenkabinett* ("Waxworks", 1924) by Paul Leni, a romantic and ghostlike series of episodes about Ivan the Terrible, Harun al-Rashid and Jack the Ripper; the *Golem, wie er in die Welt kam* (1920), mentioned before, by Paul Wegener and Carl Boese; *Torgus* (1921) by Hanns Kobe; *Schatten*, ("Warning Shadows", 1923) by Arthur Robison, a particularly fascinating film based on an idea by the painter Albin Grau, who was responsible for the decors and costumes as well. The film describes how guests at an evening party are carried away by an illusionist and a trickster to the realm of their hallucinations, from which they return "cured" at the end of the film. Two additional films by Robert Wiene use Expressionist decors: *Genuine* (1920) and *Orlacs Hände* (1924). It must be said, however, that as a director, Robert Wiene did not have the visionary strength or personal forcefulness of Lang or Murnau.

Rudolf Kurtz discovers Expressionist elements in still other films of the early Twenties, namely in those with a "literary" intent or all the films where the directors aspired beyond mere entertainment. He feels Expres-

was posted on all the advertising pillars in Berlin before the film's premiere. Overnight, after it premiered at Berlin's Marmor-Palast on February 26, 1920, the film became a raging success, which was further confirmed by triumphs abroad, especially in France and in the United States. French critics coined the term "Caligarism", which was used from that time on to designate the rest of the German films with Expressionist tendencies. There were also references to an *école allemande* that was said to have been founded by *Caligari*.

sionism can be detected "where a particular form of suppressed and alert energy must be expressed, where the sense of a situation strives to come through beyond appearances". In this connection, of course, it must be pointed out that nearly all the important German films of the time were shot in artificial settings in studios and that not only the set designers but also the lighting and camera people greatly contributed to the final result. German films of the early Twenties are not only characterized by their stylized decors but also by the way the pictures are molded sculpturally by light and dark zones of contrast. Gradually, this manner of cultivating pictorial contrasts and composition was lost to German sound film as a consequence of the naturalistic Realism that was a new esthetic requirement, and to date, it has not been recovered.

The predilection of many German films in the early Twenties for imaginary, fantastic subject matter produced a greatly differentiated codex of cinematographic modes of expression, which found their continuation in the later films of the Realist G.W. Pabst. His

contribution to Expressionism was "presenting people and objects in a luminous relief, a sort of aura with phosphorescent contours, distorting architectural perspectives, exaggerating their proportions and thus remodelling them into strange entities". [8] However, the development of a subtle pictorial instrumentation was achieved at the price of a retreat from the realm of realism (this was true at least until 1924). In this connection, Siegfried Kracauer mentions an "introvert tendency" which he traces back to "powerful collective desires", and a "retreat into a shell". He defines the postwar films of 1920 to 1924 as "a unique *monologue intérieur*. They reveal developments in almost inaccessible layers of the German mind". [9] In trying to interpret along such lines, it is interesting to note that German films of that period showed a preference for tyrants to which the individual had to submit.

The *Kammerspielfilm* ("chamber-play film") and *Strassenfilm* ("street film") are genres closely related to Expressionist film. The scenarist Carl Mayer is the connecting link (one of the most important figures in German

188   Henny Porten, Wilhelm Dieterle and Fritz Kortner in *Hintertreppe* (by Leopold Jessner and Paul Leni: 1921)
An example of the *Kammerspiel* ("chamber-play") films: the actors and decors bear the imprint of Expressionism.

189   Werner Krauss and Edith Posca in *Scherben* (by Lupu Pick: 1922)
The Expressionist author Carl Mayer wrote the scenario of this sinister "chamber play", based on the world of the petty bourgeoisie.

film during the Twenties). He wrote the scenarios for *Caligari* and *Genuine*, for the "chamber-play films" *Hintertreppe* ("Backstairs", 1921) by Leopold Jessner, *Scherben* ("Shattered", 1921) and *Sylvester* ("New Year's Eve", 1923) by Lupu Pick. He also wrote the scenarios for several of Murnau's films. The term *Kammerspielfilm* (according to Lotte Eisner) was derived from the plays for smaller theaters, by Max Reinhardt, in which the psychological finesse of the actors' performances became more intelligible to the audience. [10] By analogy, Lupu Pick's "chamber-play film", *Scherben*, (1921) is a psychological and intimate film, close to everyday life. Carl Mayer's scenarios highlight the "common run" of people, who are generally only designated as "Father" or "Mother", and, on the whole, his films adhere to unity of time, place and action. On the one hand, by 1921, they promoted the trend in German film that favored everyday, realistic and socially critical elements. On the other hand, however, they introduced the dimension of impenetrable and overwhelming destiny, fate and the pre-ordained. The role played by objects is much greater than merely being

present, for they assume a considerably enhanced symbolic function. "Chamber-play films" usually take place in the world of the lower middle class and of domestic servants and narrate melodramas with sad endings: a maidservant commits suicide after the jealous mailman kills her fiancé (*Hintertreppen*); an official kills his superior because the latter has seduced his daughter (*Scherben*); a café proprietor commits suicide because of his domineering mother (*Sylvester*). As Kracauer points out, the heroes of these films seem to be oppressed victims of their own impulses.

In these films, the actors' stylized mimicry, the oppressive elements in the decor and the density of the universe that holds the protagonists captive approximate Expressionism. Carl Mayer wrote his scenarios in a purely Expressionistic language, composed of ecstatic transports, interjections and detailed observations. It is interesting to note that the "chamber-play films" tried to avoid using any subtitles at all, which denotes a determination to condense and simplify.

The *Strassenfilme* ("street films") are related to the "chamber-play films", and Carl Grune's *Die Strasse* ("The Street", 1923) is a typical

190   *Die Strasse* (by Carl Grune: 1923)
The film that laid the foundations for the *Strassenfilm* ("street-film") genre: for the film's heroes, the Street symbolizes a dark world of temptation and danger.

example of the genre. In these films, the Street symbolizes the dark world of temptation and menace, an insidious counter image of the dismal but secure petty-bourgeois living room, to which the hero of *Die Strasse* contritely returns, after having survived several dangerous adventures and even having been suspected (although mistakenly) of murder. The film's Expressionist stylization of decor conveys this allegorical dimension of the Street, sometimes by translating the symbolic code directly into images (e.g., the enormous pair of glasses over the entrance to an optician's). The representatives of order are counterfigures in this world seething with chaotic impulses, for instance, the policemen who safely direct traffic and help children. The mythical schema of the menacing world of the Street still sets the tone of a film as realistic as Ernö Metzner's *Überfall* ("Hold-Up", 1929).

Friedrich Wilhelm Murnau and Fritz Lang were the two leading directors of the first half of the Twenties; they both worked in the Expressionist vein without actually fusing with the trend. As a screen-writer, Murnau is comparable perhaps only to Jean Renoir and Carl Theodore Dreyer, with a very personal and innovative manner of interweaving dream and reality. His *Nosferatu, eine Symphonie des Grauens* ("Nosferatu: A Horror Symphony", 1922) based on the novel *Dracula* by Bram Stoker, is a major classic of the horror-film genre. It is worth mentioning that Murnau filters reality for his poetic and macabre effects, using the cinematographic technology at his disposal, rather than resorting to studios and sets. In fact, his landscape shots are among the uncanniest passages of this film. Nosferatu, the vampire, is frightening because of the way he is integrated into real decors (the entrance of a decaying castle, the

191   Max Schreck in *Nosferatu, eine Symphonie des Grauens* (by Friedrich Wilhelm Murnau: 1921)
Murnau used camera angles and pictorial compositions masterfully to achieve spooky effects.

192   Emil Jannings in *Der letzte Mann* (by Friedrich Wilhelm Murnau: 1924)
A hotel doorman is deprived of his uniform and downgraded to the position of lavatory attendant—the camera angle underscores his humiliation.

182

193 Lil Dagover and Emil
Jannings in *Tartuffe* (by Friedrich
Wilhelm Murnau: 1925)
Murnau used the expressiveness of
decors to expose hypocrisy and
spurious morality.

194 Emil Jannings and Gösta
Ekman in *Faust* (by Friedrich
Wilhelm Murnau: 1926)
The UFA requested the author
Gerhart Hauptmann to supply the
subtitles for the film; Hans Kyser
wrote the scenario and based it on
motifs drawn from Marlowe,
Goethe and German folk tales.

facades of old warehouses in Lübeck). And a procession of people through the streets looks sinister because it is viewed through a window bearing the imprint of a cross. Certain of the film's pictorial compositions are famous, e.g., the shot of Nosferatu taken on board ship, diagonally from below, when he appears at the edge of a hatch. The performance by Max Schreck in the role of Nosferatu is particularly well adapted to the settings and movements of the frames, usually conveying the unnatural sluggishness and precision of slow motion.

The scenario for *Der Letzte Mann* ("The Last Laugh", 1924) was written by Carl Mayer; it is the story of a hotel doorman who is deprived of his uniform and downgraded to the position of a lavatory attendant. When the old man (interpreted by Emil Jannings) loses his uniform, he loses his identity as well; his world collapses. Murnau shot this film in a studio, where he had house facades, courtyards and big-city streets streaming with traffic built in the workshop hall. His cameraman, Carl Freund, used the "mobile-camera" technique for the first time, the better to convey feelings and psychic elements. This method, as well as the focusing of the camera

and the decors, made it possible for Murnau to create a subjective reality, the one seen through the eyes of his protagonist. In one and the same image, reality and unreality flow together, corroborating Kracauer's observation that, in Murnau's films, "reality... was surrounded by a halo of dreams and presentiments". [11]

Murnau improved on his methods in his later films, *Tartuffe* (1925) and *Faust* (1926). The decor mirrors the plot in *Tartuffe* and appears as a "film within a film". By contrast, *Faust* is a symphony of chiaroscuro, a procession of fantastically orchestrated visions, of lights, movements and reflections. The structure of the film, which is more reminiscent of *Golem* than of Murnau's earlier *Nosferatu*, once again shows traces of Expressionism.

Murnau left for the United States in 1926. He made four more films there before his death and, as far as the producers allowed, they were a faithful continuation of the methods used in his German films.

Fritz Lang turned from architecture to film making, which explains the importance of architectonic and spatial elements in his films. After filming several melodramas and spy films, he made a name for himself in 1921

195 *Der müde Tod* (by Fritz Lang: 1921)
Architecture was also central to Fritz Lang's films: the staircase in this film leads to the kingdom of Death.

196 Rudolf Klein-Rogge in
Dr. Mabuse, der Spieler (by Fritz
Lang: 1922)
Right from the start, Fritz Lang was
very good at picturesque
character-typing: in this scene,
Dr. Mabuse lets blind men sort his
counterfeit money.

197 Paul Richter in *Die Nibelungen*,
Part I: *Siegfrieds Tod* (by Fritz Lang:
1924)
A film that juxtaposes the
monumental and the sublime
elements of the abstract and of
kitsch and which was characterized
by its original stage sets and the
chiaroscuro of the photography.

with *Der müde Tod* ("Destiny"). In a fashion similar to *Das Wachsfigurenkabinett*, the film is composed of three episodes, which take place in exotic places. The best scene is when Death appears seated before an enormous wall; later a crevice opens in the wall and reveals a staircase that leads to infinity. The theme of *Dr. Mabuse, der Spieler* ("Dr. Mabuse, the Gambler", 1922) is related to *Caligari*, as are the painted Expressionist decors that, although they are not used as consistently as in Robert Wiene's film, create a feeling of restlessness and of hypnotism. Both parts of the *Die Nibelungen* cycle of films – *Siegfrieds Tod* ("Siegfried's Death", 1923) and *Kriemhilds Rache* ("Kriemhild's Revenge", 1924) – oscillate between kitsch, strictly ornamental stylization and the artistic effects of daring visions. Everything was built in the workshop, from the forest to the fire-spitting dragon. The conflict between exaggerated pathos and a rather dubious ideological viewpoint on the one hand, and impressive imagery on the other, appears even more flagrant in *Metropolis*. Based on a scenario by Thea von Harbou, it is a crazy, incredible story of battles and final reconciliation between the upperworld and the underworld, between the "brain and heart" of a huge city of the future. Although the ideology is laid on thick, one cannot tear oneself away from the visions and impressive crowd scenes, e.g., the scene where a gigantic

198   *Metropolis* (by Fritz Lang, 1926-27) Rudolf Klein-Rogge with one of his artificial human creations, "false" Maria.

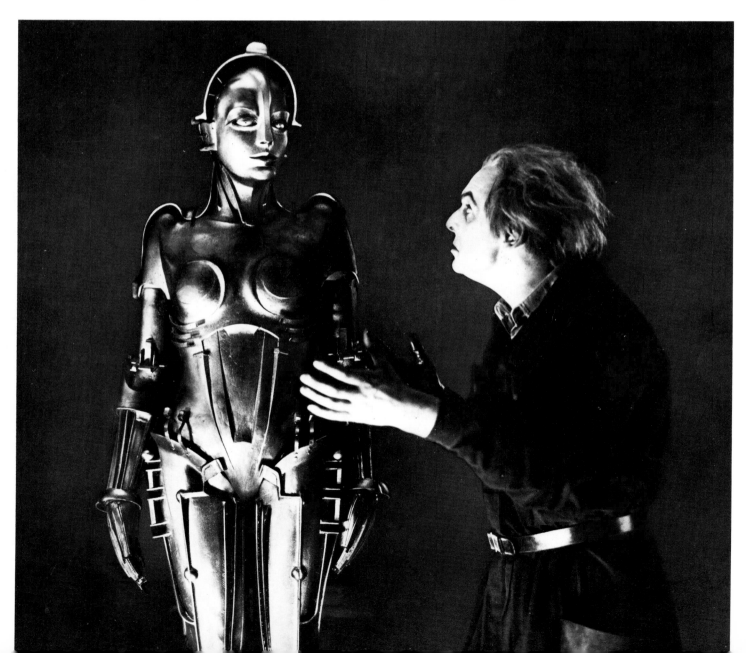

199 *Die Frau im Mond* (by Fritz Lang: 1929)
Thea von Harbou wrote the scenario for this film, one of the first science-fiction films; it is the story of an expedition that sets out for the moon to dig for gold.

200 Rudolf Klein-Rogge and Gerda Maurus in *Spione* (by Fritz Lang: 1928)
Like Dr. Mabuse, the master spy of this film leads several lives: he is also a bank director and variety-show clown.

10000 Mk.

Belohnung

Wer ist der Mörder?

Seit Montag, dem 11. Juni ds.

Der Schüler Kurt Klawitzky und

gewesen Müllerstr.

Aus verschiedene

ähnlichen

Jahres

Das unübertroffene
Meisterwerk
des deutschen
Kriminalfilms

M

von Fritz Lang
Prädikat:
Besonders wertvoll

◁ 201 *M—Eine Stadt sucht einen Mörder* (by Fritz Lang: 1931)
The shadow of Peter Lorre on an advertisement pillar is an example of the subtle treatment of decor, space, light and audio-visual counterpoint that made *M* (one of the first sound films) into one of the most fascinating films ever on fear and persecution.

machine, with workers on its many stories, operating controls, suddenly goes haywire and is transformed into a sort of Moloch that devours the workers, or the unforgettable vision of the underground city flooded with water.

In his later sound films, Lang perfected his masterful talents as director and composer of picture frames. *M – Ein Stadt sucht einen Mörder* ("M – A City Seeks A Murderer", 1921) was a high point in his career. The film tells the story of a child-killer who ends up being pursued by both the police and the underworld. Lang orchestrated his film into a fascinating mosaic of insinuations, speculations and clues, as well as a crescendo of fear, penetrated by psychological codes, frightening leitmotifs and symbols. The film also owed its success to its actors (Peter Lorre, Gustaf Gründgens), to the dramaturgical interweaving of police and underworld plots, and to the

exceptional camera angles (for instance, the staircase where the mother calls "Elsie" and the way the camera focuses, from the top of the street, on Peter Lorre when his escape is cut off on all sides).

Avant-Garde and Experimental Films

An independant "school" of avant-garde or experimental films emerged in Berlin during the postwar years. It attracted but few film makers, whose work made only a minor impact at first, but the films they created contained a multitude of precedents that made them, eventually, very important to the development of film in Germany and in the rest of the world. Avant-garde film makers like Eggeling, Richter and Ruttmann demon-

202 *Die Abenteuer des Prinzen Achmed* (by Lotte Reiniger: 1926)
As of 1918, Lotte Reiniger developed her own personal genre—"cutout" or "silhouette" films—inspired by Chinese shadow theaters.

strated for the first time that movies could offer unheard of possibilities, that "abstract" or "absolute" films could be created that were based on, and would expand, the fine arts and that, taking a step further, such films could go beyond the framework of the classical film industry and thus be accessible to individual artists as well. Above all, the versatility and daring of such films were a challenge to all the existing cinematographic arts.

The basis for experimental and avant-garde films in Germany can be traced back quite far, at least to the year 1913 (which was famous in other respects as well), when Guido Seeber, a cameraman and pioneer in special effects, completed *Trickfilm der marschierenden Streichhölzer* ("Marching Matchsticks"). He used a technique that was an innovation at the time – animation – taking individual shots that enabled inanimate objects to have the appearance of motion. But the origin of avant-garde film in a narrower sense can be dated a bit later, to 1917 or 1918. At that time, the Swedish painter Viking Eggeling and the German Hans Richter – an art and music student who "sought to discover the rhythmic laws in painting" [12] – met regularly in Ascona and Zurich. Both men were in touch with the members of the Dada movement and decided to collaborate artistically with each other. In 1919, they moved to Klein-Kölzig near Berlin and worked on a series of abstract pictures that they drew up on paper scrolls. The result was the so-called "revolving pictures", depicting abstract forms in various stages of development. Eggeling and Richter attempted to integrate motion and time into their drawings and thus were logically led to film making. In 1920, the UFA gave them permission to make use of a special-effects bench. Eggeling filmed his revolving drawings *Horizontal-Vertikal-Orchester I-III* (the film was lost) and, in 1923 and 1924, the *Diagonal Sinfonie*, which would later be considered a classic among abstract films. Whereas Eggeling (who died in Berlin in 1925) remained faithful to the original principles of his revolving pictures, Richter soon developed another technique, based on paper cutouts in the shape of squares. "The simple form of a square was by nature easily adaptable to the quadrangular

screen. I allowed my squares to grow and to disappear again, to leap and glide, all at a controlled tempo, in a systematically articulated rhythm." The film he created in this way was entitled *Rhythmus 21* (after the year of origin) and lasted some three minutes; he later filmed *Rhythmus 23* along the same lines.

Others who were experimenting in the realm of abstract or "absolute" films at the time were Werner Graeff, a Bauhaus student and a member of the group De Stijl (he drew up "scores" for films, which, however, he never managed to realize), and Walter Ruttmann, a painter and commercial artist who turned to film making in 1918. From 1919 to 1923, Ruttmann made four abstract films, which he entitled *Opus I-IV* and which already use color and music especially composed for the films. The *Opus I* premiere took place on April 27, 1921, in Berlin's Marmorhaus. Richter wrote that, on the one hand, Ruttmann's films seemed *vieux jeu* to Eggeling and himself but that, on the other, they were definitely technically superior to their own films.

In 1925, an International Avant-Garde Film Show opened in Berlin and included the films *Entr'acte* ("Intermission") by René Clair and *Ballet mécanique* ("Mechanical Ballet") by Fernand Léger. These films (and Man Ray) made an impact that provoked a gradual change in the aims of avant-garde film in Berlin: concrete forms replaced abstract, painted or drawn ones. In *Film Studie* (1926), Richter juxtaposed lines and surfaces with rotating eyes and heads multiplied through prisms; in his later films – *Inflation* (1927-28) and *Rennsymphonie* ("Racing Symphony", 1928-29) – he made montages of documentary shots. His *Vormittagsspuk* ("Guests Before Breakfast", 1927-28) described the revolt of animated objects against their everyday use. (The film was created for the German Chamber Music Festival in Baden-Baden and was coupled with Paul Hindemith's music for the mechanical piano.) In 1925, the cameraman Guido Seeber created his technically original *Kipho-Werbetrickfilm*, a publicity and special-effects film, destined for the Kino- und Foto-Ausstellung. Laszlo Moholy-Nagy had already made several documentaries on Berlin and Marseille by 1926 and 1929; he returned to abstraction with his *Lichtspiel schwarz-weiss-grau* ("Play of Light in Black-White-Gray"). It was one of the rare "absolute" films, based on Moholy-Nagy's kinetic-light sculpture, *Licht-Raum-Modulator*(cf. Pl. 160); it translated that sculpture's "actions" into film, that is to say, it enabled them to materialize for the first time through the medium of film. Finally, as of 1929, Oskar Fischinger began very intensive activities, under the auspices of the UFA, in the realm of special-effects films using abstract forms, which resulted in the *Studien* ("Studies") series. He worked on that series until 1934, basing them on specific musical compositions. Fischinger was especially interested in the relationships between sound and image, and he left behind an exceptional wealth of works; besides publicity films, he created "tonal compositions" and "light concerts". He left for the United States in 1936 and later worked for Paramount, MGM and Walt Disney.

The most important achievement of German avant-garde films during the Twenties is a film that basically transcended this genre and was accessible to a wider portion of the public, namely Walter Ruttmann's documentary film, *Berlin, die Sinfonie der Grossstadt* ("Berlin, The Symphony of a Big City", 1927). The film represented a turning point, not only for the avant-garde film movement but also for trends in German film as a whole. Frequently interpreted as an expression of *Neue Sachlichkeit* ("New Objectivity"), it was based on the ideas of the Expressionist scenarist Carl Mayer, who in turn was inspired by his encounter in 1926 with the Russian film *Battleship Potemkin* to make a film that was a "cross-section" of a big city without a narrative plot. Ruttmann's struc-

203   *Berlin, die Sinfonie der Grossstadt* (by Walter Ruttmann: 1927) Alfred Kerr wrote: "Ah, but here things flit about, flail, blaze, soar, jostle, gush, glide, stride, fade, flow, swell, die away; unfurl themselves, arch, spread, diminish, roll about, cramp up, are sharpened; split, twist, stretch; are filled, emptied, puffed up, cut down to size; bloom and are blighted: in short, Expressionism comes tumultuously alive—a feast for the eyes...."

turing of the film was starkly formally, causing Carl Mayer, whose ideas ran more to social criticism, to turn away from the project soon. *Berlin, die Sinfonie der Grossstadt* is constructed on the principle of contrasting and analogous montages. Its central theme describes the course of a spring day in Berlin, beginning with the arrival of a train at a railway station and ending with shots of the nocturnal boulevards and a firework display that eclipses all the rest. In between, the pictorial contents are separated into individual sequences and arranged according to basic principles of abstraction. Ruttmann's montages and the realism of individual shots are admirable. (It was filmed using the latest technological methods and avoiding all artificial lighting.) One can say in all truth that *Berlin, die Sinfonie der Grossstadt* is as fascinating today as ever. At the same time, however, the film reveals an indifference to the material of the film itself – to the individual images. The film's subject matter has been transformed into a function of "urban rhythm". As paradoxical as it might seem, the film can be considered a basically Expressionist work that does not reproduce reality, but follows its own inner vision and arranges the elements of reality to correspond to that vision. In fact, the film begins with an abstract sequence of surfaces and lines and then, by a formal analogy, shifts to the image of a railway barrier being lowered. The end of the film is handled in much the same way – a small tribute to Ruttmann's earlier experience with animated films, as well as a confirmation that the diversified and vibrant panorama of the big city has been developed here on the basis of an abstract premise.

"New Objectivity" in Film: Realistic and Documentary Trends

In the second half of the Twenties, trends other than Expressionism, chiaroscuro and fantastic stylization came to the forefront of the German film. The turning point can probably be traced to the showing of the Soviet film *Battleship Potemkin*, by Sergei Eisenstein, in 1926. At first the film was banned by the film censorship board on orders from the Reichswehr and then allowed to be shown in a shortened version. It hit Berlin like a bomb, provoking many artists and intellectuals into reconsidering their objectives. The film's effect was described by Feuchtwanger in his novel *Erfolg* and by Bert Brecht in his poem "An die Matrosen des Potemkin". Alfred Kerr also wrote a poem explaining why he, until then a member of the censorship board, had decided to resign after the ban on *Potemkin*. But *Potemkin* was not the only event that triggered the change in trend; the new tendencies were also favored by a stabilization of the economic and social situation after 1924. The visionary and feverish period of hopes and utopic yearnings, expressed by postwar Expressionism, was replaced by an-

204   Greta Garbo and Valeska Gert in *Die freudlose Gasse* (by Georg Wilhelm Pabst: 1925)
In this film, which was still under Expressionist influence, Pabst portrayed the decadence of the bourgeoisie in the postwar period.

192

other, more sober and often resignedly "neutral" approach to reality.

G.W. Pabst was the director whose films articulated this new basic tendency. His first film, *Der Schatz* ("The Treasure", 1924), still bore the traces of Expressionism, whereas in *Die freudlose Gasse* ("The Joyless Street", 1925), certain stylistic and thematic elements already overlap each other. On the one hand, the stylized decors of earlier German films were still in use (Lotte Eisner wrote: "*Die freudlose Gasse* is the quintessence of the Germanic approach, reflected in deeply mysterious streets, paths and stairways, which remain shrouded in zones of twilight". [13]) On the other hand, the film drew a realistically critical portrait of the despair, misery and decadence of the lower middle classes during the postwar and inflation years. The plot concerns an official's daughter, who becomes a prostitute to allay her family's misery; she is threatened by a brutal butcher and finally saved by an American. The film gained much from its excellent performers (Asta Nielsen, Greta Garbo [unknown at the time], Valeska Gert, Werner Krauss) and could already be considered distinctively significant; nonetheless, its success (even abroad), was probably due, for the most part, to the social accuracy of the subject-matter and of the characters in the film. It had been a long time since any film had so convincingly described day-to-day, contemporary life.

In *Geheimnisse einer Seele* ("The Secrets of a Soul", 1926), Pabst endeavored to transpose psychoanalytical themes; he succeeded in

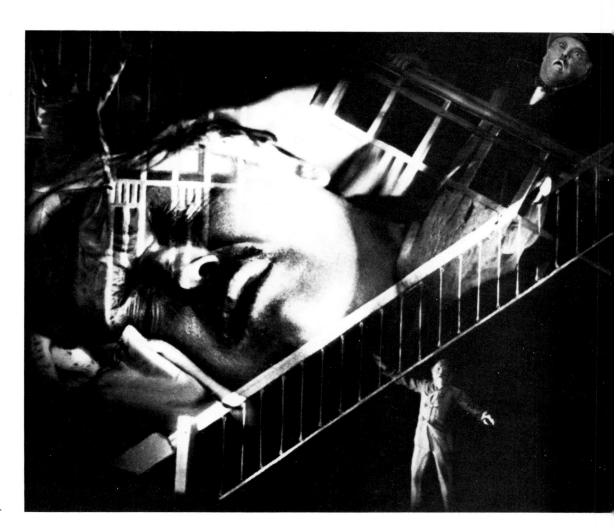

205 *Geheimnisse einer Seele* (by Georg Wilhelm Pabst: 1926) The film was presented as a "psychoanalytical chamber"; Dr. Karl Abraham, a student of Freud's, and Dr. Hanns Sachs were the "psychoanalytical collaborators".

206 Louise Brooks in *Die Büchse der Pandora* (by Georg Wilhelm Pabst: 1929)
Lotte Eisner described the "miracle of Louise Brooks... she goes through both films *[Die Büchse der Pandora* and *Tagebuch einer Verlorenen]* with enigmatic detachment".

creating interesting images but let the plot come to a rather dubious, optimistic ending. *Die Liebe der Jeanne Ney* ("The Love of Jeanne Ney", 1927) was based on a novel by Ilja Ehrenburg and described a bourgeois girl's love for a Soviet revolutionary. Pabst adapted two plays by Frank Wedekind in *Die Büchse der Pandora* ("Pandora's Box", 1928-29); the American actress Louise Brooks played the role of Lulu; she was the incarnation of the new star myth. G.W. Pabst's style defined itself in this film; it was an ornamental style with rich atmospheres, reveling in details and close-ups, lighting effects and exceptional perspectives. In contrast to Expressionist films, where such elements led to the creation of a second, metaphysical level of action, in Pabst's films they served only to accentuate the physical presence of objects and surroundings, and thus to increase the film's realism. Pabst assembled the optical details into a single continuity with flowing movements or imperceptible cuts that did not separate the audience from the action but rather pulled it into it. Admittedly, many of his films showed a preference for the picturesque as well, which took on an autonomy of its own. This was the reason Brecht did not approve of Pabst's version of the *Dreigroschenoper* ("Three-Penny Opera", 1931).

A growing social and political commitment emerged in the scripts of the sound films Pabst made before 1933, no doubt reflecting the basic tendency of many other films of the times. *Westfront 1918* (1930), which many consider Pabst's best film, was one of the severest critics of the horrors of World War I; *Kamaradschaft* ("Comradery", 1931) describes the solidarity of workers internationally, during a mine catastrophe on the German-French border. This film, in which Ernst Busch played the leading role, even included an element of the class war. To be sure, the characteristics of these last two films disappeared completely, from the work Pabst did in Germany during the Hitler era.

Several other films of the late Twenties also articulated the socially critical and realistic tendencies of German films of the time. Socially critical elements, although often reduced to the noncommittal framework of picturesque portrayals of milieu, could already be found in Gerhard Lamprecht's *Zille-Filmen*, which were based on the personal accounts of the artist Heinrich Zille, and entitled *Die Verrufenen* ("Slums of Berlin", 1925). The film's appeal and relative authenticity are products of its portrayals of milieus and types of character (which Fritz Lang developed to perfection in his films, *Mabuse* and *M*); the plot and its "morality", on the contrary, were horribly hackneyed. A real

change in the social outlook of films did not actually occur until 1928 or 1929. In 1928, several directors who were at the very start of their careers – Robert Siodmak, Fred Zinnemann, Billy Wilder and Edgar Ulmer – were responsible for creating the film *Menschen am Sonntag* ("People on Sundays"), working together on an extremely tight budget and improvising on a daily basis. The film describes a typical Sunday among low-ranking employees in Berlin; it incorporates certain documentary passages, thus embedding the plot in an everyday background and, from a documentary point of view, creating a certain similarity with *Berlin, die Sinfonie der Grosstadt*. *Menschen am Sonntag* was also characterized by the public's affectionate identification with the protagonists, by a satirical view of petty-bourgeois customs, by a "light-handed" staging and by dramaturgical accu-

209 *Kameradschaft* (by Georg Wilhelm Pabst: 1931)
International solidarity among workers at a mine catastrophe: *Die Rote Fahne* commented: "The film is an excellent description of a slice of working-class life."

210 *Die Verrufenen* (by Gerhard Lamprecht: 1925)
A film inspired by the stories and paintings of the artist-draftsman Heinrich Zille.

211 *Menschen am Sonntag* (by
Robert Siodmak, Edgar Ulmer, Fred
Zinnemann and Billy Wilder:
1929-30)
A sequence describing a provincial's
encounter with Berlin's historical
monuments is embedded in this
documentary chronicle of a
weekend spent together by four
young inhabitants of Berlin.

racy. Despite the fact that it was created as a
secondary product of the film industry, with
a virtually total disregard for the industry's
rules, the film became one of the most vivid
testimonies to everyday life in Berlin, and one
of Germany's and Berlin's best films from the
end Twenties.

Several other films, created in 1929 as well,
were characterized by their socially critical
approach. *Brüder* ("Brothers"), a recently
rediscovered film directed by Werner Hochbaum, is the story of a historical strike by
Hamburg's dockworkers. *Mutter Krausens
Fahrt ins Glück* ("Mother Krause's Journey to
Happiness") by Piel Jutzi and *So ist das Leben*
("Such is Life") by Carl Junghans (both

created in 1929) were closely connected in
theme and basic stylistic approach: they dealt
with the proletarian situation. Piel Jutzi's central character was an old newspaper vendor,
Mother Krause, whose life becomes more
miserable day by day, until the fatal moment
when she has no alternative but to open the
gas tap. The story was embedded in an
extraordinarily precise, striking yet unsenti-
mental milieu portrayal of northern Berlin.
Käthe Kollwitz and Otto Nagel collaborated
on this film, which was based on stories by
Heinrich Zille, adapted by the artist Otto
Nagel. The production firm was Prometheus-
Film which, at the time, was the leading production and distribution company for leftist

197

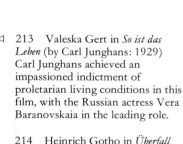

and revolutionary proletarian films, as well as
for the distribution of Soviet films. A similar
film project by Carl Junghans had been turned
down by Prometheus; so he shot his film,
about an old washerwoman (played by the
Russian actress Vera Baranovskaia) in
Prague. Whereas *Mutter Krausens* presented the
workers' movement as a possible alternative
to lower middle- and working class despair
(even if this was a secondary plot), *So ist das
Leben* was far less political and ideological. It
should be mentioned that both films and
especially Junghans's made extensive use of
"Russian" stylistic methods such as close-ups
and swift montages.

After a certain period of artistic stagnation,
German film began flourishing again in the
period from 1929 to 1932. A considerable number of films were created and contributed to the renewal of the cinematographic climate, including many which would
deserve to be analyzed in detail. Some of these
films, (all following the socially critical and
realistic trend) originated during the silent-
film period (in the years 1929 to 1930, most

movie theaters were converted to the new
sound system), and some were already filmed
as sound films. They all developed formally
new, trend-setting solutions to the problems
posed by a realistic approach to filming and
by the portrayal of everyday and social conflicts. This is true of the camera action and
work with amateur actors in *Menschen am
Sonntag*; of the use of montages in *Mutter
Krausens* and *So ist das Leben*. *Überfall* ("Hold-
Up", 1929) a short film by the architect Ernö
Metzner, was also a testimonial to the times,
in a category similar to the earlier allegorical
"street films": a petty-bourgeois finds money
on the street, goes into a bar, where he is
observed by ruffians, who later follow him as
he leaves. He takes refuge with a prostitute,
where he is tricked into an ambush, beaten
and robbed. He awakens in a hospital, to see
the world split before his eyes into a gaping
schizophrenic vision. The Street symbolized
an abysmal threat but, at the same time, was
depicted absolutely realistically, with the
detailed care of an almost documentary precision. The pursued and threatened citizen

became a caricature. The lack of dialogues or subtitles gave the film great formal coherency, which further accentuated its nightmarish effect.

Two more films belong to the same realistic context; they combine social criticism with a certain maudlin or resigned attitude; in contrast to the combative dynamism of a film like *Mutter Krausens*, the attitude that comes across in these films is formally and dramatically grayer and more monotonous. They are *Lohnbuchhalter Kremke* ("The Wages Clerk Kremke", 1930) by Marie Harder, subsidized by the German Social Democratic Party, the drama of an unemployed accountant who is then also abandoned by his daughter, which drives him to commit suicide (the film ends with a demonstration by the unemployed), and *Cyankali* ("Cyanide", 1930) by Hans Tintner, after a play of the same title by Friedrich Wolf, a strong attack on Paragraph 218 of German law, the story of a girl who dies after trying to abort with poison. The weakness of these films lies in their latent

215 Title page of *Illustrierter Filmkurier* for the film *Cyankali* (by Hans Tintner: 1930)
The film (and the original play by Friedrich Wolf) provoked public debate on the problem of abortion.

216 Marlene Dietrich in *Der blaue Engel* (by Josef von Sternberg: 1931) Josef von Sternberg projected Marlene Dietrich to stardom with this film. Although he did not keep to Heinrich Mann's novel, he created a masterpiece as far as the decors and "atmospheric" elements were concerned.

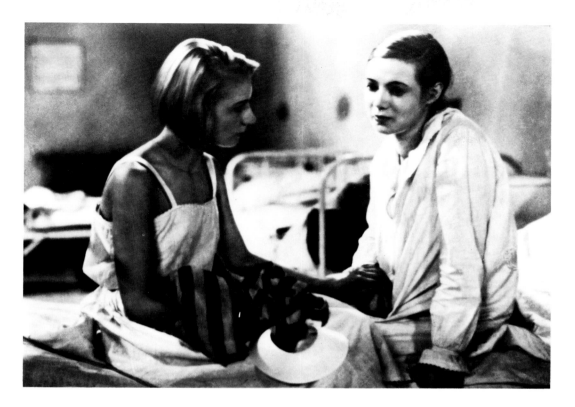

217　Hertha Thiele and Dorothea Wieck in *Mädchen in Uniform* (by Leontine Sagan: 1931)
A film characterized by the sensitivity with which its Austrian director, Leontine Sagan (who worked mainly for theater), stigmatized the repressive atmosphere of a Prussian boarding school for girls.

mawkishness, but there are many brilliant scenes in *Cyankali*, thanks to the excellent performance of Grete Mosheim in the main role, and the film is enjoying a renaissance these days, because of the theme's topicality.

Such strongly atmospheric films as Leo Mittler's *Jenseits der Strasse* ("Harbor Drift", 1929) or Josef von Sternberg's famous *Der blaue Engel* ("Blue Angel", 1930), with Marlene Dietrich, are basically more in line with the past history of German films than with its progressive trends, although both incorporate fine, highly skillful decors and photography. *Jenseits der Strasse* is situated in a milieu of beggars and jobless, which gives the film a romantic aura. *Der blaue Engel* strays far afield from Heinrich Mann's novel *Professor Unrat*, on which it was based; denunciation of the bourgeois world is replaced by personal tragedy, enhanced moods and feelings, and an evocation of pity. In this film (shot entirely in a studio) the environment seems somewhat unreal: it is transformed into a soul-scape. However, these films could not have turned out as they did if they had not adopted spe-

cific elements from the Realist movement in film.

Pacifist films like Victor Trivas's *Niemandsland* ("Hell on Earth", 1931) were more straightforward. Based on an idea by Leonhard Frank and using music by Hanns Eisler, this film describes five infantry-men of different nationalities, who are brought together among the trenches of World War I. Sagan's *Mädchen in Uniform* ("Girls in Uniform", 1931) was significant as well; it describes the authoritarian atmosphere of a Prussian girls' boarding school. The headmistress is almost an incarnation of Frederick the Great, and she directs the school so strictly that when one of the boarders has a crush on her female teacher, the schoolgirl is forced to the brink of suicide. The sensitivity with which the film is performed, the photographic perceptivity and the explicitly anti-authoritarian stand taken explain *Mädchen in Uniform*'s amazing contemporary renaissance.

Of course, German films from 1929 to 1932 were not all realistic or socially critical like the films mentioned previously or Piel

Jutzi's *Berlin Alexanderplatz* (1931), in which Franz Bieberkopf's fate was incorporated in a documentary commentary on the everyday aspects of life in Berlin. A deluge of purely "entertaining" films, some, however, ideologically distorted, were created to glorify German traditions and military values. Whereas the realistic films were produced mainly by smaller firms like Prometheus (which had connections with the German Communist Party) or Nero-Film, the light entertainment and reactionary-conservative films were almost always UFA products. Rightist films included Gustav Ucicky's *Flötenkonzert von Sanssouci* ("The Flute Concert at Sans Souci", 1930) and *York* (1931), Luis Trenker's *Der Rebell* ("The Rebel", 1932) and Friedrich Zelnick's *Der Choral von Leuthen* ("The Anthem of Leuthen", 1933): films in honor of Prussian and authoritarian values, which were consis-

218 Heinrich George in *Berlin Alexanderplatz* (by Fritz Lang: 1931) In this adaptation of Döblin's novel, faith in the "little man's" power of survival contrasts with the pessimism of *Der blaue Engel* and of *M.*

219 *S.O.S. Eisberg* (by Arnold Franck: 1932)
A search-party tries to track down an explorer who has disappeared in Greenland—a typical film of the "mountain-film" genre.

220 Olga Chekhova and Lilian Harvey in *Die Drei von der Tankstelle* (by Wilhelm Thiele: 1930) Parody and musical leitmotifs made film operetta a successful model for the new entertainment films.

221 Wolfgang Liebeneiner, Luise Ullrich and Willy Eichberger in *Liebelei* (by Max Ophüls: 1932-33) The film was based on the play of the same name by Arthur Schnitzler. Ophüls shot this film, which takes place in Vienna at the turn of the century, shortly before he emigrated in 1933.

tent with the values the Nazis promoted after 1933. Another series of films glorified war: Trenker's *Berge in Flammen* ("Mountains on Fire", 1931) and Ucicky's *Morgenrot* ("Morning Glory", 1933) — applauded at the premiere by Hitler, Hugenberg and Papen.

The *Bergfilme* ("mountain films") belonged to another genre, often magnificently photographed, which compared the solitary, masterful men of the high mountains with the plebian and run-of-the-mill people living in the valleys and lowlands: *Weisse Hölle von Piz Palu* ("The White Hell of Piz Palu", 1929) by Arnold and G.W. Pabst, *Das blaue Licht* ("Blue Light", 1932) by Leni Riefenstahl or *S.O.S. Eisberg* ("S.O.S. Iceberg", 1933) by Arnold Franck, who became the ultimate specialist of the genre along with Trenker.

All of these productions were rounded out by a great number of musicals and comedies, like the immensely successful film-operetta *Die Drei von der Tankstelle* ("Three from the Filling Station", 1930) by Wilhelm Thiele or Erik Charell's *Der Congress tanzt* ("Congress is Dancing", 1931), which portrays customs contemporary to the Congress of Vienna (1814-15): the Czar of Russia has a love-affair with a flower vendor. Ludwig Berger's *Walzerkreig* ("Waltz War", 1933) was the most subtle of these entertainment films, but May Ophül's *Liebelei* ("Playing with Love", 1932), based on the play by Arthur Schnitzler, is head and shoulders above the others; it bore the stylistic and thematic imprint of Vienna, although it was a German production. The actors and actresses were topnotch (Gustaf Gründgens, Olga Chekhova, Luise Ullrich, Magda Schneider), and the film combined all the stylistic accomplishments of German film making in the Twenties — feeling for decors, costumes and lighting — and did full justice to the bitterness of the original work of literature on which it was based.

Bertolt Brecht's and Slatan Dudow's film *Kuhle Wampe* ("Whither Germany") was the most important example of Realist-critical German film in the years 1929 to 1932 and the crowning point of that trend. The Prometheus organization initiated the project just before going bankrupt; at that point, the film's participants took over production in collaboration with the Swiss firm Praesens-

Film. The film's scenario was written by Brecht and Ernst Ottwald, the music by Eisler; it concerns the problems of the jobless in Berlin, first describing the quest for jobs (by bicycle) in impressively stylized sequences, rhythmically punctuated by music. The following sequences take place in a proletarian apartment house, where one family's son is so desperate about his lack of employment that he commits suicide, remembering to remove his wristwatch before jumping out of the window. (Brecht noted that this scene particularly offended the censorship board.) The film goes on to tell of the love between the victim's sister and a young worker (Ernst Busch). The workers' athletic movement played an important role as an activating social force among the young people. The film ends with a comical, dialectically conducted discussion, on the Berlin *S-Bahn* ("fast train"), about the social contradictions of the period. Songs (like the "Solidarity Song") often interrupt the flow of action. The alienated performances by many of the actors, the satirical elements in the portraiture of the petty-bourgeois father, the dramaturgical originality and the musical counterpoint of the film provided new criteria for the possibilities offered by cinematographic realism. *Kuhle Wampe* was not only a social commentary but also a point of comparison and a proclamation of new methods of filming. In addition, the film was entertaining for the audience; it was (and is) enjoyable to follow the dialectical development of the film's line of reasoning (which reaches its climax in the *S-Bahn* scene).

Kuhle Wampe was the subject of sharp disagreements with the censorship board of the Weimar Republic which finally allowed the film to appear only after a series of deletions. The deleted parts were never found again. The film fell into oblivion and was only rediscovered much later (at the end of the Fifties), by the German Democratic Republic; in the Sixties, the film also became known in the Federal Republic of Germany and was promoted as a cult object among the young generation of film makers, whose work was particularly centered on social goals and efficiency. As a matter of fact, *Kuhle Wampe* is one of the few links to German film history

222 *Das Testament des Dr. Mabuse*
(by Fritz Lang: 1932)
The film was banned by the Nazis immediately after they came to power and was, therefore, never premiered.

223 *Kuhle Wampe* (by Slatan Dudow: 1932)
Bertolt Brecht and Ernst Ottwald wrote the scenario for "the only German film that was openly pro-Communist"(-Kracauer)

(with the exception of films by Lang and Murnau, which clearly belong to the realm of silent films) that has lost nothing of its appeal today. The film was the high point and, unfortunately, also the conclusion of a development that brought film makers and script writers into closer touch with their surroundings, underscored their responsabilities as artists, and brought to the fore a new consciousness of form.

Fritz Lang's film *Das Testament des Dr. Mabuse* ("Dr. Mabuse's Testament", 1933) represented the final high point in film. Lang emigrated to Paris, and from there to the United States, very shortly after the film's premiere on March 29, 1933. When Hitler and the National Socialists took over, the German film industry became as still as a graveyard. The last of the leading directors still in the country also emigrated (Ophüls, Berger, Pabst – who did return later). Those who remained had to join the "Reich's Film Board", and films were subjected to a severe dose of regulations and censorship.

German film had sunk into a deep sleep, which was to remain undisturbed in 1945 (with the exception of a few experiments, which were, however, inconclusive). It was not until the years 1962 to 1965 that the Junger Deutscher Film movement managed to reawaken it.

V THEATER

Arno Paul

Preliminary Note

No period in the history of theater in Berlin since the foundation of the German Empire in 1871, when Berlin became a theatrical center as well as a political capital, has been as wealthy, stimulating and contradictory as the Twenties. Before World War I, at least twenty theaters were already active on a regular basis, and this figure rose to roughly fifty during the Twenties. Almost daily, an important premiere took place somewhere in the city, which was swarming with excellent actors, directors, stage designers, theater composers and, last but not least, playwrights

– all of whom were responsible for the exceptional brilliancy and quite inexhaustible creativity of theater life in Berlin.

This inconceivable wealth of talent is certainly one of the reasons why a comprehensive history of theater in Berlin during the Twenties, based on specific plays, has not yet been compiled. As valid and important as this task would be, we too can offer but an approximate and restricted version in this single chapter of a book. Therefore, we shall concentrate on presenting the legitimate theater, which is based on literary works. Consequently, the lyric theater – operas, ballets, revues and musicals – as well as the various

224, 225   Top critics Alfred Kerr (left) of the *Tageblatt*, drawing by Emil Orlik, and Herbert Jhering (right) of the *Börsen-Courier*, drawing by B. F. Dolbin, held sway in Berlin during the Twenties not only over reviews of plays but also over the art of acting during that period. The elegance and irony of the one and the sobriety and argumentative nature of the other provided a contrasting but indefatigable stimulus to permanent quality and improvement.

207

forms of fringe arts such as cabaret, variety and circus cannot be included. Although these stagecrafts were undeniably significant in Berlin's cultural life during the Twenties, mention of them here must remain quite parenthetical to enable us to do justice to the works of the legitimate theater central to this chapter.

We have chosen a series of productions representative of the development and activities of the diverse trends that set the style for legitimate theater in Berlin during the Twenties. Our major sources of information are reviews of plays, which surely at no other time or place were as informative, vivid and varied as in the capital of the Weimar Republic. Daily, more than a hundred newspapers published theater reviews by over fifty critics who represented the most diversified esthetic and politico-cultural points of view. As far as possible, our text relies on the words of those critics, for, from an historical point of view, their opinions are the most authentic and lasting traces of the theatrical productions that interest us.

Expressionism

In contrast to developments in other theatrical centers of the German Empire, Expressionism was a latecomer to the Berlin stage, where its stay was relatively brief. Prussian sobriety — ill-suited to the Expressionist cry *"Oh Mensch"* — had much to do with it, as did the fact that, precisely during the Twenties, an unheard of quantity of diversified esthetic trends invaded the Berlin stage and, as a consequence, thoroughly relativized the impact of Expressionism.

German theater as a whole was far slower to adopt the creative tendencies of Expressionism than were painting or poetry. Not until 1917, were several (very rare) productions in this vein put on, although the first Expressionist plays had already been in print since 1912. The main causes of this delay were the censorship regulations and the turmoil that followed World War I. But the inevitably fleeting nature of dramatic art was also responsible in part; it created a milieu more attached to conventional elements than

the other arts and hence, one more reluctant to part with tradition. The fact that at times playhouses in Berlin even lagged behind those in other parts of Germany as far as the development of Expressionism is concerned is, however, essentially connected with political conditions. No city was hit as hard as Berlin by the war Germany lost, the end of the monarchy and the birth pains of the new State. Under the circumstances, it was difficult for Berlin's passionate theater-going public to achieve the necessary sympathies and openmindedness to welcome a new stylistic tendency as basically abstract and apolitical as Expressionism.

Max Reinhardt was the first to stage the original Expressionist play, *Der Bettler* ("The Beggar") by Reinhard Sorge. With the play's premiere on December 23, 1917, at the Deutsches Theater, Reinhardt also inaugurated the matinee series initiated by his dramatic critic, Felix Hollaender; the series was entitled *Das junge Deutschland* ("Young Germany") and dedicated especially to Expressionist drama. Ten productions were staged between 1917 and 1920. Reinhardt was still favorably inclined towards reforms at the time; however, he was in no mood to become a promoter for the new trend, being far more interested in the nervous, feverish, well-contrived performances by a Jewish actor, born in Prague: Ernst Deutsch, who was at last making a career for himself as a pioneer in the role of the Expressionist Youth — the poet's son in *Der Bettler*.

Reinhardt used the private circuit of Das junge Deutschland series to stage two additional Expressionist plays: Reinhardt Goering's *Seeschlacht* ("Naval Battle", March 3, 1918) and August Stramm's *Kräfte* ("Powers", April 12, 1921). Although Reinhardt did more justice to the ecstatic cry of mankind in *Kräfte*, his staging of *Seeschlacht* three weeks after the Dresden premiere was more important from the standpoint of theater history. The stage sets (by Ernst Stern) and the performances by most of the actors (including Paul Wegener and Emil Jannings) were to a great extent reflections of Reinhardt's conventional Realism, but the performance by Werner Krauss (in the role of the fourth sailor) infused the production with a new

226   Reinhard Sorge: *Der Bettler* (premiered: December 23, 1917 at the Deutsches Theater, directed by Max Reinhardt, stage sets by Ernst Stern)
Sketches of characters by Ernst Stern: (left) the poet-son as a chastened beggar (played by Ernst Deutsch) and (right) the insane father (Paul Wegener).

energy, foreshadowing the future Expressionist style of acting: "concisely, realistically, forcefully, he tore future theatrical possibilities wide open. The style translated nuances into rhythm, descriptive details into tempo, coloration into dynamics.... Words became gestures; words were incarnated." (-Herbert Jhering, *Der Kampf ums Theater*: Dresden, 1922, p. 63).

In view of Reinhardt's preference for staging that was concretely meaningful, it is not surprising that his rare experiments with Expressionism did not make a lasting impression. Generally speaking, however, this was true of all the productions in Das junge Deutschland series, although the principal directors – Herald and Hollaender – enthusiastically encouraged Expressionism. They were even responsible for first staging a play as important as Else Lasker-Schüler's *Die Wupper* (April 27, 1919). In addition to the fact that the productions in Das junge Deutschland series were not sufficiently forceful or decisive to be influential, the leading critics did little to promote Expressionism in the capital during the years preceding and immediately following the war's end – the very period when Expressionism was taking other theatrical strongholds in Germany by storm. With the exception of Herbert Jhering, who became influential as a critic in 1918, the top Berlin critics (Alfred Kerr, Siegfried Jacobsohn, Alfred Klaar, Fritz Engel and Monty Jacobs) had made their name in the era of Realism, so it took time to change their standards. Even a masterpiece such as Werner Krauss's performance in *Seeschlacht* was not extolled in contemporary reviews, and Jhering himself only acknowledged its importance in retrospect.

Last but not least, Expressionist drama lacked the acuity and depth necessary at the time and, therefore, had difficulty adapting to the increased dynamism of an era of social changes. Fritz von Unruh's play *Ein Geschlecht* ("A Family") exemplifies this dilemma well: it was first put on as a private performance in Frankfurt, during the summer of 1918, where a war-weary audience enthusiastically acclaimed the pacifist credo on which the play was based. Six months later, however, after the November Revolution, press reviews of

the Berlin premiere of the same play, in Das junge Deutschland series, criticized the discrepancies between the author's message and the requirements of the times. The critics rejected the play and staging as pathetically distorted: "While millions of people were streaming into the streets of Berlin... to symbolize the destiny of the masses... Das junge Deutschland sat in the theater, steadfast and dutybound, lending themselves... to Fritz von Unruh's stormy and seething fantasy-world". (-Emil Faktor, *Börsen-Courier*: December 30, 1918)

Another early attempt at Expressionist theater was to prove even more inappropri-

227 Sketch by Ernst Stern of Ernst Deutsch as the son in Walter Hasenclever's *Der Sohn* (first run in Berlin: March 24, 1918 at the Deutsches Theater as a matinee performance in the Junges Deutschland series, directed by Heinz Herald, stage sets by Ernst Stern)
Hasenclever wrote, in a poem dedicated to Deutsch, "[You] beast of prey, break loose from the chains of doubt ! / The stage collapses. The scarlet dawn of cities/drops from the wound of your passion".

228　Ernst Toller: *Die Wandlung*
(premiered: September 30, 1919 by
Die Tribüne troupe, directed by
Karl Heinz Martin, stage sets by
Robert Neppach)
Stage model for the scene "In the
Barbed Wire" (4th part of the 2nd
tableau). Toller's stage instructions
read: "Clouds lash out darkly around
the moon. Barbed wire to the right
and left, with white-washed
skeletons suspended on it".

211

229 Ernst Toller: *Die Wandlung* (premiered: September 30, 1919 by Die Tribüne troupe, directed by Karl Heinz Martin, stage sets by Robert Neppach)
Photo of the stage (9th part of the 5th tableau), "Death and Resurrection": (center) the leading actor, Fritz Kortner, a prisoner whose "screams and accusations... drill into the cell doors" and "blast" them open. His pregnant wife (Olga Wojan) is kneeling in front of him.

230-32 The diversified and creative forcefulness of the Expressionist stage: ▷

230 Stage model by Emil Pirchan ▷ for Shakespeare: *King Richard III* (produced by Leopold Jessner at the Staatstheater: November 5, 1920) Pirchan's much extolled (and criticized) stepped stage, which went down in history as "Jessner's stairs", was used here to illustrate the rise and fall of a power-crazed upstart.

231 Stage-set design by César ▷ Klein ("lawyer's study") for Georg Kaiser: *Hölle Weg Erde* (produced by Viktor Barnovsky at the Lessing-Theater: January 20, 1920) The demoniacal interplay of light and shadow is especially noteworthy; it underscores the threatening aspect of the lawyer and, at the same time, makes the room oppressively narrow.

232 Stage-set design by Caspar ▷▷ Neher for Bertolt Brecht: *Baal* (performed at the Deutsches Theater as a matinee by the Junge Bühne troupe: February 14, 1926, directed by Brecht) The emphatic scenic frugality of this study for the Baal-Ekart scene (green fields, blue plum trees) confirms Brecht's break with the nature myth of previous versions of *Baal*.

ate. Since 1916, Lothar Schreyer had been using the Sturm circle (created by the publicist and art-gallery director Herwarth Walden) to present evening recitals, which led, on October 15, 1918, with the staging of August Stramm's short play, *Sancta Susanna*, to the inauguration of the Sturmbühne. Although the audience was restricted to subscribers of *Der Sturm*, their reaction was far from unanimous. Provoked by Jhering's critical review, Schreyer left to continue his theatrical endeavors in *Kampfbühne* ("theater of revolt") in Hamburg. When, in the spring of 1920, for his comeback to Berlin, his own play *Mann* ("Man", given at the Kammerspiele, the small auxiliary of the Deutsches Theater) was spurned by the theater's manager, Max Reinhardt, as esoteric and ritualistic, Schreyer returned to the provinces, where his basically Constructivist and Symbolist stage experiments met with more success.

The real breakthrough for Expressionism was not achieved until Ernst Toller's *Die Wandlung* ("Transfiguration") was performed on September 30, 1919, ten months after the end of World War I. The play was staged by Karl Heinz Martin at Die Tribüne, a recently founded, activist, avant-garde theater, which, according to its own proclamations, worked "without bustle and technology", without "the artificial separation between stage and audience" and, instead, tried to "bare the soul and meaning" of the stage. Not until Toller's play was produced was theatrical Expressionism liberated from all the dross of conventionally psychological Realism, as well as from the impasse of empty exaltation — the two pitfalls of the attempts that had been made to that date. Although Toller's "play in tableaux" bears the imprint of his own biography and is laced with pathetic language, moralizing symbolism and embellished banalities, it was transformed into an event of epic theater by the concentrated efforts of the director, Karl Heinz Martin, of his stage designer, Robert Neppach, and by the compelling performance of Fritz Kortner in the main role: "Words clustered together rhythmically and fell apart. Screams broke out and died away. Movements pushed forewards and back. It was more concentration and momentum than psychology and development, more punctuation than description, more forcefulness than gestures... never moods or background but always essence, always expres-

KAISER: HÖLLE WEG ERDE   CESAR KLEIN

sion". (-Herbert Jhering, *Der Tag*: October 2, 1919).

It was, however, more than the esthetic qualities of the inaugural version of *Die Wandlung* in Berlin that made it fit in with the times far more than any other Expressionist play. Most Expressionist plays were not staged until several years after they had been written, when the heat of the emotional and linguistic imagery had cooled down, whereas Toller's play was produced at the most auspicious moment. He wrote it in the spring of 1918, while in military prison, and described his own transformation from a patriotic, volunteer soldier to a pacifist and, finally, a revolutionary. At the time the play opened, Toller was already considered a martyr to the cause of the very revolution he evoked, since he had just barely escaped being condemned to death as a champion of the leftist movement to create a Soviet state in Munich and was serving a severe prison term (five years' confinement in a fortress) in Bavaria. His tragic fate and his many camarades who had died violent deaths lent authenticity to the play's subject matter and gave both the performers and the audience the possibility of participating in something tangible, even if it was partially based on abstract dramatic material.

A long series of plays followed the sweeping success of *Die Wandlung*; however, in view of the great number of rival directors, troupes and theaters, no uniquely definable style crystallized in Berlin, as it had over the years in Frankfurt-am-Main, Mannheim or Darmstadt, for instance. Even in stage design, a tremendous expressive and creative variety existed, from the classically strict spatial organization of Emil Pirchan to the strange, demoniac lighting effects and play of contours of César Klein or the childishly scribblish, linear images of Caspar Neher. None of the stage directors were willing to explore systematically, in a series of productions, the possibilities of Expressionist theater that were formally inherent in the dramatic contents of the plays. The leading directors preferred to dip into the new genre and use some of its elements and approaches, which they expanded and transformed, without committing themselves stylistically.

When Toller's *Die Maschinenstürmer* ("The Machine Wreckers") was first staged under Karl Heinz Martin's direction at the Grosses Schauspielhaus (June 30, 1922), it no longer depended on Expressionist effects, despite the corresponding elements in the script. For, in addition to the stage sets (by John Heartfield) that realistically reproduced a machine-room "with a red-hot boiler, revolving fly-wheels and clattering looms" (-an unidentified review: July 7, 1922), which the actors used properly, the production's main ideological tendency rejected Symbolism decisively in favor of a heartfelt materialization of reality meant to produce direct political agitation. "Four thousand people fill 'Reinhardt's circus' to the eaves... in a veritable frenzy! The basics of a mass demonstration. Repeated salvoes of applause interrupt the performance. During intermissions, popular speeches attacking the Bavarian government, to which the stage director responds after the final act... completely turning the stage into a platform". (-Hermann Kienzl, *Steglitzer Anzeiger*: July 1, 1922).

At the end of 1919, Reinhardt was joined by a young director from Mainz, Ludwig Berger who, in the autumn of 1918, had already presented an abstract and soulfully pathos-ridden Expressionist staging of Immermann's *Merlin* at the Volksbühne. Berger achieved his most Expressionist results with Johan August Strindberg's *Advent* (at the Kammerspiele: December 9, 1919) and the premiere of Paul Kornfeld's *Himmel und Hölle* ("Heaven and Hell" at the Deutsches Theater: April 21, 1920). The "fantastic, hushed decorations of the room" (-Jhering) were designed by Berger's brother, Rudolf Bamberger. Agnes Straub played the part of the prostitute Maria, performing "with the willpower of inner vision and the forcefulness of expressivity. She played her role with innate emotionalism. She was a prostitute and the incarnation of holy illumination. She was a clown and an ecstatic. She set everything on fire. She was possessed by rhythm. She personified a new dramatic art". (-Herbert Jhering, *Der Tag*: April, 23, 1920) Agnes Straub followed in the footsteps of Deutsch, Krauss and Kortner — an actress who also developed the stylistically character-

233 Agnes Straub in the leading role of Hans Henny Jahnn: *Medea* (premiered by the Junge Bühne troupe: May 4, 1926, directed by Jürgen Fehling)
Straub, more than any other Berlin actress, was the very personification of Expressionist ecstasy; until the late Twenties, she continued to develop new expressive features in this line, without, however, allowing herself to be stereotyped in such roles.

istic forcefulness to convey creatively the spirit of a poetical work and to incarnate a role. Heinrich George and Gerda Müller also belong to the select circle of great Expressionist performers; both had already fully developed their overwhelming talents for incarnating roles in the provinces (above all in Frankfurt-am-Main under the direction of Weichert) and only made a name for themselves in Berlin as of 1922. There they participated in the change in dramatic art to Realism and social motivation.

Another high point of Expressionist theater was staged at the Lessing Theater by its manager and director, Viktor Barnovsky, and his stage designer, César Klein (both of whom were perfectionists rather than pioneers of the new trend). Barnovsky was, above all, a masterful and style-conscious craftsman who proved that "Expressionist technique... can be learnt" (-Jhering); Klein's sets had an

234 Photo of the stage for Georg Kaiser: *Hölle Weg Erde* (produced by Viktor Barnovsky at the Lessing-Theater: January 20, 1920)
The procession of liberated prison inmates on the way from "hell" to "earth", led by the artist (Theodor Loos) and the lawyer (Curt Goetz): "The stage setting was extraordinary,... because a sculptural bridge... dissolved into the infinite and immaterial". (-Herbert Jhering, *Börsen-Courier*: January 21, 1920)

innate dramatic forcefulness. For Georg Kaiser's *Hölle Weg Erde* ("Road from Hell to Earth", January 20, 1920), inaugurated six weeks previously in Frankfurt under Arthur Hellmer's direction, Klein created ingeniously simple scenic solutions, nuanced by novel lighting, color and surface values that shaped the actual directing: "César Klein's stage sets were text illustrations; they did not play up to the actors but to the pictorial tone of the scene. One did not so much hear the play in them as read it". (-Herbert Jhering, *Der Tag*: January 22, 1920) During the premiere, the public vociferously indicated its opinions by whistling, pounding, applauding and making catcalls, although the performers managed to continue. The test thus withstood by no means settled the argument over Expressionism, which was rekindled whenever the basic tendency to scenic concentration and spiritual cogency broke through a purely stylistic framework. By the spring of 1921, progressive critics such as Jhering had already noted that the Expressionism of distorted perspectives and hammered-out dialogues was *passé*. "But the Expressionism that aspires to great theater of spiritual release and rhythmic mastery is just now beginning to develop – even if it is no longer labelled as such". (-Herbert Jhering, *Der Tag*: April 16, 1921)

Leopold Jessner was the best representative of the Expressionist label and fashion. Since the autumn of 1919, he had assumed the position of the first Republican intendant of the "state" (formerly royal) theater: the Staatliches Schauspielhaus on the Gendarmenmarkt. An active Social Democrat and a devout Jew, Jessner, who had worked as a stage director in Hamburg before the war and directed the Neues Schauspielhaus in Königsberg during the war, was not related to the generation or methods of the inner circle of Expressionists. His roughly ten years of thoroughly controversial tenure in Berlin were based on an anti-naturalistic conception of theater that heightened reality. The unheard-of tempo and sharply accentuated rhythm characterizing his work were well suited to Expressionism, as were the concentrated language and image worlds he created to convey the essence of a work. Jessner totally rejected

the subjective arbitrariness and egocentrism that characterized Expressionist style; his stagings were aggressive not destructive, pathetic not plaintive, demoniac not grotesque, political not agitational or zealous.

In keeping with his aloofness from current fashion, Jessner produced hardly any Expressionist plays. His field was the Classics. He freed and updated their powerful historical potential in a fashion unheard of previously and also furnished outside plays with new expressive forcefulness, e.g. Frank Wedekind's satire of an imposter, *Der Marquis von Keith* (March 12, 1920) and Christian Dietrich Grabbe's exaggerated historical drama, *Napoleon oder die Hundert Tage* ("Napoleon or the Hundred Days", May 5, 1922). Jessner stripped both plays of all elements of psychology and genre, and concentrated on conveying the network of human relationships, which was developed into a frenzied but thoroughly choreographed dance of characters and speeches with social implications. In a fashion typical of his work, Jessner accomplished a contradictory but fertile coupling of the highest degree of expressivity with a well-contrived abstractness, which not only liberated Expressionism sty-

236 César Klein: Elba scene from ▷ Christian Dietrich Grabbe: *Napoleon oder die Hundert Tage* (produced by Leopold Jessner at the Staatstheater: May 5, 1922)
Audiences marvelled at the "exceptional harmony" between Jessner and his stage designer Klein "in the scene on Elba, where the jagged twilight glides over the mysterious silhouettes of Napoleon and his loyal cohorts, greatly intensifying the luminous energy of the dialogue". (-Emil Faktor, *Börsen-Courier*: May 6, 1922)

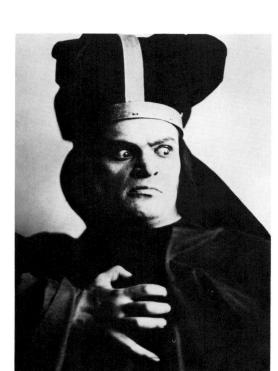

237 Fritz Kortner as Richard III in Shakespeare's play: "Richard's ravenous rise to power... at a frenzied tempo that tramples down conscience, men and obstacles with galloping, unreined language". (-Fritz Kortner, *Aller Tage Abend:* Munich, 1969, p. 235)

238 The idealistic and activist period of Expressionism was followed by a scorched and sadistic period that critics characterized as "cruelly lustful". Photo of the stage for Arnolt Bronnen: *Anarchie in Sillian* (premier: April 6, 1924 by the Junge Bühne troupe at the Deutsches Theater, directed by Heinz Hilpert), (from left to right): Walter Franck as the technician, Maria Eis as the secretary, Hans Heinrich von Tvardovski as the engineer, Franziska Kinz as the stenotypist; setting: the engineer's office at the Sillian power station.

239 Ernst Toller: *Masse Mensch* ▷ (first public performance: September 29, 1921 at the Volksbühne, directed by Jürgen Fehling, stage sets by Klaus Strohbach) Photo of Scene 6 (dream scene): Josef Bunge as Begleiter (guardian), Mary Dietrich as Sonja Irene L. (captive). Stage instructions: "Unlimited space. In the center, a cage, illuminated by a flashing spotlight.... The captive: 'Where am I ?'; the guardian: 'In a human showcase.' "

240 Ernst Barlach: *Die Sündflut* ▷▷ (performed at the Staatstheater: April 4, 1925, directed by Jürgen Fehling, stage sets by Rochus Gliese) Photo of Part 2, scene 2: "At Noah's tents". (From left to right) Albert Steinrück (Calan, the blasphemer), Lucie Mannheim (Awah), Heinrich George (Noah), Fritz Valk (God, disguised as a beggar). "Heavy gray clouds frame the stage that mirrors the primeval world: a bare landscape with a huge sun and pale hovering moon... a giant brush has feverishly painted a dream of fear.... Amidst thunder and lightning and a howling storm the inferno opens". (-Ludwig Sternaux, *Lokal-Anzeiger:* April 6, 1925)

218

listically but also laid the foundations for *Neue Sachlichkeit* ("New Objectivity") in the theater in Berlin during the later Twenties.

In addition to the actor Fritz Kortner, whose wide vocal range and powerfully dynamic gestures made him a major element of Jessner's creations, Emil Pirchan's stage designing made an impressive contribution to Jessner's work: Pirchan replaced cluttered stages with lucid, pregnantly symbolic spatial structures that went down in theatrical history as "Jessner stairs". Pirchan's tiered stages were not decorative elements; they fulfilled a dramatic function, for they were used by the actors to channel and intensify the line of reasoning of the plot. In the staging of Shakespeare's *Richard III* (November 5, 1920), Richard's better days and tragic ending were played up (and down) the staircase; this was the climax of endeavors to dramatize space and heighten expressivity: "... a staircase. It is here that everything transpires. The staircase is the Tamworth plain. The same steps are the throne room. The same steps become the tent. The steps remain a battlefield". (-Alfred Kerr, *Berliner Tageblatt*: November 6, 1920) Jessner and his leading actor Kortner worked on the death scene particularly. Using the symbolic imagery of the staircase, they created a new and graphically convincing version of the scene: "Shakespeare has Richard die backstage. Jessner sends him, with a naked torso... slowly down the red staircase into the spears of the white enemy. During the descent, he lets out the famous cry for a horse three times, four times. Actually he sings it. Differently each time. Not more and more shrilly but more and more hopelessly, more and more resignedly. It wrenches [the spectator] to the core". (-Siegfried Jacobsohn, *Das Jahr der Bühne*, Vol. 10: Berlin, 1921, p. 42)

The other source of inspiration that was a seedbed for Expressionism was Moritz Seeler's matinee series, *Die junge Bühne* ("Young Stage"), which produced eleven plays from May, 1922 to May, 1927, including seven premieres. Like its predecessor Das junge Deutschland, this series was primarily a platform for new authors, i.e. for those whose plays had not yet been staged. Arnolt Bronnen's work, including his scandalizing *Vatermord* ("Parricide", at the Deutsches Theater, May 14, 1922, directed by Berthold Viertel) was staged four times. The only one of Bertolt Brecht's plays staged in this series was *Baal* (at the Deutsches Theater, February 14, 1926, directed by Brecht, stage sets by Caspar Neher), but Brecht was substantially involved in choosing and rehearsing various plays in the series. Other trailblazing authors of Die junge Bühne series include Marieluise Fleisser (*Fegefeuer in Ingolstadt* ["Purgatory in Ingolstadt"] at the Deutsches Theater, April 25, 1926, directed by Paul Bildt and Brecht), Carl Zuckmayer (*Pankraz erwacht* ["Pankraz Awakens"] at the Deutsches Theater, February 14, 1925, directed by Heinz Hilpert) and Hans Henny Jahnn (*Die Krönung Richards III* ["The Coronation of Richard III"] at the Theater am Schiffbauerdamm, December 12, 1926, directed by Martin Kerb). From Expressionism all of these plays derived the nervous egocentrism of the main characters, their rebelliousness representing protest, and the conflict that resulted between generations. But the rage that permeates the productions in Die junge Bühne series is cynical – propelled by lust, bloodthirstiness and perverted impulses. Idealistic revolt is replaced by brutality and nihilism; the emphasis on man's capacity for renewal is replaced by the certainty of his downfall; cathartic jolts by provocative shocks. When the series ended, Brecht coolly dismissed the whole experience as pseudo-revolutionary and qualified it as an easy target for both the scandal-hungry press and the conservative theatrical industry. He noted that it provided an occasion for the latter, wary of assuming any risks, to avoid paying royalties and other costs of trial-periods, and thus to take over a successful production in the repertory virtually "free of cost". The ostensible scandals involving Die junge Bühne probably caused both its contemporaries and historians of the theater to overrate the experience. But the series did serve as a catalyst and laid the foundations for diverse post-modernist works of the present day, beginning with the renaissance of early works by Brecht and Fleisser in the Sixties and continuing to the theater of cruelty.

Jürgen Fehling, the other outstanding director of Berlin's Staatstheater during the Twenties, had even less to do with Expressionism in the strict sense than Jessner. But as Jessner's energy began to wane, it was Fehling who promoted and accentuated, in his fashion, the trend towards visionary, emotional and intensively expressive productions. He first made a name for himself with comedies but gradually shifted over to a pathos that, in contrast to Jessner, allowed room for mystic and magic elements and that (in its mixture of dreams, spectres and reality) represented a freer, more condensed and new form of expressivity. In his first, and perhaps most direct, confrontation with Expressionism – Toller's *Masse Mensch* ("Man and the Masses"), which was staged at the Volksbühne on September 29, 1921 – Fehling transplanted the disparate elements of the plot to the visionary realm of dreams, thus producing a coherent whole and the "soulful spirit" intended by the author. Next he staged plays by Ernst Barlach – *Der arme Vetter* ("The Poor Cousin", May 23, 1923), *Die Sündflut* ("The Deluge", April 4, 1925), *Der blaue Boll* ("Blue Boll", December 6, 1930) – in line with his Expressionist-oriented conceptions and brilliantly conveying impassioned pathos and transcending reality. Fehling was the first director, and indeed the only one, to capture the whole scope of fervor, phantasy and populism contained in plays by Ernst Barlach. In the same fashion that Jessner used Kortner to portray his expressive visions, Fehling relied on the help of the actor Heinrich George to translate his delusive, yet down-to-earth dream images: "His voice could break loose like the scream of stones... there was something in his voice like boiling ice water, a sweet bee-like tonality and the rumbling sound of a scree slope. Always he was a human being, driven and tortured by too many faces". (-Jürgen Fehling, *Nachruf auf Heinrich George*: 1946) All

241   Emil Pirchan: stage model with the *hohle Gasse* ("high gulley") for Friedrich Schiller: *Wilhelm Tell* (performed at the Staatstheater: December 12, 1919, produced by Leopold Jessner)
"Tell: 'Through this high gulley must he pass.' 'Where is it?' was screamed out shrilly by someone unsatisfied with the gulley suggested [by the scenery]. This was followed by laughter from opponents [of the performance] and cries of resentment from its partisans.... 'Jewish Hoax' was cried out in chorus. Then blows began to fly". (-Fritz Kortner, *Aller Tage Abend*: Munich, 1969, p. 229)

242   William Shakespeare: *Othello* (performed at the Staatstheater: November 11, 1921, directed by Leopold Jessner, stage sets by Emil Pirchan)
Final scene: Desdemona (Johanna Hofer) and Othello (Fritz Kortner). Jessner's fourth Classical production in Berlin surmounted the eccentricities of Expressionism with clarity and nuance. Kortner "tempers the hero into a suffering lover... and the high points were the moments with quieter feelings". (-Paul Fechter, *Deutsche Allgemeine Zeitung*: November 12, 1921)

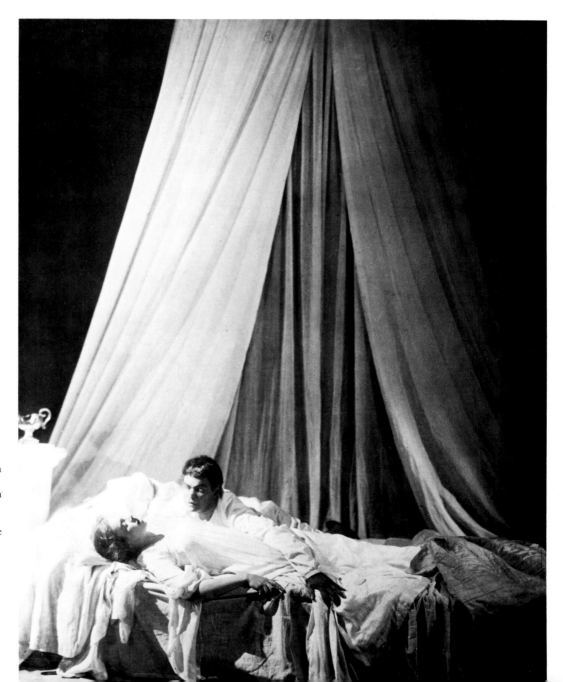

243   William Shakespeare: *Julius
Caesar* performed at the Grosses
Schauspielhaus: May 28, 1920,
directed by Max Reinhardt)
Stage-set design by Ernst Stern:
funeral speech by Marcus Antonius
(Alexander Moissi [Caesar: Werner
Krauss]). Like its predecessors,
Reinhardt's last large-scale classical
production in Berlin, before leaving
for Vienna, comes alive especially in
the drama of the mob scenes.

222

„Danton". v. Romain Rolland
Im Grossen Schauspielhaus.
Regie Max Reinhardt.

244   Romain Rolland: *Danton*
(performed at the Grosses
Schauspielhaus: February 14, 1920,
directed by Max Reinhardt, stage
sets by Ernst Stern)
Sketch of the stage: the
revolutionary court, (center left) the
defendants, with Danton (Paul
Wegener) at the balustrade, which
he overturns at the end. The hordes
of red-capped *sans culottes* surge in
front of the balustrade. In the
foreground to the right, on the
spectator seats, the judges, with
Werner Krauss as Robespierre.

the other leading directors influenced by Expressionism shifted over to New Objectivity or socially critical plays during the last years of the Twenties. But Fehling's work at that period acquired, for the first time, what is termed "Magic Realism", through the inherent concentration of atmosphere and abstractness in stagings and by relying on the support of settings by the pragmatic stage designer Rochus Gliese and later by César Klein and, as of 1933, on empty space as accentuated by Traugott Müller. Fehling's work of this period prolonged into the Thirties and Forties the impassioned aspect of Expressionism, as well as that part of it which transcends time and reality.

Classical Productions

Although the first productions of Expressionist protest theater appeared even before the downfall of the German monarchy and then extended their call to the "New Man" throughout Germany during the postwar years, Republican theater proper began by producing an adaptation of the Classics, namely Leopold Jessner's staging of Friedrich von Schiller's *Wilhelm Tell* at the Staatliches Schauspielhaus (premiere: December 12, 1919). Renouncing the traditional, syrupy, antiquated style of court theater, the stage designer (Emil Pirchan) stripped the play of its scenic Swiss frills and replaced mountains, lake and the "high gulley" by a large surface of strictly organized, symbolic space, dominated by steps and curtains that provided new dramatic possibilities for emphasizing tempo and allegory. Jessner's break with the nationalist-patriotic traditions of *Tell* was as decisive as the scenic transformation and brought to the fore the liberating, revolutionary aspect of the murder of High Bailiff Gessler. Fritz Kortner, who had just transferred from Die Tribüne theater to the Staatstheater, gave the most outstanding performance of the cast in his role as Gessler; he whipped up totally expressive aggressivity to personify the most absolute of tyrants. The revolutionary tone of all the aspects of the production created an immense uproar that,

to be sure, was also directed against Jessner, who was both a Jew and a Socialist. The regular battle that ensued in the audience, provoked even an actor as mature and wise as Albert Bassermann into responding from the stage and was the beginning not only of years of controversy over Jessner's methods at the Staatstheater but also of debate concerning the political role of the theater. Even before the Nazis came to power, the battle, spearheaded by Berlin on behalf of the entire Weimar Republic, was lost by those favoring a democratization of culture.

Jessner relied especially on the Classics in his fight in favor of a democratization of culture; he chose ideas of topical interest from them, which he used as leitmotifs in his productions. The plays with a political slant that Jessner staged were mainly dramas by Schiller and Shakespeare; some were even staged twice over the years (*Wilhelm Tell*: 1919, 1923; *Othello*: 1921, 1932; *Wallenstein*: 1924, 1931; *Don Carlos*: 1922, 1929). Jessner's production of *Tell* was meant essentially to convey the idea of liberty; power was the central theme of *Richard III* (1920); *Fiesco* (1921) focused on treason to the Republic, and *Hamlet* (1926) was concerned with corruption in monarchist circles.

The new principle of updating the Classics shaped theater under the Weimar Republic at least as conclusively as the fundamental changes implicit in Expressionism. In the development of the theater, it was, in fact, even more decisive than Expressionism: even abroad, German-language theater today allots the most prestigeful place in its repertories to the demanding and problematical staging of the Classics and is justifiably lauded for doing so by the press and the public alike. By updating great plays, Jessner did not mean to "modernize" them outwardly; his aim was rather to update the spirit of the Classics, to provide an understanding of the ancient dramatic conflicts and their ideological foundations so that they could stand on their own for all times, and hence be valid for a modern audience.

The leading stage directors in Berlin responded to Jessner's challenge concerning the Classics in their own personal fashions. Max Reinhardt was perhaps the most

affected; several weeks before the premiere of *Tell*, he had inaugurated his "theater for 3,000", called the Grosses Schauspielhaus and located in the Schumann Circus (which had been transformed by Poelzig), with the staging of *Orestes* by Aeschylus. Between 1910 and 1914, Reinhardt had already staged Classics in the circus as folkloristic festivities in an arena, so that the Grosses Schauspielhaus was less new departure than continuation in institutionalized form of previous tendencies. In order to fill the tremendous building with spectators, Reinhardt even attempted to apply the principles of his suggestive "spectacles for the masses" to a play as politically slanted as Romain Rolland's *Danton* (February 14, 1920). The result was conflictive total theater, which effaced the boundary between acting and reality and the one between actors and audience, producing an effect that was as confusing as it was overwhelming.

Aside from plays already recognized as spectacles for the masses, Reinhardt undertook only two new Classical productions at the Grosses Schauspielhaus: Shakespeare's *Hamlet* (January 17, 1920) and *Julius Caesar* (May 28, 1920). Whereas, in the enormous theater, his production of *Hamlet* failed to come across, his *Julius Caesar* represented an all-time high in choral and spatial staging: "while, on a tremendously long stage divided into three levels, the mass of spectators down in the arena and those above on the revolving stage suddenly – with a single jolt – form an intimate continuity with the central stage, where the bald skull of Julius significantly... tries to catch the wind of the times and of the environment". (-Emil Pirchan, *Börsen-Courier*: May 28, 1920) Despite the effective acting (by Werner Krauss as Caesar) and the structural apparatus, with this play Reinhardt had exhausted his interest in monumentalizing the Classics and in the theatrical development of the Grosses Schauspielhaus as well. In October, 1920, Reinhardt resigned as director of his theaters in Berlin to work mainly in Vienna and Salzburg for the next decade. The fact that in plays he directed later in Berlin he no longer planned to update Classics was most significantly demonstrated by the opening of his new boulevard theater, Die Komödie (constructed by Oscar Kaufmann).

The theater's boxes and distinguished elegance were proof of Reinhardt's intention to continue exclusively along the lines of court theater. An illustrious circle of top politicians, financiers and industrial leaders attended Carlo Goldoni's *Diener zweier Herren* ("Servant of Two Masters", November 1, 1924) – a frothy, light-hearted and playfully gay production that even turned the multiple,

246, 247 Two generations—two versions of the Classics:

246 *Bertolt Brecht*, drawing by B. F. Dolbin

247 *Max Reinhardt*, drawing by Autori
Although Brecht polemized against Reinhardt's "monumentalized style", he adopted its scenic concreteness and theatrical individualism.

"nuanced hunger pains" of the servant Truf-faldino into a delectable farce. (-Norbert Falk, *BZ*: November 3, 1924)

It was Bertolt Brecht, a young man from Augsburg, who did the most to encourage continued work on the Classics. Since the early Twenties, his exotic plays and heretic speeches had had an unsettling effect on the theater scene. At first, Brecht could not get a foothold in Berlin; over the years, his plays premiered everywhere else in the Reich (as the Weimar Republic continued to be known), but they were repeatedly imported to Berlin as guest productions. Consequently, Brecht lacked professional connections in the capital. He was brilliantly defended by the leading critic Herbert Jhering, but another major critic (Alfred Kerr) was against him. The openly contentious rivalry over Brecht between these two renowned critics thwarted his breakthrough in Berlin. Inspired by Jessner's Shakespearean productions, Brecht wrote an adaptation of Marlowe's *Edward II*, which he produced himself at the Kammer-spiele in Munich on March 19, 1924. His adaptation was basically novel in that it sought neither to mitigate discreetly nor to over-emphasize the chaotic idiosyncrasy of the original, but rather to explore it soberly, one might almost say scientifically. Brecht's attempt at structuralization and accuracy was hardly understood at the time, not even by the play's director in Berlin, Jürgen Fehling, who produced *Das Leben Eduards des Zweiten von England* at the Staatstheater (December 4, 1924) without doing justice to the dramatic lucidity and objectivity of the play. Fehling, who was innately and ideologically the oppo-site of Brecht, obscured and mystified the story.

Despite Fehling's misinterpretation, Brecht's epic *Eduard* brought the debate over the Classics back on the carpet in Berlin. Responses came from four directions: firstly, from Brecht's circle of friends, through the director Erich Engel, who left Munich in 1923 to become the most important producer besides Reinhardt at the Deutsches Theater; secondly, from the radical-leftist camp of Erwin Piscator who was seeking, energeti-cally and capably, to create a politically oriented "topical theater" (*Zeittheater*) that embraced all the artistic elements available; thirdly, from Leopold Jessner, who was beginning to adapt his politically slanted Clas-sical models into epics, and finally, from the growing counter-current of Irrationalism, impressively exemplified by Jürgen Fehling.

Erich Engel tried out his realistic concep-tion of the Classics (in line with Brecht and performed by Kortner) by staging Georg Büchner's *Dantons Tod* ("Danton's Death", February 29, 1924), before going on to an analytically restrained, anti-heroic version of Shakespeare's *Coriolanus* (February 27, 1925). Again, the latter production relied on Kort-ner in the leading role; his portrayal divested Coriolanus of all heroism and ardor, accentu-ating the character's consciously political nature. This attempt at an epic approach was an innovation that restricted the success of the actor's performance and — a drawback — attracted some negative reviews: Kortner was thought to have been miscast in the role, and his performance during the war scenes was judged dull and lacking in pathos. The production was only truly appreciated in ret-rospect, when it was used as a model and its epic nature was finally understood. As Jher-ing put it in 1929: "Kortner portrayed an aus-tere, almost taciturn Coriolanus, not as if he identified with the heroic image of the char-acter but as if he were detached from the role, almost as if he were impartially narrating.... There is no doubt that the colorfulness and splendor, the whole development and atmos-phere of the tragedy disappear when por-trayed in such an inappropriate manner. No doubt as well, however, that the impact of a Classical play can only be truly conveyed beyond the fleeting moment if it is integrated into a new perception of the world".

Erwin Piscator undertook the most far-reaching attempt at an ideological integration of the Classics. Since the early Twenties, he had spearheaded the radical-leftist wing of the theatrical scene in Berlin; the brutal changes, deletions and reorganizations he operated on the text of Schiller's *Die Räuber* ("The Rob-bers") turned the production by the Staats-theater of that play (September 12, 1926) into a manifesto for the Socialist revolution. Pis-cator's Karl Moor wore the "official Com-munist outfit" (-Paul Fechter, *Deutsche Allge-*

meine Zeitung: September 13, 1926), while the robber Spielgelberg was made up as Trotsky. But no modernistic "renovation" in the widespread fashion of the conventional theater was intended: there Hamlet appeared in tails and Franz Moor with a monocle. But Piscator wanted to sound the essence of the class war that remained in Schiller's early seditious play, created barely 150 years previously. At the expense of portraying Karl Moor as a "revolutionary for private reasons" (-Herbert Jhering), Piscator centered attention on Spielgelberg, who was portrayed as a man turned revolutionary out of inner necessity, which, in Piscator's terms, produced the following results: "How he accomplished his revolution!... having no rich father in a grand castle to rely on, not being... an 'appealing' hero.... What a severe and pitiless destiny forces him... to follow his path to the bitter end, regardless of the consequences. He came to represent our difficult social situation, a link between today and yesterday". (-Erwin Piscator, *Das politische Theater*: Berlin, 1929, p. 86) The leftist and liberal press in general rated the production unsuccessful but noteworthy; the rightists railed against the "bolshevizing" of Schiller and got the Prussian parliament *(Landtag)* to cancel the production. But the staging of *Die Räuber* did accomplish something; it brought to the fore the gap between the contemporary historical potential of the Classics and the concrete, socially critical demands being made on dramatic art.

Leopold Jessner made a personal crusade of transforming the Classics into realistic, politically oriented productions. His adaptation of Christian Hebbel's *Herodes und Mariamne* (March 26, 1926) took up the critical, analytical conceptions of *Coriolanus*, shattered the image of Herod (again played by Kortner) as a war hero and embedded private tragedy in a politico-historical context. Jessner's *Hamlet* (December 3, 1926) was a direct reply to Piscator's *Die Räuber*, and conceived in terms of an attack on still virulent "Wilhelm-ism" and reactionary German nationalism. Although this production is also in the same vein as his first *Tell* production in Berlin, the political implications in the staging of *Hamlet* were far more incisive, direct and comprehensive, as evidenced, for example, by the

way the king was patterned in detail on William II. Jessner's *Hamlet* was cited in the Landtag as well, but legal action against the Social Democrat intendant of the Staatstheater was averted.

Jessner's final production in the phase when he was revising the Classics was the

Hamlet als politisches Tendenzstück

Der Geist von Hamlets Vater: „Jeßner, das ist mein Hamlet nicht, du hast mein Kind getötet! — Schaudervoll, höchst schaudervoll!"

248 Paul Bildt with Trotsky make-up, as Spiegelberg the robber in Friedrich Schiller: *Die Räuber* (performed at the Staatstheater: September 12, 1926, directed by Erwin Piscator, stage sets by Traugott Müller) "Spiegelberg, who was a cowardly, slanderous, destructive, vane, phrase-thrashing Jew in Schiller, this Spiegelberg is rehabilitated by Piscator". (*-Die Rote Fahne:* September 19, 1926)

249, 250 William Shakespeare: *Hamlet* (performed at the Staatstheater: December 3, 1926, directed by Leopold Jessner, stage sets by Caspar Neher)

249 Caricature by Arthur Johnson from *Kladderadatsch* (vol. 79, no. 32), (left) Fritz Kortner as Hamlet. Conservative circles were especially shocked by Jessner's satire of the royal "Wilhelm-ish" household and went so far as to provoke a debate in the Prussian parliament.

250 The "mousetrap scene", the high point of the satirical concept of Jessner and Neher: in a play-within-the-play, the king's murderer and the decadence and intrigues of the monarchy are both laid bare.

great production of *Oedipus* (January 4, 1929) that combined both of Sophocles' plays into one production and "acknowledged that *Oedipus* is not the sentimental or pompous tragic spectacle of a king.... It, therefore, maintains its distance from any painfulness, avoiding a directly solicitous representation.... The tone is calm; the chorus narrates, ... convulsive denouement is replaced by epic peace and coherency". (-Herbert Jhering, *Reinhardt, Jessner, Piscator oder Klassikertod?*: Berlin, 1929) *Oedipus* was the culminating point of Jessner's long and controversial intendancy in Berlin. About a year later he resigned, somewhat unexpectedly, from his positions, after having proven himself equal to the most difficult

artistic and managerial crises. Although Jessner retained his title as a director at the Staatstheater, his originality and forceful creativity were exhausted. Billinger's *Rosse* ("Steeds"), the last play Jessner directed in Berlin, opened to the public one month after Hitler had come to power (March 1, 1933). Thereafter, Jessner, like so many others, was forced to leave Germany. During the last major crisis that Jessner weathered before resigning, Alfred Kerr described the Jessner era as the "Periclean Age of the Republic" (-*Tageblatt:* April 5, 1929) – his appraisal was to be confirmed.

With the exception of Max Reinhardt whose voluptuously Baroque and Classical

251 Heinrich von Kleist: *Das Kätchen von Heilbronn* (performed at the Staatstheater: February 1, 1923, directed by Jürgen Fehling, stage sets by Caspar Neher)
Photo of the stage with Carl Ebert (Wetter vom Strahl) and Lucie Mannheim (Kätchen). Fehling transformed this traditional, old-Franconian, chivalrous play into an ironic fable. Whereas Fehling's first Staatstheater production was a success, the performance by his favorite leading actress, Lucie Mannheim—more at ease in comedies—was a failure.

252 Jürgen Fehling: portrait in 1928
Fehling first succeeded with Classical comedies and local farces, but during the Twenties he progressively turned to tragedies.

253 Gustaf Gründgens as Mephisto in both productions of *Faust* by the Staatstheater (*Faust I:* December 2, 1932, directed by Lothar Müthel, stage sets by Hermann Zweigenthal; *Faust II:* January 22, 1933, directed by Gustav Lindemann, stage sets by Teo Otto)

"The make-up itself is sensational: the bald skull is powdered white like the face; the eyebrows are arched grotesquely and the blood-red mouth extended in a fixed smile".
(-Klaus Mann: *Mephisto, Roman einer Karriere:* Amsterdam, 1936)

254   Teo Otto: stage-set design for
Faust II, Act 3: shaded grove
(Euphorion scene)
Lindemann's production of *Faust II*
was generally considered the swan
song of the Weimar Republic's
theater; the scenes in Greece are
notable for "large-scale picturesque,
brown landscapes with temples,
created for the projector by Teo
Otto". (-Paul Fechter, *Deutsche
Allgemeine Zeitung:* January 23, 1933)

231

productions ignored social changes, Jürgen Fehling, more than any other director, represented the position opposed to the tendency of critical detachment when producing the Classics, a tendency that had served as a yardstick for modern dramatic art since the mid Twenties. Fehling's reaction to the new intellectualism was to promote excessively emotional acting, forcefully and unreservedly, pushing it to its ardent limits. While Engel, Jessner and later Hilpert as well forged on to New Objectivity, Fehling persisted in following (especially in Classical tragedy) the opposite path of intuitively discovered visions and secrets conjured up from the dark. He even turned Chekhov's tenderly ironic *Three Sisters* (December 21, 1926) into a production "greatly spun-out, infinitely oppressive, filled with penetrating outbreaks of despair... Russian ecstatic agony". (-Franz Servaes, *Berliner Lokal-Anzeiger*: December 22, 1926) Compared to the rich and powerful imagination evident in his staging of Classical comedies, there was a heaviness and imbalance to Fehling's style in tragedies until the end of the Twenties. It was only with Jessner's decline that Fehling gained his full measure as a tragedian, with the result that political aspects were brought more to the fore in his work. Hence, under the Nazis, Fehling more or less followed in Jessner's footsteps as a politically engaged director, delivering truths to the government, across the footlights, in a more forcible and radical manner than any other director dared attempt (especially in Schiller's *Don Carlos* in Hamburg, 1935, and in Shakespeare's *Richard III* in Berlin, 1937).

The theater of the Weimar Republic began and ended with a Classical production. On December 2, 1932, the centennial year of Goethe's death, the Staatstheater produced *Faust I*, literally at the last minute; the second part (*Faust II*) followed seven weeks later, on January 22, 1933. The reason for this disgraceful delay at Germany's leading theater was the permanent management crisis that lasted from Jessner's resignation in 1930 until 1934 when Gustaf Gründgens took over. Ernst Legal, the theater's intendant as of 1931, started the rehearsals for *Faust*. He had trouble with the casting and resigned from the intendancy, so that Heinz Tietjen, general director of the Prussian theater, became in turn deputy manager. The actor whom Tietjen proposed to Lothar Müthel (pinch-hitting as stage director for *Faust*) for the role of Mephisto had hardly been able as yet, in Berlin, to prove his worth as a Classical actor. The man was Gustaf Gründgens, whom Reinhardt had engaged at the Deutsches Theater in 1928 and who had made a name for himself in the capital since then acting the role of lounge lizard on stage, acting in films and directing operas. Gründgens's portrayal of Mephisto was that of a first-rate character-actor, and this role of a lifetime personified his own dazzlingly dramatic existence as well, which was enhanced by the conflict between professional pride and its political consequences, especially under Facism. Gustav Lindemann (together with Louise Dumont the long-established directors of the Schauspielhaus in Düsseldorf) was imported from the provinces to direct *Faust II*. That production was the last time that the deeply divided and harassed politico-cultural parties achieved mutual recognition and common resolution. The entire German press celebrated the opening of *Faust II* as the most significant theatrical event of the season; and the public at large in Berlin, who sought only the lightest entertainment at the time, came in droves and continued to be enthralled by the play even though the performance lasted five hours.

Revolutionary Leftist Theater

In the summer of 1919, around half a year after the November Revolution aborted, the Spartacist uprising was unsuccessful and Rosa Luxemburg and Karl Liebknecht were assassinated, a group of artists and intellectuals in Berlin called for the founding of a League for Proletarian Culture whose first aim — before the liberalization of schools, the introduction of Soviets and the phasing-out of cities — was to create a proletarian theater. By November, this League, which was oriented along the lines of the Russion cult of the proletariat, set up a first "proletarian theater" under Rudolf Leonhard and Karl Heinz

255 Cover page to the first program of the Proletarisches Theater, under the direction of Erwin Piscator and Hermann Schüller, drawing by George Grosz. Inauguration on October 14, 1920, in Kliem's banquet halls in a workers' district of southeastern Berlin (Neukölln), with three one-act plays that took a stand for the Soviet or Red Russians and against the Whites, supported by the West.

Proletarisches Theater
Bühne der revolutionären Arbeiter Groß-Berlins
Geschäftsstelle: Halensee, Karlsruher Str. 27.   Telefon: Pfalzburg 4515

Genossen und Genossinnen!

Die Seele der Revolution, die Seele der kommenden Gesellschaft der Klassenlosigkeit und der Kultur der Gemeinschaft ist unser revolutionäres Gefühl.

Das proletarische Theater will dieses Gefühl entzünden und wach halten helfen.

Die Erlebnisse, die sozialistische Kunst in uns hervorruft, stärken das Bewußtsein vom Ernst und von der Größe der geschichtlichen Sendung unserer Klasse.

I. Programm-Ausgabe.   20 Pfg.

Martin. The two men had recently left the privately managed avant-garde theater, Die Tribüne, disillusioned by the management's refusal to allow them to stage Toller's *Die Wandlung* for strikers.

The Proletarian Theater's only production, *Freiheit* ("Liberty") by Herbert Kranz, staged on December 14, 1920, on the platform of Philharmonic Hall, is the story of a group of pacifists who have been sentenced to death. To prove their human dignity they refuse an opportunity to escape from their prison cells. Although the play was given to a capacity audience whose reaction was encouraging, for unknown reasons it was not repeated nor did the two men continue their work together. In any case, the Communist newspaper *Rote Fahne* considered the group and the play unrevolutionary (nos. 74 and 75: December, 1920). Although the group itself was intended as a collective (all the members received the same salary and performed anonymously), it seemed to lack the necessary cohesion. Only ten days after *Freiheit*, Martin produced Carl Sternheim's *Die Hose* ("The Knickers") for a private theater, and by February, 1920, he had become general stage manager for Reinhardt's theater. At that time too, the League for Proletarian Culture disbanded.

However, that was not the end of the cult-of-the-proletariat movement in Berlin. Erwin Piscator stepped into the picture to infuse the movement with new energy and talent. For a short time after the war, he had belonged to Berlin's Dadaists. In the spring of 1920, he directed his own politically conceived theater (Das Tribunal) in Königsberg and, on October 14, 1920, he inaugurated the second Proletarian Theater – Stages of the Revolutionary Workers of Greater Berlin, with a sequence of scenes entitled *Gegen den Weissen Schrecken – für Sowjetrussland* ("Down with the white threat – Long live Soviet Russia"). Although he only managed to stage five productions before his Proletarian Theater was closed down by the police in April, 1921, Piscator's attempt was the first serious step towards Socialist theater in Germany. Basically, Martin's "proletarian" approach had been a mere continuation of the radical Expressionist trend of the Tribüne group, whereas Piscator contributed fundamentally new elements to the art of dramatics. Despite his lack of plays with forceful political impact, the acting already surpassed Expressionism and had the beginnings of an epic, detached and soberly realistic dramatic style, in line with the acting style that would be systematically adopted at the end of the Twenties, especially by Brecht. The stage designs by that artist of montage, John Heartfield, also represented a break with Expressionist conceptions; they were not created for esthetic purposes but to serve as dramaturgical elements in narrating the story. "In *Russlands Tag* ["Russia's Day"], a map of the world, in a single stroke, went beyond the geographical location to define the political symbolism of the place of action". (-Piscator, *Das politische Theater*: Berlin, 1929, p. 40) For propaganda reasons as well as for practical monetary ones, Piscator strove to obtain the collaboration of all parties and associations politically to the left of the Social Democratic Party of Germany. In addition, he created a theater-goers' association which is said to have included over 5,000 members at the end; however, bourgeois critics were not admitted to his plays.

Too few press reviews exist to provide much of an idea of the group's actual accomplishments. Early accounts in the *Rote Fahne* are, for the most part, unflattering. On the one hand, the intention was to "punish" such overly political and dogmatic theatrical evolution and, on the other, the accounts reflected the prejudiced, bourgeois conception of art represented by the critic Gertrud Alexander, who conceived of art as a "holy matter" and denigrated Piscator's scenes of Russia as "tritest propaganda". (-*Rote Fahne*: no. 210, October 17, 1920) Looking back, Piscator himself stressed the artlessness of his Proletarian Theater, which did not mean a lack of creativity. Although Piscator worked primarily with amateur actors in an attempt to enlighten and agitate, he used artistic methods exclusively, systematically and with purpose; he brought them to the fore, tried them out and changed them, and even drew them together into a basic theory of esthetics.

In order to reach the working classes in particular, the plays were performed in public banquet rooms and school auditoriums of working-class districts. But the performances did not manage to attract the desired number of proletarians, who showed little response when implored to avoid the movies and other capitalistic entertainments. Therefore, the police's refusal to prolong the franchise was not the only reason for the premature dissolution of the second Proletarian Theater: it was inadequately financed by the theatergoers' association (entry was free for the unemployed), leaving the group on precarious grounds economically.

In 1923, after staging three significant plays at the Central Theater, Piscator's lease was revoked, forcing him to abandon this latest attempt at a socially critical "Popular Theater" (*Volkstheater*). More or less by coincidence, he ended up as a director of the Volksbühne, which, until that time, had hardly been touched by the social and cultural upheavals of the postwar years. Although the Volksbühne had served as a platform for activist Expressionism (e.g. Toller's *Masse Mensch*, directed by Jürgen Fehling; Georg Kaiser's *Gas*, directed by Paul Legband), there was never a conscious decision to take a politico-cultural stand. From his first production, Piscator emphasized this aspect with great incisiveness and artistic competence. On May 26, 1924, Piscator premiered Alfons Paquet's *Fahnen* ("Banners"), a play depicting the bloody fight of late nineteenth-century workers in Chicago for an eight-hour day. Piscator's version of the play took a provocative, radically leftist stand in an atmosphere of acute socio-political conflict (increase in hours of work and cuts in salary brought on by inflation and the payment of war reparations). His stylistic methods were equally provocative — especially dialogues and inserts of photographic film — and so unusual that, at first, they alienated most of the critics, including the most progressive among them, whereas the audience was positively electrified by them.

The success of *Fahnen* established Piscator as a permanent and important director of the Volksbühne. It was there that he developed his far-reaching "political theater", chronicling the times and using all the imaginative technological innovations available — until the tremendous uproar over his staging of Ehm Welk's *Gewitter über Gottland* ("Storm over Gotland", March 23, 1927).

Welk's old-fashioned text and crudely

256   Edward Suhr: design for final scene of Alfons Paquet: *Fahnen* (premier: May 26, 1924 at the Volksbühne, directed by Erwin Piscator)
Banners are lowered from the fly gallery over the coffin with the Soviet star; they symbolically link the death of the five Chicago anarchists (who were executed in 1888) with the triumph of the Russian October Revolution.

"FAHNEN"

SUHR 24.

257 Alfons Paquet: *Sturmflut* (premier: February 20, 1926 at the Volksbühne, directed by Erwin Piscator, stage sets by Edward Suhr) Photo of the stage. The literary weakness of this production was compensated for by its esthetic impact, based on the innovative integration of film inserts, including documentary sequences as well as acting sequences made especially for the film.

258 Alexander Granach in *Gewitter über Gottland*: 1927, as the primitive Communist *Vitalienbruder* Asmus made up as Lenin, a make-up which Granach enjoyed using after performances as well, to create a sensation in the Berlin pubs. Granach played Lenin again in Piscator's production of *Rasputin*; rightist critics mocked him as a "professional Lenin", but the audience did not spare their applause.

236

structured, oversize slice of history, which dealt with a battle in the late Middle Ages between primitive Communists, the *Vitalien-brüder* (medieval pirates who provided the Swedish king with food during the siege of Stockholm from 1389 to 1392), and the Hanseatic League, was thoroughly overhauled by Piscator. Moreover, he made the line of reasoning more revolutionary and used film sequences to update the historical context with references to the Soviet Union and the latest popular uprisings in China.

This production caused opinions to become more dramatically divided than at any other time during the turbulent Twenties: the critics of *Der Tag* felt they had been victimized, the unwilling guests of a "Lenin celebration"; Paul Fechter — an author and chairman of the Volksbühne — railed against Piscator and demanded that he be liquidated; Alfred Kerr and Manfred Georg, on the other hand, noted that the production (which was enriched by film sequences) was particularly in tune with the times and praised its "totally novel visual impact" and "rare forcefulness".

However, there was more to the causes and consequences of the controversy than the production itself: the cohesion of the Social Democratic Volksbühne and the impartial artistic values on which it was based, were being called into question. Even before the scandal about *Gottland*, an opposition group pledged to supporting the socially revolutionary beginnings of the Volksbühne emerged from the youth division of the Communist Party of Germany (KPD). The board of directors of the Volksbühne, however, clung resolutely to their conservative esthetic conceptions. The production of *Gottland* provided a chance to appease the opposition, but it created a stir because Piscator, consciously counteracting the occasion to furnish an alibi for his work, accentuated Socialism to the farthest limits of critical development instead. The theater's board of directors had already begun to censor the play during the last stages of rehearsals; after the premiere, they insisted on more serious deletions and changes, which finally led to their cancelling the play altogether. A letter of protest, signed (as was to be expected) by renowned leftist intellectuals, as well as by Thomas Mann, Jessner, Fehling, Rowohlt, Pechstein, Polgar and others, was drawn up to proclaim solidarity with Piscator, and a meeting on his behalf was attended by 2,000 more or less prominent "Berliners". Since the management of the Volksbühne refused to revoke

259 Felix Gasbarra, Erwin Piscator: *Revue roter Rummel* (premier: November 22, 1924 at the Pharus Halls)
This "living tableau", which nowadays seems involuntarily funny, is the only remaining document of this epochal election-campaign production for the German Communist Party; it foreshadowed many of the elements that shape popular political theater to the present day.

260-265   Productions of the Piscator-Bühne at Nollendorfplatz and at the Wallner-Theater

260-261   Two photomontages:

260   Ernst Toller: *Hoppla, wir leben !* (premier: September 3, 1927, stage sets by Traugott Müller) Collage for the scene "In the Prison": (upper left) portrait of the author, Ernst Toller, beside an overall view of the tiered stage, (bottom center) "The last cigarette before execution", (on the right) "Escape Attempt" (Alexander Granach in the leading role as Karl Thomas). "Theater had become uninteresting. The shabbiest film was more topical... than the stage with its clumsy dramatic and technical machinery." (-Erwin Piscator: *Das politische Theater:* Berlin, 1929, p. 122)

261   Profile of Piscator, mounted on a background of the tiered stage, which was divided into sections corresponding to the framework of society under the Weimar Republic. The synchronized performances were completed by film and slide projections on canvas backdrops in each section.

262   Jaroslav Hasek: *Die Abenteuer des braven Soldaten Schwejk* (stage adaptation: Max Brod, Hans Reimann; premier: January 23, 1928, directed by Erwin Piscator, stage sets by George Grosz) Photo of the stage: On the way to the front lines. Schweik (Max Pallenberg) vaunts his lieutenant, Lukasch (Anton Edthofer), to the hilt. A real freight car moved on a track on the stage. The cardboard figures by George Grosz, caricaturizing the *K[aiserlich] und K[öniglich]* ("imperial and royal") monarchy played an essential role.

263 *Rasputin, die Romanows, der Kreig und das Volk das gegen sie aufstand* by Tolstoy and Shchegolev (in an adaptation by the dramaturgical collective [authors Felix Gasparra, Leo Lania, Bert Brecht], premier: November 10, 1927, directed by Erwin Piscator, stage sets by Traugott Müller) Collage of a scene by Sascha Stone. (Top center and right) Alexander Granach (Lenin), Oskar Sima (Trotsky); (center, left) Gerhard Bienert (the minister Dobrovolski), Tilla Durieux (Czarina Alexandra), (below) Erwin Kalser (Czar Nicolas II), (right) Anton Edthofer (Prince Yousoupoff), Paul Wegener (Rasputin), (bottom) Paul Wegener (Rasputin), (diagonally below) Leonhard Steckel (Protopopoff), who is next to Sybille Binder (Vrobava, the Czarina's confidante).

264 Karl Arnold: caricature for *Simplicissimus* (vol. 32, no. 43, January 23, 1928)

265 Friedrich Wolf: *Tai Yang erwacht* (premier: January 15, 1931 at the Wallner-Theater, directed by Erwin Piscator, stage sets by John Heartfield) Banners fly above the stage and auditorium; their mottoes are intended to instill a revolutionary communion between the audience and the actors. Conceived as a didactic play, without a stage-curtain or scenic technology, the production linked social problems in China with those in Germany.

their decision, Piscator had no choice but to resign. It would seem, however, that he had already thought of resigning, for within six months he inaugurated his own, first Piscator-Bühne at Nollendorfplatz.

Both *Roten Revuen* ("Red Revues") produced by Piscator for the German Communist Party in 1924 and 1925 were as significant as his work with the Volksbühne. The *Revue roter Rummel* (November 22, 1924), specially conceived for the third election campaign to the Reichstag, was played in a great many reunion and banquet rooms throughout Berlin. *Trotz alledem!* ("In Spite of Everything") on the other hand, was a one-night performance for the tenth anniversary of the German Communist Party at Reinhardt's Grosses Schauspielhaus (July 12, 1925). The first *Rote Revue* was a loosely constructed sequence of socially satirical sketches, intended as campaign propaganda; the second revue was a more historical panorama, having the evolution of the KPD, from the beginning of World War I to the assassination of Luxemburg and Liebknecht, as its central theme. By combining the unpretentious and colorful aspects of union evenings and the sharply satirical possibilities of cabaret with the refined dramatic efficacy of bourgeois light-entertainment theater, Piscator achieved a new dramaturgical dimension: montage that was instructive and entertaining at the same time. It became a model for the entire agitprop theater movement during the Weimar Republic and has continued to influence popular theaters in Germany and abroad to the present.

Piscator could scarcely hope to surpass the successful combination of actors and audience, technical apparatus and human performances, politics and esthetics that he accomplished in his *Roten Revuen*. When he took over the direction of his own theater from 1927 to 1931, he shifted his focus, for financial reasons, from the proletariat as a target group to the bourgeois public, which was

266   Walter Mehring *Der Kaufmann von Berlin* (premier: September 6, 1929, directed by Erwin Piscator, stage sets by Laszlo Moholy-Nagy) A projection of Berlin: "What a contrivance !... the tempo of the street... troops of soldiers,... whores,... policemen, porters, stockbrokers, [men in] caftans, [men with] swastikas. A thoroughfare on stage. Reality now." (-Bernard Diebold, *Frankfurter Zeitung:* September 11, 1929)

adverse effect on the development of the art of dramatics itself. As of 1930, after going bankrupt twice, Piscator decided to continue his work in a strictly Socialist and collective form and to appeal to radical-leftist organizations to provide a public; this included the Junge Volksbühne, a left-wing group that had split away from the Volksbühne earlier. In line with Brecht's didactic plays, the productions became more instructive and the scenery far less lavish, for instance in Credé's § 218 and Wolf's *Tai Yang erwacht*; nevertheless the effects were as technically and rousingly effective as ever. Piscator continued, however, to have trouble finding plays of the necessary political and literary calibre. In 1931, he left for the Soviet Union to do some film work, and in 1936, he emigrated from there, via France, to the United States. At first, his collective theater continued its work under the auspices of the Junge Volksbühne but was dissolved in June, 1932, for internal as well as external reasons.

The Socialist speaking-chorus movement and Piscator's *Roten Revuen* inspired the actor Maxim Vallentin to create the First Agitprop Troupe of the Communist Youth Association (KVJD) in 1926. His aims were to avoid the static and declamatory aspects of the chorus by creatively enhancing gestures, dialogues and music, and to provide the Party with useful and effective means of attracting the attention of the public that could be staged in the streets and at meetings at little expense — something the Partiy was hard-pressed to do. Due to the success of the First Agitprop Troupe, more troupes shot up all over Germany and in Berlin within no time; they were inspired by the Muscovite Blue Blouses, a satirical agitprop group created in 1923, that came into fashion during its tour through Germany in 1927.

In 1927, the young avant-garde composer Hanns Eisler joined Vallentin's KVJD troupe, which was renamed *Das rote Sprachrohr* ("The Red Megaphone") in 1928. Unlike most of the agitprop theaters, the Rote Sprachrohr did not entirely adopt the satirical cabaret style of the Blue Blouses; it preferred to retain certain aspects of the chorus and of emotional dramaturgy. Eisler soon became a leading Communist songwriter — even the

economically more interesting; however, the result was detrimental to the lively communication between stage and spectators. Nevertheless, together with his stage designer, Traugott Müller, Piscator continued to think up the most amazing technical solutions for his ingenious scenic ideas, in particular his stages: a stage in tiers for Toller's *Hoppla, wir leben!* ("Hoppla, Such is Life!", September 3, 1927), a hemispherical stage for *Rasputin* (November 10, 1927), and a treadmill stage for *Schwejk* (January 23, 1928). But the technical difficulties of such constructions and the shortage of rehearsal time owing to a lack of funds had a noticeably

Nazis adopted his melodies. Due to the large number of new agitprop groups and their organizational efficiency, the Communists took over the management of the Social Democratic Arbeiter-Theater-Bund or ATB, which was ten years old. The new management systematically expanded the federation during the early Thirties in order to turn amateur acting which, until then, had remained politically indifferent and stylistically traditional, into an instrument of the proletarian class war. The districts of Berlin played a decisive part in this development. By 1931 almost thirty troupes had sprung up there, including, among the most important, Rote Raketen, Sturmtrupp Alarm, Kolonne links, Roter Wedding (in the district of that name), Junge Garde, Tempo Truppe, Rote Blusen and Rote Trommler.

As the influence of agitprop groups increased, the counter trend also gained influence. Since the early 1930's, the government's "emergency decrees" had stifled Red theater troupes increasingly by resorting to methods that went from searching homes, confiscation and censorship to barring the performances, arrests and severe prison terms (nine months for Max Vallentin). In mid 1931, the central organ of the magazine *Arbeiterbühne und Film* was obliged to cease publication, despite a circulation of about 6,000 copies, because growing unemployment curtailed the payment of subscriptions. Reprisals continued; the federal headquarters of the ATB in Berlin was forced to stop its administrative duties; these were transferred to the districts, thus enabling limited regional activities to continue until the Fascists took over. As late as 1932, the Rote Sprachrohr troupe was enlarged to fifty actors, who were divided into four units, each with its respective artistic function (a children's unit, a touring unit, an active and a reserve unit). The children's productions continued (illegally) even after the wholesale arrests that occurred in the wake of the burning of the Reichstag. Despite the growing number of emigrations, some troupes in Berlin clandestinely kept up their activities until the wave of arrests in 1936 put a great number of the members of workers' troupes into concentration camps or penitentiaries.

The year 1929 ended in an international economic crisis that was provoked by the crash on the New York Stock Exchange on October 24; however, during the rapid economic decline at the beginning of that year, the proletarian agitprop movement continued to grow, and leftist "bourgeois" playwrights also radicalized their thinking. This was especially true of Bertolt Brecht, who had long since adopted the role of *enfant terrible*. He began studying Marxism in 1926; as of 1927, he became a leading member of the

268-269 Bertolt Brecht and Kurt Weill: *Die Dreigroschenoper* (premier: August 31, 1928 at a performance inaugurating Aufricht Productions at the Theater am Schiffbauerdamm, directed by Erich Engel, stage sets by Caspar Neher)
Two impressions of the final scene:

268 Photo of the stage (from left to right): Erich Ponto (Peachum) Roma Bahn (Polly), Harald Paulsen (Macheath), Kurt Gerron (Tiger Brown).

242

269 Stage design by Caspar Neher: arrival of the messengers on horseback. Bad luck followed this inaugural production right into the first performance. By mistake, even the enemy critics Kerr and Jhering were seated side by side. Up until Scene 3, everyone on stage felt very insecure, while audience response was unfavorably cold. But after the "Canon Song" the play's international success was guaranteed.

dramaturgical collective that formed Piscator's theaters, and in 1929, Brecht witnessed the "Bloody May" incident in Wedding, when the police opened fire on unarmed workers who, despite the ban, had gathered to make their traditional May Day demonstration. As a result, Brecht abandoned his tactic of scandalizing the bourgeoisie, which he had adopted in a rather playful spirit, to give his allegiance to Socialism.

Brecht's second play, *Trommeln in der Nacht* ("Drums in the Night"), written in Augsburg and Munich when he was barely twenty-one (1919), already centered on a revolutionary theme: the Spartacist uprising. But he had hardly intended the play to be instructive, let alone an instrument of class war. It contained the same traces of nihilism and anarchism as the rest of his plays from that early period, in a predominantly crazy and jesting tone, although socially critical passages began to emerge more distinctly and incisively. Such productive ambivalence also characterized the international success *Die Dreigroschenoper* ("Three-Penny Opera") by Bertolt Brecht and Kurt Weill. The production, which was thrown together in just a few months and premiered on August 31, 1928 at the Theater am Schiffbauerdamm (with Erich Engel as director and stage sets by Caspar Neher), captured the bittersweet, self-consciously coquettish frivolity of the Twenties as no other play did. Despite certain ideological and dramaturgical weaknesses, which allowed the public as a whole to enjoy the play without feeling personally concerned, the "Three-Penny Opera" was a masterpiece: it combined traditional and progressive elements, music and speech, subtle metaphors and obvious topicality, dramatic tension and epic caesura, shrewd wisdom and catching popularity. The play's continued success is not only due to its dissolute theme and thrilling songs, but also to its critical verity with regard to the system: "What is Dietrich worth compared to a stock certificate? What is a bank robbery compared to the founding of a bank?" (Scene 9).

Following this phase of "choice plays", Brecht produced a series of puritanically severe didactic plays, culminating in *Die Massnahme* ("The Measures Taken"), on the eve of 1931. His didactic plays are a singular

if arbitrary attempt to incorporate Marxist philosophical and political ideas into plays as esthetic and dramatic elements. The first didactic plays were staged in the summer of 1929, at the Baden-Baden Music Festival (*Lehrstück vom Einverständnis* ["Cantata of Acquiescence"], *Flug der Lindberghs* ["Lindbergh's Flight"], music by Paul Hindemith and Weill), but the scenic and politico-cultural effects really materialized in Berlin with the staging of a school opera, *Die Jasager* ("He Who Said Yes", with music by Weill) and *Die*

270   Three vignettes from the newsmagazine for members of the Arbeiter-Theater-Bund; the Communist party held a majority in this federation as of 1928 and transformed it into a "Proletarian Revolutionary Mass Organization". They countered Nazi propaganda with the battle cry: *Die Strasse ist unser !* ("The street is ours !").

271 Bertolt Brecht: *Die Massnahme* (premier: December 13, 1930 at the Philharmonic Hall, directed by Slatan Dudow, music by Hanns Eisler)
Photo of the stage: the four agitators, in alphabetical order—Ernst Busch, Alexander Granach, Anton Maria Toplitz, Helene Weigel. Conductor: Karl Rankl. "Three choruses in one group, a brass band..., a singer and three speakers, explaining the action on the podium. Text projections... create a whole new style of performance... [which] will perhaps be the form of future proletarian art." (-*Welt am Abend:* December 15, 1930)

272 Bertolt Brecht: *Die Mutter* (premier: January 16, 1932 by the Gruppe Junger Schauspieler at the Komödienhaus, directed by Emil Burri and Bert Brecht, stage sets by Caspar Neher)
Photo of the stage: (outer right) Ernst Busch as Pavel in Scene 5: report on May 1, 1905
Pavel: "We had our flag still. Smilgin was carrying it...."
Masha: "At this moment a police officer called to us: 'Hand over the flag !...'"
Smilgin: "I won't give it up !...'"
Ivan: "Yes, he said and he fell forward upon his face, for they had shot him."
Andre: "... at that moment our Pelagea... bent down and reached for the flag."
Pelagea [the mother]: "Let me have the flag, Smilgin, I said, give it here. I will take it. All of this must be changed !"
(From *The Mother* Reprinted by permission of Grove Press, Inc. Translated from the German by Lee Baxandall. Copyright © 1965 by Lee Baxandall.)

Massnahme (with music by Eisler). Both productions were discussed after the performance by the author and the composer, who made certain changes. *Die Massnahme*, which was premiered on December 13, 1930 at the Philharmonic Hall and staged in its revised version on January 18, 1931 at the Grosses Schauspielhaus, especially excited tempers. Since, with the exception of Jhering, the bourgeois press was generally unflattering or uncomprehending, the debate over the play took place among the Communists. The majority of the latter greatly praised the attempt made at using proletarian choruses with politically conscious professional actors; however, they denounced the script — especially the execution of an unreliable agitator by his own comrades, which was its major theme — as "unmarxist" (-*Rote Fahne*: December 16, 1930) and as "untypical of revolutionary tactics" (-Otte Biha, *Die Linkskurve*: no. 1, 1931). The plot concerns three illegal Communist agitators in China, who shoot their young comrade because he was repeatedly guilty of negligeance that seriously endangered their mission. When they return to Moscow, they confess the shooting to the Party's control group, which, after thorough explanations and debate, gives its sanction to their decision.

Debate continues even today on how to interpret *Die Massnahme*: as an attempt to re-establish the ethical precepts of tragedies or as a prefiguration of Stalinist terrorism; was it meant to glorify the inspirational ideas of Marx, Engels and Lenin concerning the inevitable universal revolution, or was it rather the work of a "leftist-deviate idealist", who based its development on abstract teachings of the Communist classics with disregard for the actual living conditions of struggling proletarians. In fact, Brecht in his second version incorporated many changes as a result of Communist objections; yet until his death, he refused to stage any more performances on grounds which, taken by themselves, seem virtually to destroy the play's effective power. Yet the conflicts inherent in *Die Massnahme* correspond best to the purpose of didactic plays, which are meant to "depict politically incorrect attitudes as a means of inculcating correct attitudes". (-Brecht, *Anmerkungen zu den Stücken*) For what more can a play accomplish than to give rise to sustained reflection?

At the time, Brecht was not only his own best pupil but, going a step further, also wanted to understand and influence the opinions of his new Communist audience. This was clearly evidenced by the next premiere, on January 16, 1932: *Die Mutter* ("The Mother", co-directed by Emil Burri, music by Eisler, stage sets by Neher); it was based on Gorki's novel and adapted by Brecht with the Gruppe Junger Schauspieler and some amateur actors from agitprop theater, under the auspices of the Communist-managed Junge Volksbühne. Several private performances for members of different proletarian organizations preceded the premiere in order to test reactions, to discuss the performance and to make the necessary changes. In contrast to the didactic plays, scenic symbolism and the plot were accorded a certain importance here, although the story of a working-class mother and her son was not handled in the same manner as the bourgeois Classics but appeared in narrative form, broken into epic episodes. The structure of *Die Mutter* lacks much of the dialectic tension and multi-dimensional scope that characterize Brecht's plays. However, the play was not primitively or clumsily constructed, as many bourgeois critics have alleged, in particular Alfred Kerr, who was generally receptive to radical-leftist theater (see Piscator) but who harbored a deeply rooted and unsurmountable antipathy to Brecht that literally blinded his dramaturgical outlook. Kerr was, however, more perceptive about Helene Weigel's outstanding performance in the role of the Mother; a role that placed her in the forefront of character actors in Berlin.

Communist critics tended to interpret epic theater less in terms of its technical aspects than as a pragmatic means of stimulating spectators into mentally participating in the plays, whereas Jhering went a step further and considered the style itself to be substantively valid. This discrepancy in sociocultural appreciations came to the fore in the reactions to the unbelievably grotesque and, of course, anticonstitutional censorship to which a guest performance of *Die Mutter* at the Moabit community house was submitted:

273, 274 Gustav von Wagenheim: ▷
Die Mausefalle (premier:
December 22, 1931 by Truppe 31
at the Kleines Theater directed by
Wagenheim, stage sets by Alice Lex
and Oscar Nerlinger)
While Germany was in the midst of
festive preparations for Goethe's
anniversary year, there were five
and a half million unemployed
roaming the streets, appealing in
ever growing numbers to the
Fascists to "rescue" them so as to
avoid falling prey to "Socialist
depersonalization". Those people,
who, *statt die Faust zu ballen* ("instead
of clenching their fists"), sought
solace in Goethe's *Faust*, witnessed
the fate of their hero, the employee
Fleissig, depicted by Truppe 31.

273 Photo of the stage: ▷
"Capitalistic Witches' Sabbath",
(left) Mephisto, (center) the
wholesalers on their heaps of goods,
(right) Fleissig, played by Curt
Trepte

274 Photo of the stage: "Zeppelin ▷
scene", where the airship is used to
demonstrate the advantages and
disadvantages of technological
achievements

246

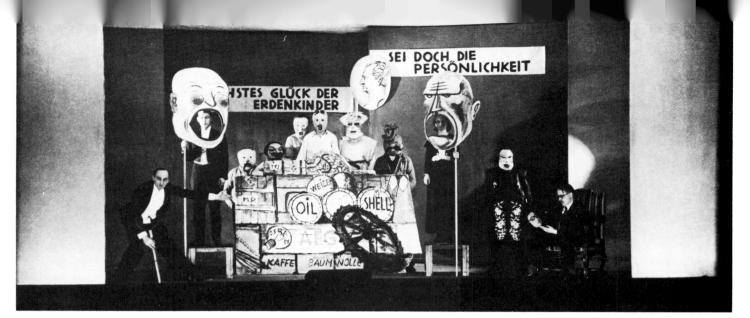

the Building Police used "security measures" as a pretext first to ban scenery and costumes, then movements and gestures and finally to interrupt the play during the performance, demanding that the actors "sit in a row and read off their roles" (-*Rote Fahne*: March 1, 1932). While Jhering noted that the success of the "performance", despite the interruption, testified to the particular efficacy of "Brecht's epic dramatic style" (-*Börsen-Courier*: February 29, 1932); the *Rote Fahne* added a note of class conflict, stating that "through their 'participation', the police... [had] essentially heightened the effect [of the drama] even more".

Die Mutter was Brecht's last production before leaving for exile. At the time, a new Socialist collective appeared, Truppe 31; instead of focusing on workers, the group tried to appeal to the hordes of employees who were defecting to Nazism, in an attempt to win them over to Communism. It emerged from a Party cell of young artists who had created a revue program in January, 1931, for the traditional Lenin-Luxemburg-Liebknecht demonstration. The success of their program incited them to continue working together and to link up with an experienced professional actor and author, Gustav von Wangenheim, a Communist Party member since 1922, who had been especially active in setting up the agitprop movement. Contrary to the other professional dramatic troupes of the period, Truppe 31 strove to create an all-encompassing collectivity that decided in common on themes and material and on cultural and political indoctrination, and analyzed together their role in society as a theatrical troupe. Having reached the conclusion that the theater attracts the middle classes above all, which in the event represented their own origins as well, Truppe 31 took over three months to put together a petty-bourgeois satire, *Die Mausefalle* ("The Mousetrap"), based on a text written by Wagenheim during rehearsals, with the assistance of the collectivity. The play appeared for the first time on December 29, 1931, the first day of an eight-day trial period of guest performances at the Kleines Theater Unter den Linden; it was such a hit that it turned into a series of 317 performances. Based on the

controversial methods introduced in the shoe industry (Bata, Salamander, etc.) to increase output, the play focused on an employee, Fleissig, a typical individualist eager for culture (1932 was the anniversary year of Goethe's death). Fleissig's resolutions turn from gold to dust when confronted with the economic crisis; he surrenders his petty-bourgeois ideals piecemeal throughout the performance, until finally he "realizes that he must march shoulder-to-shoulder with the 'prolos' ". (-*Rote Post*).

Die Mausefalle had more to contribute than its innovative Marxist-revolutionary standpoint on the contingencies of the petty-bourgeois question. The montages were also an innovation; they ingeniously complemented a wealth of very diversified creative means and levels of acting. Even competent critics lacked a yardstick for this: Bernard Diebold described montage, which until then had only been used in theater in Piscator's revues and by the Russian avant-garde (Meyerhold, Majakovski, Trejakov), as a mixture of "dramatics, epic, sketch, operetta and song-cabaret". (-*Frankfurter Zeitung*: January 14, 1932) In addition to those elements, the acting itself was a blend of comical, serious, realist and detached modes of expression, so that the spectators had to really concentrate on what was happening. Employee Fleissig was the only universal; he did not typify agitprop activism but represented such diversified and realistic characteristics that he could be accepted as a point of reference by the audience. But even Fleissig (Curt Trepte) is detached at all times, since he is prone to drop his actor's role and become himself, commenting on and analyzing his performance, usually at the most tensely emotional or dramatic moments, which are thus heightened by his reflections.

Truppe 31's *Mausefalle* was the high point of revolutionary leftist theater under the Weimar Republic. From a literary point of view, the play is overshadowed by Brecht's *Die Mutter* and *Die Massnahme*, but as a genuine theatrical event it surpassed both of them in artistic and creative terms as well as on a socio-political level. Artistically, because *Die Mausefalle* was an original product of joint collaboration by all those involved in creating

theater, and politically because the apprentice hero is won over by his own social experience and can in turn affect those around him. The play's effectiveness was not only proven by the enormous number of performances but also by the tangible reactions of those sections of the public that composed the target group: the white-collar proletarians.

Taking into consideration the unknown risk factors and the more stringent demands inevitably involved in such novel and uncompromisingly collective modes of staging, the achievements of Truppe 31 are doubly praiseworthy. Their first crisis occurred right after the production of *Die Mausefalle* when, inspired by the success of their first attempt, they tried to write the next play collectively. Not only were they incapable of agreeing on a formula for a story based on all the material they had collected and sifted through – which led to frustation and tension – but they also had to deal with their author Wagenheim, whose services were no longer needed. They survived this and other rending trials and continued to work together as a collective until the end of the Weimar Republic. They emigrated *en bloc* to Paris, where they rehearsed their first "exile drama", Friedrich Wolf's *Professor Mamlock*; nevertheless, for financial reasons, they were obliged to disband.

Popular and Topical Theater

As far as one can speak in chronological order at all, the "popular play" (*Volkstück*) and "topical play" (*Zeitstück*) represent the last genuine genres of theater to emerge during the Weimar Republic. Both genres were not innovations but rather renovations and evolutions. The popular play of the Twenties links up with relevant plays by Gerhart Hauptmann, Ludwig Thoma and Ludwig Anzengruber; the topical play harkens back to the Naturalist dramas of Zola and Ibsen most especially. Both types of plays came to the fore more or less at the same time, and their aims overlapped right from the start. Nevertheless, they represent two specific forms of theater in the Twenties, and it was particularly in Berlin that they were able to retain their unique

characters and from there to continue to make an impact up to the present.

The premiere of Kaiser's *Nebeneinander* ("Side by Side") on November 3, 1923, by the actors' association Die Truppe, under the direction of Berthold Viertel, marks the break with Expressionism and the shift to contemporary popular plays. Kaiser's play, which appeared at the Lustspielhaus two weeks before the currency reforms and was subtitled by the playwright *Volkstück 1923*, explores the effects of inflation on three social classes. Despite the aura of tragedy surrounding the pawnbroker and his daughter, who are central to the plot, and the remaining examples of the "New Man", Expressionist pathos yields to a very great extent to coldly dissected and socially critical observations.

The stage design and costumes by George Grosz were essential props in this process of cooling-down; contrary to the aggressivity that usually characterized his style, Grosz sought to produce analytically sober contents and form, without impeding the critical impetus. Toller's *Hinkemann* ("Broken Bow") was

a less significant earlier example, more inclined to the topical-play genre; it illustrated post-revolutionary disillusionment as symbolized by the helplessness of a war cripple. Since the staging of the play was not stylistically trailblazing, it owed its explosive impact to organized nationalist rowdiness, especially in the provinces.

Another nationalistically provocative 'folk' production, Zuckmayer's *Fröhlicher Weinberg* ("The Merry Vineyard"), opened on December 22, 1925 under the direction of Reinhard Bruck, at Saltenburg's Theater am Schiffbauerdamm; it became the top comedy of the Twenties. Though the acting was not exceptional, the production had overwhelmingly triumphed by the intermission: "It provoked a contagious laughing sickness, an epidemic of gleeful ecstasy, such as the transports of the medieval masses." (-Carl Zuckmayer, *Als wär's ein Stück von mir*: Frankfurt-am-Main, 1969, p. 346) The play was staged hundreds of times in the provinces, where it aroused opposition from radical rightists: the figure of the dissolute corps brother and dowry-chaser

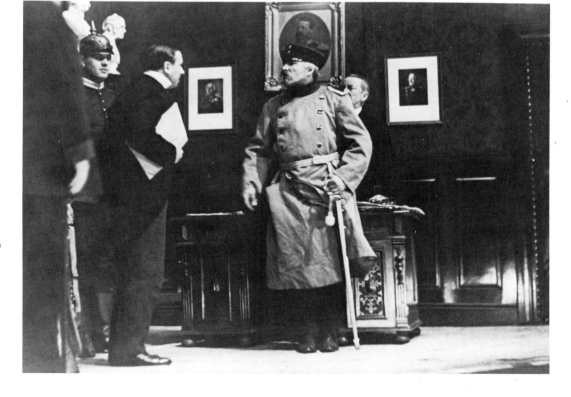

Knuzius, who thrashes out radical-right expressions and ends up drunk on a dunghill, was considered an insult by students and Nazis alike. Zuckmayer's play' and the performance itself, corresponded to the need for an intact world, for simple homespun and sensuous pleasures in a context devoid of any racial or nationalistic overtones. It aroused rightist reactions against the "totally unbelievable filth... that in every aspect shames Christian concepts, German customs, German women, German war cripples, German officialdom". (intervention by the National Socialist fraction at the Bavarian Landtag in 1926)

Der Hauptmann von Köpenick ("The Captain from Köpenick"), which premiered on March 5, 1931 at the Deutsches Theater under the direction of Heinz Hilpert, was Zuckmayer's most important contribution to the popular social-satire genre. Basically, three mutually determining factors made this play the last successful comedy under the Weimar Republic. In the first place, the public had had their fill of critical topical plays by the late Twenties; and as a result, in the second place, in view of the depressing conditions then prevailing, they wanted more than just criticism: plays should furnish food for conversation in a more positive sense, for truthful observations with which the public could identify. Finally, the identification thus provoked should not be tinged with the flavor of one trend or the other, so that it could lead to the desired communal experience. Zuckmayer used a uniform fetish in the play, which served as a pattern for audience identification, so that "one person can take it as a military farce, another as a social critique and the third as a satire". (-Herbert Jhering, *Börsen-Courier*: March, 6, 1931) Nevertheless, the Nazi press was enraged, especially Goebbel's *Angriff*, which threatened to have Zuckmayer jailed and/or deported under the coming "take-over". No disturbances were created during the performances themselves, due in no small measure to the competent direction and the knockout casting in almost all seventy-three roles, including Werner Krauss as the Captain, in a performance that was the high point of his career. All that was intended and acknowledged as political during the shattered Weimar Republic's final moments,

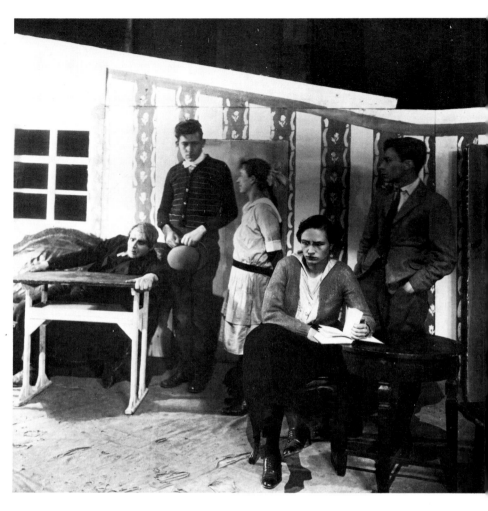

later took on an innocuousness that clairvoyant critics like Jhering had already sensed at the time. Nowadays, all that is left of *Der Hauptmann von Köpenick* is an amusing evening, altogether enjoyable even for dyed-in-the-wool militarists.

The "popular plays" from the small Bavarian town of Ingolstadt by Marieluise Fleisser were of an entirely different nature, although they too frayed a passage somewhere between popular and topical theater. Whereas Zuckmayer belongs to a long traditional line of narrating folkloristic tales in a solid and clear-cut manner, Fleisser writes in a more complicated and naive fashion; she is halting yet incisive, disorganized yet more precise than Zuckmayer. *Fegefeuer in Ingolstadt* ("Purgatory

281 Marieluise Fleisser: *Fegefeuer in Ingolstadt* (premier: April 25, 1926 by the Junge Bühne at the Deutsches Theater, directed by Paul Bildt, with the collaboration of Bertolt Brecht, stage sets by Traugott Müller) Photo of the stage (Act 1, scene 6): Berotter's living room, (from left to right) Walter Franck (Berotter), Matthias Wiemann (Roelle), Helene Weigel (Clementine), Maria Koppenhöfer (Olga), Martin Koslek (Christian). "No light shines into this darkness; no pure breath of air blows through the mold and stink of this small town, and religion throws all those who are miserable and humiliated ... into devilish confusion." (-Kurt Pinthus, *8-Uhr-Abendblatt:* April 26, 1926)

282, 283 Marieluise Fleisser: *Pioniere in Ingolstadt* (premier: March 30, 1929 at the Theater am Schiffbauerdamm, directed by Jacob Geis, with the collaboration of Bert Brecht, stage sets by Caspar Neher)

282 Caricature by Linne (from left to right): Leo Reuss (sergeant), Lotte Lenya (Alma), Albert Hoerrmann (Korl), Hilde Körber (Berta), Peter Lorre (Fabian). "Engineers come to Ingolstadt, to ... build a bridge. They create disturbances among the townsfolk and the maid servants .... There are quarrels, flirtations, reciprocal unhappiness and separations. The bridge is finished. The engineers leave." (-Herbert Jhering, *Börsen-Courier*: April 2, 1929)

Reuß   Lenia   Hoerrmann   Körber   Lorre

283 Peter Lorre as Fabian Benke. "A new face appeared, a horrible face: the hysterical petty-bourgeois son, whose goggle-eyed, bloated head yellowly bobs over his suit." (-Kurt Pinthus, *8-Uhr-Abendblatt*: April 2, 1929)

in Ingolstadt"), premiered as a private matinee on April 25, 1926 by Moritz Seeler's Junge Bühne (with Brecht's help on the staging), represents the beginning of the modern popular play both in form and substance. It neither accuses nor embellishes but plainly lays bare conditions such as they are, without delineating them naturalistically. Instead, Fleisser develops a new scenic poetry that uses the unspoken dialogues under the surface of tangible appearances to reveal the unconscious. Uninfluenced by Büchner and the Expressionists, yet reminiscent of them in their inner and external existential torments, Fleisser's characters live in small-towns — a suffocating and unenlightened world — and obey their instincts. At first glance, their world seems strangely anachronistic and comparatively rural; however, its topical relevance is finally revealed: the god-forsaken setting is a metaphor for the inner strife that also torments simple, unintellectual people today. The "utmost brutality is juxtaposed with the greatest diffidence. Hysterical outbursts with grim taciturnity.... Whatever hampers these people, whatever strangles them, whatever makes them narrowminded is, at the same time, an unconscious awe of Creativity.... One understands Hitler". (-Jhering, *Börsen-Courier*: April 26, 1926)

It is no wonder that Fleisser's plays did not become popular on their own, or even as a result of censorship scandals and rightist protests. This was the case in Berlin at least, where *Pioniere in Ingolstadt* ("Engineers in Ingolstadt") was produced at the Schiffbauerdamm Theater under the direction of Brecht's friend, Jakob Geis, on March 30, 1929, one year after its uncontested premiere in Dresden. The police censored certain "indecencies" and wanted to prohibit the play, despite the fact that the constitution guaranteed freedom for art, and the nationalistic German press was incensed at the "kind of hysterical brazenness and blunders involved in this arbitrary, womanly phantasy" (-Franz Servaes, *Lokal-Anzeiger*: April 2, 1929) and threatened that "Nazis by the hundred" would put out a "dragnet" to stop the "naked fun" of those "retired Democrats" whose "political extermination" was "inevitable". (-Richard Biedrzynski, *Deutsche Zeitung*: April 2, 1929)

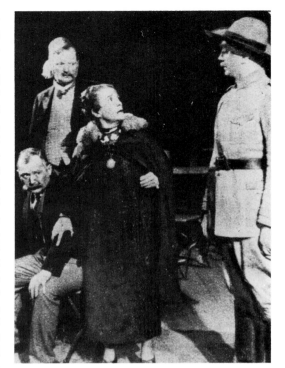

The reaction over Fleisser's portrayal of "what goes on between maid servants and soldiers in Bavaria" (-Alfred Kerr, *Tageblatt*) when they are "under the hazy spell of beer and a spring evening" (-Paul Wiegler, *BZ*) was so strong that the real point of the play — the problem of the communication among the "little people" — was missed. "This helplessness in expressing themselves moves us deeply.... It is precisely because... their dialogues and behavior are at cross-purposes, that these helpless creatures are unhappy and tragic". (-Kurt Pinthus, *8-Uhr-Abendblatt*: April 2, 1929) Fleisser strings such exceptionally complicated and radical ties between her lowland characters that big-city theater had a great deal of trouble creating the appropriate dramatic tone and at times resorted to grotesque representations. The result was inadvertently laughter-provoking, a "hick" context to which the people of Berlin could not relate personally. However, they did relate to the familiar figure of the babyish bourgeois son — a role that provided Peter Lorre, who had been unknown up until then, with an instant breakthrough.

284 Ödön von Horvath: *Italienische Nacht* (premier: March 20, 1931 at the Theater am Schiffbauerdamm, directed by Francesco von Mendelssohn) Photo of the final scene: the garden restaurant, (from left to right), Oskar Sima (the town councilor), Hans Adolfi (Betz), Elsa Wagner (Adele, wife of the city councilor), Hans Alva (major, leader of the SA storm troopers, in an imperial colonial uniform).
Adele: "Take all that stuff off, the war is finally over, you buffoon! You would do better to do without your pension and hand it over to the war cripples...." Ernst Josef Aufricht, the producer, in his memoirs: "I invited the *Gauleiter* [a Nazi title] Hinkel ... to the premiere. The ... Nazis refused to be provoked. They applauded." (-*Erzähle, damit du dein Recht erweist*: Frankfurt and Berlin, 1966)

285 Ödön von Horvath: *Geschichten aus dem Wiener Wald* (premier: November 2, 1931 at the Deutsches Theater, directed by Heinz Hilpert, stage sets by Ernst Schütte)
Photo of the stage (from left to right): Peter Lorre (Alfred), Lucie Höflich (Valerie), Frieda Richard (the grandmother), Carola Neher (Marianne), Heinrich Heilinger (Oskar), Hans Moser (magic king). "The entire bizarre performance is enacted with such ice-cold wit that any bit of warmth that one character or the other emits from time to time condenses immediately into frosty steam." (-Alfred Polgar, *Die Weltbühne*: Vol. 27, no. 46, November 17, 1931)

The Austrian Ödön von Horvath, who had taken up residence in Berlin in the mid-Twenties, used criticism of speech in popular plays to analyze social conditions even more emphatically than the Bavarian Marieluise Fleisser. He tended to resort to satire in a fashion similar to Zuckmayer, but he did not spare the simple people whose "sound popular instinct" he unmasked without mercy as coarse and self-deluding. Instead of focusing on their lack of communication, he expounded on their jargon, criticizing its syrupy sentimentality and destructive apathy that entrap men in a cage. Von Horvath surpassed all other playwrights during the Weimar Republic with his descriptions of the fertile ideological grounds so propitious to the rise of Fascism, but he persisted in limiting himself to the circumstantial and theoretical aspects of the question, without furnishing either political or economic facts to substantiate his social critique, nor proposals for social changes.

Despite the urban themes and social relevancy of the *dramatis personae* for the theater audience, Von Horvath's plays encountered staging problems akin to those created by Fleisser's work. Surprisingly, it was one of his plays which depicted Nazis in their most threatening and ridiculous element that met with the greatest success in Berlin. Von Horvath's *Italienische Nacht* ("Italian Night"), his first mature popular play, was produced by Ernst Josef Aufricht and premiered at the Theater am Schiffbauerdamm on March 20, 1931; there were over forty uncontested performances, although the play's central theme concerned a surprise attack on a garden party, during the Weimar Republic, by a Fascist "flying squad" whose leader was exposed to ridicule by a woman. But Von Horvath had a harder time with *Geschichten aus dem Wiener Wald* ("Tales from the Vienna Woods"), premiered a good six months later by Heinz Hilpert at the Deutsches Theater (November 2, 1931) and featuring an Austrian cast of stars (Hans Moser, Paul Hörbiger). The play was misinterpreted as a local parody, and the rightist press noted that "vulgar derision sullies... the Vienna we love" (-Ludwig Sternaux, *Lokal Anzeiger*: November 3, 1939), while liberal critics praised the way it unmasked the "sentimental lies about Austria" (-Alfred Kerr, *Tageblatt*: November 3, 1931). Only a few recognized that the play transcended regionalism and was a satire on the philistine mentality, but significantly, those few included the Austrian legation, which considered it unnecessary to undertake steps on a diplomatic level against the production. Despite the unfortunate combination of light satire and milieu portrayal, the critics were most sensitive to Carola Neher's

Skadek Eysoldt

die Angeklagten

286 A real "topical play" occurred in 1921 with the lawsuit against the performance of Arthur Schnitzler: *Reigen* (premier: December 23, 1920 at the Kleines Schauspielhaus, directed by Hubert Reusch) Both theater directors, Maximilian Sladek and Gertrud Eysoldt (drawn by Emil Orlik), were accused "on grounds that the play alludes several times to the accomplishment of sexual intercourse" (court records). The spectacular case ended with an acquittal, after a special performance was scheduled for the court—a visit to the scene of the "crime".

excellent performance as Marianne, a leading role in which she accentuated the inevitable spiritual destruction of a lowly salesgirl, rather than trying to convey the authenticity of the character in terms of local color.

The last of Von Horvath's plays to be premiered before he emigrated was *Kasimir und Karoline*, which was tested on audiences in Leipzig before it was premiered, as an Aufricht production, in Berlin on November 25, 1932 at the Komödienhaus. The play was a success that was even more misunderstood than *Wiener Wald*, although people were beginning to realize that "a universal perceptivity exists behind the Bavarian hoax" (-Alfred Kerr, *Tageblatt*: November 26, 1932). Unfortunately, the director, Francesco von Mendelssohn, did not manage to make a coherent whole of Von Horvath's specific dialectical combination of irony and folklore, which would have enabled the audience to

relate self-critically to the characters. Instead the element of parody came to the fore, and "everyone screams with amusement" (-Kerr).

The rather run-of-the-mill reactions that Fleisser's and Von Horvath's work induced in contemporary audiences was no coincidence, nor were the reactions uniquely the fault of the entertainment-hungry, cynical Berlin "asphalt parquet", which was always ready for a good laugh over provincial obtuseness. At the time, the necessary ideological and critical distance was lacking, not only in terms of social consciousness but more precisely, in terms of artistry as well. When conditions lent themselves to such an understanding (a result of the social criticism of the New Left during the late Sixties and the mature analytical esthetics produced by epic theater), there was such a powerful and significant Fleisser and Von Horvath revival in German-speaking countries that a potent new gener-

287 Günther Weisenborn: *U-Boot* ▷ *S4* (premier: October 16, 1928 at the Volksbühne, directed by Leo Reuss, stage sets by Edward Suhr) Photo of the stage: Heinrich George as Sailor Pep. "At the end ..., when the six sailors in the torpedo room... have suffocated, a 'man in black' ... invites the public to observe a moment's silence in honor of the sailors who went down with their ships last year." (-Arthur Eloesser, *Vossische Zeitung:* October 17, 1928)

256

ation of popular playwrights came to the fore, notably Martin Sperr, Franz Xaver Kroetz and others. However, despite their initial popularity, there has been no similar revival of Zuckmayer's popular plays.

While the popular or *Volk* genre is rooted in local milieus and its chiefly humoristic plots are less argumentative than illustrative, the "topical play" (*Zeitstück*) rejects parochial and humoristic aspects in favor of relating to

contemporary problems and their causes. Topical plays do not portray; they point out. They take a stand and attempt to motivate the audience to do likewise. The themes do not necessarily have to stem from the present, but are related to a contemporary situation in order to enlighten the public; these plays protest, try to incite changes or simply revel in sensationalism. There have always been topical plays in this sense, but they emerged as a genre in Berlin as Expressionism declined, and were in competition with the new mass media of cinema, radio, sports and revues. The topical play is quite unpretentious, since it is written and staged for a specific moment. This is its main difference with the work of Piscator and Brecht, whose socially engaged theater maintained high esthetic standards. Topical plays can also be differentiated from the agitprop movement, since that movement generally had no literary basis for their productions except what emerged directly from rehearsals.

Actual "topical theater" (*Zeittheater*) did not appear before 1928, when a wave of explosive productions were staged in Berlin within just a few weeks of each other, beginning on October 16 with the *U-Boot S4* ("Submarine S4", directed by Leo Reuss, stage design by Edward Suhr) by a twenty-six-year-old newcomer, Günther Weisenborn. The burning actuality of the play was not only due to the fact that with it a world-shaking naval catastrophe that had occurred barely a year before reached the stage but also to the fact that Weisenborn used this tragic and sensationalist example to engage in national politics himself, directly and vehemently. The coalition under Hermann Müller (SPD), which was to be the Weimar Republic's last government under parliamentary law, had been vacillating for months over the question of rearmament. Just a few days before the play's first run, when its political significance would be enhanced by other premieres throughout Germany, a large-scale popular referendum against the manufacture of armored tanks had failed to be accepted, and it is perhaps due to Weisenborn and his play that the argument on that question, so cleverly contrived in the play, once again became a subject of public debate. The sinking of an American subma-

288, 289   Ferdinand Bruckner: *Die Verbrecher* (premier: October 23, 1928 at the Deutsches Theater, directed by Heinz Hilpert, stage sets by Rochus Gliese)

288   Photo of the stage: overall view of the apartment house (synchronized acting, partially posed). "It's as if Bruckner, who opens all the rooms in a house, wants to uncover every type of art-with-a-purpose at the same time." (-Monty Jacobs, *Vossische Zeitung:* October 24, 1928)

289   Photo of the stage: Hans Albers (waiter), Lucie Höflich (cook). "For the handsome waiter ... they brought in Hans Albers.... His brash ... mood cured of the worst symptoms of smugness this time." (-Monty Jacobs, *Vossische Zeitung:* October 24, 1928)

rine is the central theme of the play, which included a dramatic rescue attempt and a harrowing outcome for the crew; the theme was thoroughly exploited as an indictment of militarism and of sensationalist newspaper reporting. There is a formal connection between this production and Piscator's multimedia theater, especially the film inserts from real life conceived for the play and assembled and filmed by Piscator's collaborators, Leo Lania and Curt Oertel, which substantiated the direct connection with German policies of rearmament.

Exactly one week later, on October 23, another play which also became the talk of the town was premiered at the Deutsches Theater: Ferdinand Bruckner's *Verbrecher* ("Criminals", directed by Heinz Hilpert, stage designs by Rochus Gliese). Based on recent murder cases and the accompanying judicial scandals, the play is an attack on criminal law, on the people who carry it out and on the State that was ultimately responsible in such matters. Bruckner, whose real name is Theodor Tagger, founded and directed the Renaissance-Theater in Berlin (1922-28), after having created several unsuccessful Expressionist plays; he was more of a moralist than a social critic, although he is not even clearly that. The plays he wrote under his pen name tend to be rather sensationalist. The impact of *Verbrecher* was softened by the fact that he widened the social focus to include the everyday imbroglios that lead to criminality as well as the different aspects of the judicial machinery. These complex themes were translated theatrically by refined montage for synchronized action, reminiscent of the tiered stages Piscator used for *Hoppla, wir leben!* "In the First and Third Acts, we see a cross-section of a middle-class apartment house over a disreputable bar on the ground floor; in the Second Act, we are presented with the interior of a courthouse divided into four courtrooms. It barely suffices; even the stage experiences the 'housing shortage', but the action is brisk; never a dull moment. One would want a swivel chair to follow the action from left to right and from top to bottom". (-Fritz Engel, *Berliner Tagblatt*: October 24, 1928)

The critics were very divided in their assessments of the political utilitarianism of the *Verbrecher*: some considered the play banal and insignificant (Jhering, Fechter); others praised it as a "successful sort of artistic trend" (-Monty Jacobs, *Vossische Zeitung*). But they were unanimously taken with the high-level acting, which Norbert Falk of the *BZ* labelled as the joint achievement of a fictitious "Berlin ensemble", which was not only intended to apply to the stars such as Gründgens, Ilka Grünig, Erwin Faber, Maria Fein, Hans Deppe, Leonard Steckel, Matthias Wiemann and others who were cast in secondary roles; the label was also a tribute to the performance as a whole, a demonstration of the unique capacities of regeneration and integration inherent in Berlin's dramatic corps: an actor as spoiled as the movie star Hans Albers found his way back to the joint responsibilities and fastidiousness of group work; an actress as important as Lucie Höflich, who had not played a leading role for almost ten years, got back into harness without ado and with overwhelming forcefulness – "In the role of a goofy, blond, aging old maid, totally involved in herself, yet a victim of inner strife, Lucie Höflich gave a fantastic, exceedingly interiorized, and hence simplified, performance that surpassed the portrayals of women of the last ten years". (-Kurt Pinthus, *8-Uhr-Abendblatt*: October 24, 1928)

By the third premiere of a topical play, Peter Martin Lampel's *Revolte im Erziehungshaus* ("Uprising in a Reformatory", December 2, 1928, Thalia-Theater), politically engaged topical theater had already become a considerable factor in society. Although it had a rather obscure opening as a Sunday matinee at a third-class theater, this play made a terrific impact. It was performed by a group as unknown as the author, the Gruppe Junger Schauspieler – an *ad hoc* formation that was projected by the success of its performance in this play into becoming the first and most enduring theater collective of the Weimar Republic. Lampel's ideas for the play came from news coverage on Prussian houses of correction; he adapted them into a play especially for the troupe. The setting was a reformatory on the outskirts of Berlin; the plot is about a group of youngsters who are

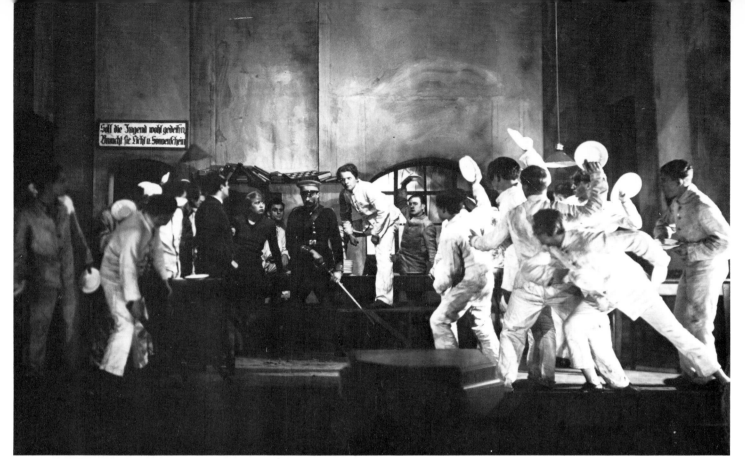

◁ 290 Peter Martin Lampel: *Revolte im Erziehungshaus* (premier: December 2, 1928 by the Gruppe Junger Schauspieler at the Thalia-Theater, directed by Hans Deppe, stage sets by Wolfgang Böttcher)
Photo of the end of Act 2: beginning of the revolt, (center left) Renée Stobrava (Viktoria), (to the right of the guardian) Fritz Genschov (Fritz). "One is shattered into wondering what remedial measures could be taken. One would want... the entire Reichstag to take a look at this hair-raising monument to education and instruction." (-Bernard Diebold, *Frankfurter Zeitung:* December 14, 1928)

◁ 291 Peter Martin Lampel: *Giftgas über Berlin* (premier: March 5, 1929 by the Gruppe Junger Schauspieler at the Theater am Schiffbauerdamm, directed by Bertolt Brecht, stage sets by Wolfgang Böttcher)
Photo of the stage: Max Schreck (fourth from left) as "His Excellence", made up as General von Seeckt. Under pressure from the army, Berlin's chief of police, Zörrgiebel (SPD), at first allowed only a single private showing for the police and military, members of parliament and the press, and other public figures; then he banned any repeat performances as a "danger to public security". The ban was not repealed despite manifold protests.

deprived of their rights and self-respect, and turn into a gang of pillagers who end up in a reformatory. The theme was handled from a new point of view that turned its back on the conventional development of themes in plays, which would have depicted educators and parsons as villainous sadists. Instead, they are characterized as respectable, well-intentioned officials whose commitments to duty reveal the inhuman aspect of State reformatories. Consequently a terrifying pathos of *fait accompli* emerges, emphatically underscored by the boundless dramatic ardor of the actors. "The youngsters [are] completely out of hand; cushions flutter about on the stage, which is covered with straw and dust, before an appalled audience. Genschow [the leader of the uprising] tinkers around with a fuel tank held under his arm and floods the whole whirling chaos like a maniac. The audience seeks protection behind their handkerchiefs.... Renée Stobrava [playing the kitchen girl] lunges towards Fritz in pure panic and tears the match from his fingers; then the police break in to save the house". (-*Börsen-Courier*: no. 603, 1928)

Political and pedagogical discussion groups followed the performances. The problematical nature of rehabilitation centers became a central theme of the reviews, which linked the problem to the State's responsability. The topic gained ground, moving from feature articles to editorials, and resulted in vehement debates in the Berlin and Prussian Chamber of Deputies and even in the Reichstag. In September, 1929, the Welfare Ministry enacted certain reforms in the field of juvenile rehabilitation, and even in the early Thirties this production of Lampel's play remained a reference point for left-of-center parties and organizations interested in youth welfare.

The publicity surrounding Lampel and the Gruppe Junger Schauspieler provoked opposition as well. Their next joint endeavor, *Giftgas über Berlin* ("Poison Gas over Berlin") was banned by the police after a single private performance at the Theater an Schiffbauerdamm (March 5, 1929, Aufricht production, directed by Brecht). The play was a take-off on a real-life incident and discredited the army doubly by going beyond the poison-gas

scandal into the question of secret rearmament policies. The leftist press stood behind the production almost to a man, and a special Association Against the Re-Establishment of Censorship was created, supported by the majority of prominent artists and intellectuals. Nevertheless, the army prevailed upon the Minister of the Interior, Severing (SPD), to intervene because the army chief-of-staff, General von Seeckt, and his *éminence grise*, General von Schleicher, appeared in the play *in persona*. As a result, Lampel reverted to the youth question and continued his own artistic development, but he never again earned the same success as with *Revolte im Erziehungshaus*.

Friedrich Wolf's *Cyankali* ("Cyanide") represents the high point of this spate of topical plays. Once again, the play (premiered on September 6, 1929 at the Lessing Theater, directed by Hans Hinrich) was performed by the Gruppe Junger Schauspieler. After several internal problems, the group had developed into a Socialist collective. The play took up arms against the unpopular Paragraph 218 of the law which banned abortion; the campaign in favor of a legal change came at the perfect time: the play opened just a few weeks before the Great Depression when unemployment and shortages of housing and food wreaked havoc with the lives of a great portion of the population for whom another child was the final stroke. A meeting of the German Medical Association estimated that there were over half a million illegal abortions in 1929, resulting in over 10,000 deaths.

Inevitably, *Cyankali* stirred up a veritable wasps' nest. Public demonstrations erupted constantly after each performance — sometimes even during performances when exasperation reached such a point that the political debate flowed right over onto the stage. Yet *Cyankali* was not a theme-play in the agit-prop sense, nor was it an analytically structured epic play, modelled on Brecht or Piscator. Wolf's work was distinctly naturalistic, and the actors strove to make the acting and setting as realistic as his lifelike plot. While the rightist press vehemently attacked the "hackneyed poor-man's Naturalism" (-Franz Servaes, *Lokal-Anzeiger*: September 7, 1929), Communist reviews were very impressed with the artistic validity of the acting and with

292   Friedrich Wolf: *Cyankali*
(premier: September 6, 1929 by the
Gruppe Junger Schauspieler at the
Lessing-Theater, directed by Hans
Hinrich, stage sets by Wolfgang
Böttcher)
Photo of Scene 5: the newspaper
stand (from left to right): Reinhold
Bernt (Kuckuck), Adolf Fischer
(Max), Renée Stobrava (Hete),
Gerhard Bienert (Paul). While
Kuckuck calls out the headlines of
the scandal-sheet, Hete is doubled
over in pain after just having
attempted an abortion.

293   Friedrich Wolf, the author of
Cyankali, was well acquainted with
the problems of birth control from
his experience as a general
practitioner, panel and welfare
physician. Here he discusses the
social and medical implications of
Paragraph 218, in an address to
Berlin's Upper Chamber of
Parliament.

294　Friedrich Wolf: *Die Matrosen von Cattaro* (November 8, 1930 at the Volksbühne, directed by Günther Stark, stage sets by Nina Tokumbet)
Photo of the stage. Wolf's play stands above the spate of revolutionary naval plays that followed Eisenstein's *Battleship Potemkin*, because it not only refers to past history but also updates the thwarted Austrian uprising of 1918, on which it was based, as a lesson for contemporary times.

the realism: "Life is so close here, so real, so impetuous that at times one finds oneself in Mother Fent's kitchen, at Kuckuck's newspaper stand, in the doctor's office... and the people who talk and live there, who are condemned as victims of capitalist shortcomings, have... nothing to do with the performers Stobrava, Bienert, Krahn, for they are the worker's Widow Fent, her daughter Hete, the boilerman Paul.... They all infuse [their roles with] life, real, real life". (-Durus, *Rote Fahne*: September 8, 1929)

It was Jhering who most explicitly defined the artistic value of a topical play in terms of

the actual political purposes it fulfilled. Referring to the pragmatic effects of *Revolte im Erziehungshaus*, he expected *Cyankali* "to have a similar practical impact" and to "contribute to changing Paragraph 218" (-*Börsen-Courier*: no. 7, September, 1929), although he also warned against the counter-dynamics of reaction, "because every new triumph of topical theater provokes the reactionary vanguard into tightening their ranks". In Berlin *Cyankali* played for over three months, more than any other play of the season, provoking "combative demonstrations", press campaigns, academic and moral/theological discussion groups. However, the major goal – to change the law – was not reached because for the Christian, bourgeois and authoritarian State more was at stake in Paragraph 218 than the legalization of abortion. Wolf himself made a tactical "mistake" in putting the political and economic implications openly into words. For his play is an attack – albeit indirect – on capitalism, and it was inevitable that the organs of the capitalistic system would strike back. The point was brought home to Wolf (a panel doctor) when he was arrested in 1931 for an alleged offense against Paragraph 218.

Topical plays remained popular until around the end of 1931, when interest began to ebb. With the aggravation of political conflicts, it became progressively more difficult for leftist theater producers to stage topical plays and attract enough people to cover their expenses. But problems with the authorities and fear of growing Nazi terrorism were not the main obstacles. The difficult economic situation and the dulled political and moral senses of the masses made it increasingly difficult for such progressive, engaged, topical plays to reach their target audiences. Inadequate box-office receipts forced the Gruppe Junger Schauspieler to cancel the last of their own productions in autumn, 1931 – Katajev's *Avantgarde* – after a mere five-night run, because they could not continue paying rent to the Reinhardt concern. In mid January, 1932, the group managed to put on Brecht's *Die Mutter*, but it was less of a collective venture than a question of star appeal, for Brecht filled the majority of the leading roles with his own people. Like the Piscator collective, all

295 Sigmund Graff and Carl
Ernst Hintze: *Die endlose Strasse*
(performed at the Schiller-Theater:
February 23, 1932, directed by
Leopold Lindtberg, stage sets by
Traugott Müller)
Sketch by F. Hänsel (from left to
right): Bernhard Minetti (Corporal
Jansen), Walter Franck (the captain),
Fritz Genschov (the lieutenant),
Alexander Granach (Musketeer
Richter), Veit Harlan (Musketeer
Heller). "The martyrdom of a
company relieved from duty in the
front-line trenches, but ... which
must return to the front again. Joint
destiny. Resignation. No way out."
(-Herbert Jhering, *Börsen-Courier*:
February 24, 1932)

traces of the Gruppe Junger Schauspieler disappeared during the summer of 1932.

Towards the end of the Weimar Republic, topical theater exhausted its reserves for simulating reality and sacrificed informative and argumentative aspects in favor of those calculated exclusively to excite the audience, all of which progressively turned to the advantage of the political right. Although the Nazis failed three times in a row in their attempt to found their own nationalist and topical theater in Berlin, reactionary topical plays that glorified patriotism, sacrifice, heroism and militarism continued to gain grounds. Menzel's *Toboggan* (1928) was the first of a series of war plays that corresponded to the swing to the right. At first these plays continued to be anti-militaristic, but gradually they came to focus ever more distinctly on the communal and heroic facets of war. The first major success of this trend, *Die endlose Strasse* ("The Endless Street") by Sigmund Graff and Carl Ernst Hintze, equated the death of a company of frontline soldiers with deliverance from the agony and senselessness of war. The play had already been written in 1929 but was not premiered until the end of 1930 in Aachen; that was the starting point for a circuit of unprecedented triumph throughout Germany, which ended in Berlin, where the play was staged at the Schiller-Theater on February 23, 1932, (director Leopold Lindtberg) with an eye to the greatest possible objectivity. Jhering, more than anyone, saw through and criticized the attitude of resignation promoted by the play: "And that is the danger of this play which, in the last analysis, strains the nerves without, however, appealing to either willpower or reason. It cripples". (-*Börsen-Courier*: February 24, 1932)

In the end effect, the astounding public triumph of *Die endlose Strasse* was a sign of a general acceptance of current bans and hence also a sign that a large part of the population was prepared to submit to the threat of Fascist dictatorship. Consequently, the right sought to win the public over to a Third Reich by offering more militant, topical plays. *Schlageter* by Hanns Johst, was the major work of this genre; it became the foundation for the future official National Socialist theater. The play, written in 1930 and 1931 under the influence of a nationalistic celebration of Schlageter, is a tribute to the people's volunteer corps and to a fanatic slayer of Communists named Schlageter. He was executed by a French military court in 1923 for important acts of sabotage committed in the French-occupied sector of the Rhineland. He was glorified in the play as the "first soldier of the Third Reich" to die with the Nazi slogan *"Deutschland erwache!"* ("Germany, wake up!") on his lips.

Only a few days after the Fascists came into power, the new Chancellor and Führer, Adolf Hitler, had Franz Ulbrich, the Nazi intendant at Weimar, appointed as stage director of the Staatstheater in Berlin. *Schlageter*, dedicated to Hitler, opened on the Führer's birthday (April 20, 1933). Circumstances had changed abruptly and in a particularly eerie fashion: there was not a peep from the leftist press nor, for that matter, from the great majority of the liberal-bourgeois press represented by Jewish critics such as Arthur Eloesser, Emil Faktor, Manfred Georg, Monty Jacobs, Alfred Kerr, Ludwig Marcuse, Max Osborn, Kurt Pinthus, Alfred Polgar, Hermann Sinsheimer (most of whom had lost their jobs and many of whom were already living in exile). The irreverence, bravado and brutality of "brown barbarism" set a new tone: "Criticism in literary terms would be inappropriate. The play and performance are an appeal, a slap on the shoulder, a [means of] pulling down and pushing forward. Comrade... give me your hand!... Schlageter is the new, the young German man. His death is resurrection; his possessions are comradery, loyalty, brotherhood.... The character Schlageter is authentic. It stands there as a warning until ALL is fulfilled. It contains the grail of all that is new in transparent purity.... What more can one say of a performance... than that it captures, obliterates, rends and tramples underfoot and once again reassembles, to cul-

296   Hanns Johst: *Schlageter* (premier: April 20, 1933 [the Führer's birthday] at the Staatstheater, directed by Franz Ulbrich, stage sets by Benno von Arent)
Before the final curtain (from left to right): Maria Koppenhöfer (Frau Thiemann), Albert Bassermann (the general), Lothar Müthel (Leo Schlageter), Hanns Johst (making the Hitler salute), Emmy Sonnemann [later Goering] (Alexandra Thiemann), Hans Leibelt (President Schneider). "An audience is always made up of followers .... They are creatures who are enthusiastic followers, for better or for worse." (-Hanns Johst *Standpunkt und Fortschritt:* Munich, 1933, p. 44)

minate in a heroic and creative communion of sensitivity?" (-Keienburg, *Tägliche Rundschau*: April 22, 1933) Even a judge formerly as objective and independent as the conservative Paul Fechter declared his relentless satisfaction with the radical changes in the theatrical world and went on to pay a highly respectful tribute to the new despots: "A totally new public has invaded the parquet and balconies; the former premiere society of the previous Staatstheater has almost completely disappeared. One catches a glimpse of the Minister, Dr. Goebbels and of State Commissioner Hinkel, representing the Reich's administration. At the end of the play, after the execution scene, no one applauds – there is a short silence, and then the public stands to sing the first stanza of the national anthem, followed by the first stanza of the 'Horst-Wessel Song'. Only then does the house come down with applause". (-*Deutsche Allgemeine Zeitung*: April 22, 1933)

Paradoxically enough, *Schlageter* (directed by Intendant Ulbrich) was premiered with the Jewish actor Albert Bassermann in a main role, opposite Emmy Sonnemann – Goering's mistress, who was to become a sort of "first lady". This premiere was supposed to have inaugurated the National Socialist era at the Staatstheater and also to have opened the way for new, heroic-cult plays. But Nazi theorists were wrong on both counts. After one and a half years, Ulbrich, who was a mediocre intendant, was obliged to yield to Gustaf Gründgens, an undaunted republican. Johst's *Schlageter* was not the beginning but the climax of National Socialist theater. Under Gründgen's icily tactical direction, torn back and forth as it was between cynical vanity and altruistic magnanimity, the Staatstheater managed to conserve more of the humanist spirit of the Weimar Republic than any other German theater during the era under Fascist domination.

NOTES

City, Architecture and Habitat

1 Sonja Günther, "Raumkunst und Kunstgewerbe auf den Weltausstellungen Paris 1900, St. Louis 1904, Brüssel 1910", in *Zwischen Kunst und Industrie*, Vol. 2 [Werkbund Archives] (Lahn-Giessen, 1977), pp. 55 ff., cat. I, nos. 3, 5, 23

2 Max Osborn, "Erster Rundgang durch die deutsche und österreichische Abteilung", in *Deutsche Kunst und Dekoration* 5 (1899/1900): 538

3 Henry van de Velde, *Renaissance im modernen Kunstgewerbe*, Berlin, 1901, p. 148

4 Friedrich von Thiersch, "Architektur und Kunstgewerbe auf der Welt-Ausstellung in St. Louis", in *Kunst und Handwerk* 15 (1904–05): 96

5 Hermann Muthesius, "Das Kunstgewerbe, insbesondere die Wohnungskunst", in *Amtlicher Bericht über die Weltausstellung in St. Louis 1904* [by the Reichskommissar] (Berlin, 1906): 289

6 Günther, *op. cit.,* cat. II, nos. 9–10, 12, 25–26

7 Hermann Muthesius, "Die Wohnungskunst auf der Weltausstellung in St. Louis", in *Deutsche Kunst und Dekoration* 15 (1904–05): 213

8 "Der Deutsche Werkbund", in *Deutsche Kunst und Dekoration* 22 (1908): 337

9 Ibid.

10 Interior decoration of the ship "Kronprinzessin Cecilie" after designs by Joseph Maria Olbrich, Bruno Paul and Richard Riemerschmid in 1907; Richard Riemerschmid's designs for the interior decoration of railroad cars (1908) and those by Peter Behrens (employed by AEG) for household appliances

11 "Haus Westend" by Bruno Paul; see: Hermann Post, "Bruno Paul als Architekt", in *Deutsche Kunst und Dekoration* 25 (1909–10): 165 ff. [fig.]

12 Julius Posener, "Hermann Muthesius: Vortrag zur Eröffnung der Ausstellung", in *Hermann Muthesius: Ausstellung in der Akademie der Künste*, Berlin, 1977–78, p. 7

13 Ibid.

14 Richard Hamann and Jost Hermand, *Stilkunst um 1900*, Berlin, 1967, p. 486

15 Karl Scheffler, "Kultur und Geschmack des Wohnens", in Eduard Heyck [ed.], *Moderne Kultur: Ein Handbuch der Lebensbildung und des guten Geschmacks*, Stuttgart/Leipzig, 1906, Vol. I *Grundbegriffe: Die Häuslichkeit*, p. 182

16 Vereinigte Werkstätten für Kunst im Handwerk A.G., *Typenmöbel für Stadt und Land von Professor Bruno Paul*, Berlin, 1913, p. 5

17 Robert Breuer, "Der Einkauf als kulturelle Funktion", in *Deutsche Kunst und Dekoration* 21 (1907–08): 79

18 Max Osborn, "Bruxelles Kermesse", in *Kunstgewerbeblatt* new series, No. 21 (n.d.): 202 f.

19 Hans Maria Wingler, *Das Bauhaus*, Bramsche, 1962, p. 39

20 *Ein Versuchshaus des Bauhauses in Weimar*, compiled by Adolf Meyer [Bauhausbücher, Vol. 3] Munich, 1925, pp. 16 f.

21 Hannes Meyer, "Die Neue Welt", in *Das Werk* 13 (1926): 221 ff.

22 *Der Cicerone* 13 (1921): 361

23 Walter Riezler, "Qualität und Form: Betrachtungen zur Deutschen Gewerbeschau München 1922", in *Die Form* 1 (1922): 31 [issue 1]

24 Deutscher Werkbund [ed.], *Bau und Wohnung*, Stuttgart, 1927, p. 7

25 Quotation from: *Zwischen Kunst und Industrie—Der Deutsche Werkbund*, Munich, 1975, p. 284

26 *Innendekoration* 42 (1931): 174

27 Ibid., p. 259

28 Heinrich Tessenow, *Die kleine und grosse Stadt: Nachdenkliches von Heinrich Tessenow*, Munich, 1961, p. 32

29 Julius Cohn, "Wohnungsnot und Krankenkassen", in *30 Jahre Wohnungsreform 1898-1928* [memorandum on the occasion of the 30th anniversary of the Deutsche Verein für Wohnungsreform e.V.], Berlin 1928, pp. 192

30 See: *Berlin und seine Bauten*, Vol. IV A, Berlin/Munich/Düsseldorf, 1970, p. 8

31 Wilhelm Lotz, *Wie richte ich meine Wohnung ein?*, Berlin, 1930, p. 192

32 This quotation and the following verses by Scheerbart are from *Tendenzen der zwanziger Jahre*, Berlin, 1977, pp. 2; 62

33 Ibid., pp. 2; 86

Painting

1 Wolf Dieter Dube, "Zeichen des Glaubens—Expressionismus", in Wieland Schmied [ed.], *Zeichen des Glaubens—Geist der Avantgarde: Religiöse Tendenzen in der Kunst des 20. Jahrhunderts*, Stuttgart, 1980, p. 101

2 Exhibition catalogue *Der Sturm: Herwarth Walden und die europäische Avantgarde Berlin 1912–1932*, Berlin: Staatl. Museen Preussischer Kulturbesitz, Nationalgalerie, 1961, p. 10

3 Hans Maria Wingler [ed.], *Der Sturm: Zeichnungen und Graphiken*, Feldafing, 1955, p. 7

4 Kurt Pinthus [ed.], *Menschheitsdämmerung: Symphonie jüngster Dichtung*, Berlin, 1920; new ed., Rheinbeck b. Hamburg, 1969

5 Exhibition catalogue *Ernst Ludwig Kirchner 1880–1928*, Berlin: Staatl. Museen Preussischer Kulturbesitz, Nationalgalerie, 1980, p. 217

6 Ibid., p. 218

7 Hans Richter, "Begegnungen in Berlin", in exhibition catalogue *Avantgarde Osteuropa 1910–1930*, Berlin: Deutsche Gesellschaft für Bildende Kunst und Akademie der Künste Berlin, 1967, pp. 13 f.

8 Eberhard Steneberg, *Russische Kunst Berlin 1919–1932*, Berlin, 1969, p. 9

9 Ibid. pp. 13 f.

10 Ibid. p. 25

11 Richter, *op. cit.*, p. 18

12 Helga Kliemann, *Die Novembergruppe*, Berlin, 1969

13 Carl Zuckmayer, *Als wär's ein Stück von mir*, Frankfurt-am-Main, 1966, pp. 388 f.

14 Ibid., p. 389

15 Exhibition catalogue *B.F. Dolbin*, Dortmund: Institut für Zeitungsforschung, 1975

16 Eberhard Roters, "Der Bruch", in exhibition catalogue *Jeanne Mammen*, Bonn: Bonner Kunstverein, 1975

17 Zuckmayer, *op. cit.*, p. 446

Sculpture

1 Cf. exhibition catalogue *Abbilder—Leitbilder: Berliner Skulpturen von Schadow bis heute*, Berlin: Neuer Berliner Kunstverein, 1978

2 Cf. Kurt Reutti, *Ernst Barlach in Berlin (Ausstellung im Haus am Lützowplatz)*, Berlin, 1974, p. 19

3 For Kolbe's portrait of Ebert, cf. Hella Reelfs, "Die Bildnisse Adolf von Harnacks und Max J. Friedländers von Georg Kolbe", in *Jahrbuch preussischer Kulturbesitz 1977* 14 (Berlin, 1979): 293 ff.

4 Cf. Dietrich Schubert, *Die Kunst Wilhelm Lehmbrucks*, Worms, 1981, p. 130

5 Trans. of a quotation from: exhibition catalogue *Ernst Barlach/Käthe Kollwitz*, London: Marlborough Fine Art Ltd., 1967, p. 10

6 L. de Marsalle, "Über die plastischen Arbeiten von E.L. Kirchner", in *Der Cicerone* 17 (1925): 695

7 Marsalle, *loc. cit.*

8 Kasimir Edschmid, "Hoetger", in *Die Sammlung der Werke von Bernhard Hoetger*, Leipzig: Galerie Erich Cüpper, 1916, p. 15

9 Donald E. Gordon, *Ernst Ludwig Kirchner*, Munich, 1916, p. 81

10 J. Hermand, in Richard Hamann and Jost Hermand, *Expressionismus (= Epochen deutscher Kultur von 1870 bis zur Gegenwart)*, Munich, 1976; also Jost Hermand and Frank Trommler, *Die Kultur der Weimarer Republik*, Munich, 1978

[11] Manfred Schneckenburger, "Bemerkungen zur 'Brücke' und zur 'primitiven' Kunst", in exhibition catalogue *Weltkulturen und moderne Kunst*, Munich, 1972, p. 460

[12] Cf. U. Boccioni, "Die Futuristische Bildhauerei", in Christa Baumgarth, *Die Geschichte des Futurismus*, Reinbek b. Hamburg, 1966, pp. 194 ff.

[13] Cf. Paul Westheim, *Wilhelm Lehmbruck*, Postdam-Berlin, 1919: trans. of a quotation from Dieter Honisch, "Neuerwerbungen der Nationalgalerie 1979", in *Jahrbuch preussischer Kulturbesitz* 16 (Berlin, 1980): 216

[14] Cf. Albert Elsen, *Modern European Sculpture 1918–1945: Unknown Beings and Other Realities*, New York, 1979, pp. 62 f. Roland Schlacht ("Archipenko, Belling und Westheim", in *Der Sturm*, 14, no. 5 [1923]: 76) already noted in a review of the book *Architektonik des Plastischen*, Westheim's fashionable over-glorification of Belling's work and his consequent under-estimation of the historical importance of Archipenko's prewar work.

[15] Paul Westheim, in *Das Kunstblatt* (1921): 32

[16] Raoul Hausmann, "Der Geist unserer Zeit" (1919); text of September 14, 1967, trans. of a quotation from the exhibition catalogue *Tendenzen der zwanziger Jahre: 15. europäische Kunstausstellung*, Berlin, 1977, pp. 3; 50

[17] Ibid. pp. 1; 106

[18] Quotation from John Willett, *Art and Politics in the Weimar Period 1917–1933*, New York: Pantheon Books, 1978, p. 76; first published by Thames and Hudson Ltd., under the title *The New Sobriety: Art and Politics in the Weimar Period 1917–1933*

[19] Cf. Fritz Schmalenbach, *Die Malerei der Neuen Sachlichkeit*, Berlin, 1973

[20] Quotation from Willett, *op. cit.*, p. 117

[21] Trans. of a quotation from the exhibition catalogue *Ewald Mataré*, Kaiserslautern/Heilbronn, 1981

[22] W.S. [Wilhem Michel], "Das Bildnis — eine neue Möglichkeit", in *Deutsche Kunst und Dekoration* 57 (1925-26): 33 ff.

[23] On the revalorization of "painting-like sculpture" in the late Twenties: W.M. [Wilhelm Michel], "Das plastische Werk von Edgar Degas", in *Deutsche Kunst und Dekoration* 60 (1927): 97 ff.

[24] Georg Kolbe, "Randbemerkungen zur Entstehung meines Rathenau-Brunnens", in *Museum der Gegenwart* (1930–31): 140 ff.

[25] Trans. of a quotation from Will Grohmann, "Der Bildhauer Gerhard Marcks", in *Die Kunst* 75 (1936–37): 328 ff.

[26] Ibid.

[27] Cf. Werner Haftmann, *Der Bildhauer Ludwig Kasper*, Berlin, 1978, pp. 55 f.

[28] Adolf Behne, "Alexander Calder (USA)", in *Das neue Frankfurt* 3, no. 6 (1939): 121

FILM IN BERLIN

[1] Alfred Döblin, "Das Theater der kleinen Leute", in *Das Theater* 1 (1909). Quoted from Ludwig Greve, Margot Pehle, Hedi Westhoff [eds.], *Hätte ich das Kino !*, Marbach a.N., 1976, pp. 32 f.

[2] Egon Friedell, "Prolog vor dem Film", in *Blätter des Deutschen Theaters* 2 (1912): 511; quoted from Greve, Pehle, Westhoff, *op. cit.*, p. 125

[3] Kurt Pinthus, *Das Kinobuch* (new edition of *Kinobuch* [1913–14]), Zurich, 1963, pp. 9 f.

[4] Ibid., p. 16

[5] Siegfried Kracauer, *From Caligari to Hitler*, Princeton: Princeton University Press, 1947; reprinted 1966, p. 28

[6] Rudolf Kurtz, *Expressionismus und Film*, Berlin, 1926; reprinted Zurich, 1965, pp. 65 f

[7] Ibid., pp. 82 f.

[8] Lotte Eisner, *Die dämonische Leimwand*, Wiesbaden-Biebrich, 1955, p. 21

[9] Kracauer, *op. cit.*, p. 60

[10] Eisner, *op. cit.*, p. 81

[11] Kracauer, *op. cit.*, p. 78

[12] Hans Richter, "Der avantgardistische Film in Deutschland (von 1921-1951)", in *Cinéaste* [special issue for Deutsche Filmtage] (Göttingen, 1953): 14

[13] Eisner, *op. cit.*, p. 113

THEATER

The numerous references to theater reviews in newspapers of the period are included in the text of the chapter within parentheses.

GUIDE TO PERSONS MENTIONED IN THE BOOK

ANKER, ALFONS (Berlin) 1872–1958 (Stockholm): architect

ARCHIPENKO, ALEXANDER (Kiev) 1887–1964 (Paris): sculptor

ARP, HANS or JEAN (Strasbourg) 1887–1966 (Basel): painter, sculptor, poet

AUFRICHT, ERNST JOSEF: stage director

BAADER, JOHANNES (Stuttgart) 1875–1956 (Adldorf, Bavaria): architect, tombstone designer

BALUSCHEK, HANS (Breslau) 1870–1935 (Berlin): painter and stage designer

BARLACH, ERNST (Wedel, Holstein) 1870–1938 (Rostock): sculptor, graphic artist, playwright

BARNOVSKY, VIKTOR (Berlin) 1875–1952 (New York): actor, director and theater manager

BARTNING, OTTO (Karlsruhe) 1883–1959 (Darmstadt): architect

BASSERMANN, ALBERT (Mannheim) 1867–1952 (Zurich): actor, emigrated in 1934, returned to Germany after the war

BECKMANN, MAX (Leipzig) 1884–1950 (New York): painter and graphic artist

BEHRENS, PETER (Hamburg) 1868–1940 (Berlin): architect, designer

BELLING, RUDOLF (Berlin) 1886–1972 (Munich): sculptor

BERGER, LUDWIG [Ludwig Gottfried Heinrich Bamberger], 1892–1969: director, made films from 1920, emigrated after 1933

BERGNER, ELISABETH (Drogobych, Galicia) 1897–: actress

BERLEWI, HENRYK (Warsaw) 1894–1967 (Paris): painter

BILDT, PAUL: actor

BLUMENTHAL, HERMANN (Essen) 1905–1942 (d. in action in Russia): sculptor

BRECHT, BERTOLT (Augsburg) 1898–1956 (Berlin): dramatist and poet, emigrated in 1933, lived in East Berlin from 1948

BREKER, ARNO (Elberfeld) 1900– (lives in Düsseldorf): sculptor

BRONNEN, ARNOLT [Arnold Bronner] (Vienna) 1895–1959 (East Berlin): author

BROOKS, LOUISE (b. in the USA) 1906–: dancer, film actress, made films in Germany in 1928–29

BRUCKNER, FERDINAND [Theodor Tagger] (Vienna) 1891–1958 (Berlin): author, emigrated in 1933, lived in Paris and Berlin from 1951

BUCHHOLZ, ERICH (Bromberg) 1891–1972 (Berlin): painter, stage designer

BUSCH, ERNST (Kiel) 1900–: actor

CALDER, ALEXANDER (Lawnton, Pennsylvania) 1898–1976 (New York): sculptor, painter, graphic artist

CHAGALL, MARC (Vitebsk, Belorussia) 1887– (lives in St-Paul-de-Vence, France): painter, graphic artist

CORINTH, LOVIS (Tapiau, East Prussia) 1858–1925 (Zandvoort, Holland): painter

DEUTSCH, ERNST (Prague) 1890–1969 (Berlin): actor (mainly on stage), film roles from 1916, emigrated in 1933, lived in Vienna and Berlin from 1947

DIETERLE, WILHELM or WILLIAM (Ludwigshafen) 1893–1972: actor, director, author, film roles from 1923, moved to Hollywood in 1929, made films in Germany in 1959–60, played in Hersfelder Festival in 1961–65

270

DIETRICH, MARLENE [Maria Magdalena von Losch] (Berlin) 1901– (lives in the USA): film actress and singer, film roles since 1923

DIX, OTTO (Untermhaus near Gera) 1891–1969 (Hemmenhofen on the Bodensee): painter, graphic artist

DOLBIN [Benedikt Fred Pollack] (Vienna) 1883–1971 (New York): civil engineer, stage designer, composer, reporter and draftsman

DORSCH, KÄTHE (Newmarkt, Oberpfalz) 1890–1957 (Vienna): actress

DUDOW, SLATAN (Bulgaria) 1903–1963: director, emigrated to the USSR from 1933–46, after 1946 made films for the Defa in East Germany

DUNGERT, MAX (Magdeburg) 1896–1945 (Berlin): painter

DURIEUX, TILLA [Ottilie Godeffroy] (Vienna) 1880–1971 (Berlin): actress, emigrated in 1933, returned to Berlin as guest performer in 1952

EBNETH, LAJOS D' (Hungary) 1902–(lives in Chaclacajo, Peru): painter, architect

EGGELING, VIKING (Sweden) 1880–1925: painter, developed abstract films

EISLER, HANNS (Leipzig) 1898–1962 (Berlin): composer, emigrated to the USA in 1933, returned to East Berlin in 1945

EMMERICH, PAUL (Berlin) 1876–1958 (Berlin): architect

ENDELL, AUGUST (Berlin) 1871–1925 (Berlin): architect

ENGEL, ERICH (Hamburg) 1891–1966 (Berlin): theater and film director

FAKTOR, EMIL: critic

FECHTER, PAUL (Elbing) 1880–1958 (Berlin): author, journalist, literary historian

FEHLING, JÜRGEN (Lübeck) 1885–1968 (Hamburg): director

FELIXMÜLLER, CONRAD (Dresden) 1897–1977 (Berlin): painter, graphic artist

FISCHINGER, OSKAR, 1900–1967: made animated films, attempted to interpret music optically, worked in the USA from 1936

FLEISSER [Haindl], MARIELUISE (Ingolstadt) 1901–1974 (Ingolstadt): playwright and author

FORSTER, RUDOLF (Gröbming, Steiermark) 1889–1968 (Bad Aussee): actor

FRANCK, ARNOLD (Frankenthal, Pfalz) 1889–1974: made mountain and nature films from 1913

FRANCK, WALTER (Hüttensteinach) 1896–1961 (Garmisch): actor

FREUND, CARL, 1890–1969: cameraman, worked in films from 1913, in the USA from 1930

FREUNDLICH, OTTO (Stolp, Pommerania) 1878–1943 (Lublin–Maidanek): painter, sculptor

FRITSCH, ERNST (Berlin) 1892–1965 (Berlin): painter

GABO, NAUM [Naum Pevsner] (Bryansk, Russia) 1890–1977 (Waterbury, Connecticut): sculptor

GALEEN, HENRIK (Holland) 1882–1949: actor, scriptwriter, director, from 1910 active mainly in German films, emigrated to the USA in 1933

GARBE, HERBERT (Berlin) 1888–1945 (in prison in France): sculptor

GEORGE, HEINRICH [Georg Heinrich Schulz] (Stettin) 1893–1946? (interned in a Soviet camp at Sachsenhausen): stage and film actor

GERT, VALESKA [Gertrud Anderson], 1909–1978: dancer, singer, actress, know for Expressionist dances

GLIESE, ROCHUS, 1891–: stage and film-set designer, director

GRANACH, ALEXANDER: actor

GRENANDER, ALFRED (Sköfde, Sweden) 1863–1931 (Berlin): architect

GROPIUS, WALTER (Berlin) 1883–1969 (Boston): architect

GROSZ, GEORGE (Berlin) 1893–1959 (Berlin): painter, graphic artist, guest professor in New York in 1932, in the USA from 1933–59, then returned to Berlin

GRÜNDGENS, GUSTAF (Düsseldorf) 1899–1963 (Manila): actor, director (mainly for the stage, but also worked in films in both capacities)

GRUNE, CARL, 1885–1962: actor, film director from 1919, worked in films in France from 1931

GÜLSTORFF, MAX: actor

GUTFREUND, OTTO (Königinhof) 1889–1927 (Prague): sculptor

HARBOU, THEA VON (Tauperlitz near Hof) 1885–1954 (Berlin): author and scriptwriter, wrote scripts for Fritz Lang's films from 1920–32

HARTH, PHILIPP (Mainz) 1885–1968 (Bayrischzell): architect, sculptor

HARTMANN, PAUL (Fürth) 1889–1977 (Munich): actor

HARTUNG, KARL (Hamburg) 1908–1965 (Hamburg): sculptor

HASENCLEVER, WALTER (Aachen) 1890–1940 (Les Milles): author, emigrated to France

HAUPTMANN, GERHART (Ober-Salzbrunn) 1862–1946 (Agnetendorf): dramatist, novelist and poet, received Nobel Prize in literature (1912)

HAUSMANN, RAOUL (Vienna) 1886–1971 (Limoges): painter, graphic artist, sculptor, founder of Dada in Berlin, emigrated via Paris to Ibiza in 1933, lived in Limoges from 1944

HEARTFIELD, JOHN [Helmut Herzfeld] (Berlin) 1891-1968 (Berlin): graphic artist, stage designer, emigrated via Prague to London from 1933–50

HECKEL, ERICH (Döbeln, Saxony) 1883–1970 (Radolfzell on the Bodensee): painter, graphic artist

HEEMSKERCK, JACOBA VAN (The Hague) 1876–1923 (Domburg, Holland): painter

HELDT, WERNER (Berlin) 1904–1954 (Sant'Angelo, Ischia): painter

HERZFELDE, WIELAND (Berlin) 1896– (lives in East Berlin): publisher, literary historian

HERZOG, OSWALD (Haynau, Silesia) 1881– (missing): sculptor

HILBERSEIMER, LUDWIG (Karlsruhe) 1885–1969 (Chicago): architect, urban planner

HILPERT, HEINZ (Berlin) 1890–1967 (Göttingen): actor, director

HÖCH, HANNAH (Gotha) 1889–1978 (Berlin): painter

HOCHBAUM, WERNER, 1899–1946: journalist, actor, film director, made films from 1929–39; his film *Brüder* (1929) was rediscovered recently

HOETGER, BERNHARD (Hörde near Dortmund) 1874–1949 (Unterseen near Interlaken): sculptor, painter, architect

HOFER, KARL (Karlsruhe) 1878–1955 (Berlin): painter

HÖFLICH, LUCIE (Hanover) 1883–1956 (Berlin): actress

HOMOLKA, OSKAR: actor

HORVATH, ÖDÖN VON (Fiume) 1901–1938 (Paris): author, emigrated in 1934

HUBBUCH, KARL (Karlsruhe) 1891–1980 (Karlsruhe): graphic artist, painter

HUELSENBECK, RICHARD (Frankenau, Hesse) 1892–1974 (Minusio, Switzerland): author, poet, psychoanalyst

JACOBS, MONTY: theater critic

JACOBSOHN, SIEGFRIED (Berlin) 1881–1926 (Berlin): theater critic

JANNINGS, EMIL (Rorschach) 1884–1950 (Strobl): actor, worked in films from 1914, in the USA from 1926–29, then returned to Germany

JAHNN, HANS HENNY (Hamburg) 1894–1959 (Hamburg): author, organ maker, biologist, in exile in Norway from 1915–18, lived on Bornholm from 1934–50

JESSNER, LEOPOLD (Königsberg) 1878–1945 (Los Angeles): director, stage manager in Hamburg, Königsberg, Berlin, also made films

JEHRING, HERBERT (Springe) 1888–: theater critic, publicist, chief theater critic in East Berlin after 1945

JUNGHANS, CARL, 1897–: film director, also made montage and documentary films, emigrated to the USA in 1939, returned to Germany in 1963

JUTZI, PIEL, 1894–1945: director, cameraman, made his own films from 1920, worked in German films until 1942

KAISER, GEORG (Magdeburg) 1878–1945 (Ascona): dramatist

KALSER, ERWIN: actor

KAMPMANN, WALTER (Elberfeld) 1887–1945 (Berlin): painter, sculptor

KAUFMANN, OSKAR (Neu St. Anna, Hungary) 1873–1956 (Budapest): architect

KAYSSLER, FRIEDRICH (Neurode, Silesia) 1874–1945 (Berlin): actor, author

KERR, ALFRED [Alfred Kempner] (Breslau) 1867–1948 (Hamburg): theater critic, emigrated in 1933

KIRCHNER, ERNST LUDWIG (Aschaffenburg) 1880–1938 (Frauenkirch-Wildboden near Davos): painter, graphic artist

KLEIN, CÉSAR (Hamburg) 1876–1954 (Pansdorf near Lübeck): painter, stage designer

KLIMSCH, FRITZ (Frankfurt-am-Main) 1870–1960 (Freiburg im Breisgau): sculptor

KLÖPFER, EUGEN (Thalheim-Rauenstich near Heilbronn) 1886–1950 (Wiesbaden): actor, theater intendant, in Berlin from 1918

KOKOSCHKA, OSKAR (Pöchlarn) 1886–1980 (Villeneuve, Switzerland): painter, graphic artist

KOLBE, GEORG (Waldheim, Saxony) 1877–1947 (Berlin): sculptor

KOLLWITZ, KÄTHE (Königsberg) 1867–1945 (Moritzburg near Dresden): graphic artist, sculptress

KOPPENHÖFER, MARIA: actress

KORNFELD, PAUL (Prague) 1889–1942 (Lodz: concentration camp): author

KORTNER, FRITZ (Vienna) 1892–1970 (Munich): actor, director, emigrated in 1933, worked mainly as director in Berlin and Munich from 1948

KRAUSS, WERNER (Gestungshausen, Upper Franconia) 1884–1959 (Vienna): stage and film actor

KUBICKI, STANISLAV (Ziegenhain near Kassel) 1886–1943 (Poland): painter

KULVIANSKI, ISSAI (Janova, Lithuania) 1892–1970 (London): painter

LAMPEL, PETER MARTIN [Joachim Friedrich Martin Lampel] (Schönborn, Silesia) 1894–1965 (Hamburg): author, emigrated during the Nazi era

LAMPRECHT, GERHARD, 1897–1974: film director and film historian

LANG, FRITZ (Vienna) 1890–1968 (Beverly Hills): studied architecture and painting, film director and scriptwriter, made his own films from 1919, emigrated via France to the USA in 1933

LASKER-SCHÜLER, ELSE (Wuppertal-Elberfeld) 1869–1945 (Jerusalem): poetess, emigrated in 1933

LEMBRUCK, WILHELM (Duisburg-Meiderich) 1881–1919 (Berlin: suicide): sculptor, graphic artist

LENI, PAUL, 1885–1929: film director, before that made posters and built stage sets, specialized in horror films, lived in the USA from 1927

LENK, FRANZ (Lagenbernsdorf, Vogtland) 1898–1968 (Schwäbisch Hall): painter

LENYA, LOTTE (Vienna) 1900–: actress, singer, emigrated via France to the USA in 1933, returned to Germany in 1955

LINGEN, THEO (Theodor Schmitz) (Hanover) 1903–: stage and film actor

LISSITZKY, EL [Lasar Markovich Lissitzky] (Polschinok) 1890–1941 (Moscow): architect

LORRE, PETER [Laszlo Löwenstein] (Rosenberg, Hungary) 1904–1964 (Hollywood): actor, director, emigrated to England in 1933, to the USA in 1935

LUBITSCH, ERNST (Berlin) 1892–1947 (Hollywood): film actor, scriptwriter and film director, in the USA from 1924

LUCKHARDT, HANS (Berlin) 1890–1954 (Wiessee): architect

LUCKHARDT, WASSILY (Berlin) 1889–1972 (Berlin): architect

MACK, MAX, 1884–1973: film actor, scriptwriter and film director from 1911, emigrated to England in 1933

MALEVICH, KASIMIR (Kiev) 1878–1935 (Leningrad): painter, art historian

MAMMEN, JEANNE (Berlin) 1890–1976 (Berlin): painter, graphic artist

MANNHEIM, LUCIE: actress

MARCKS, GERHARD (Berlin) 1889–1981 (Cologne): sculptor, potter, graphic artist

MARTIN, KARL Heinz: stage designer and film director

MAYER, CARL, 1894–1944: from 1919 the most important scriptwriter for German films, emigrated to England in 1932

MEBES, PAUL (Magdeburg) 1872–1938 (Berlin): architect

MEIDNER, LUDWIG (Bernstadt, Silesia) 1884–1966 (Darmstadt): painter, graphic artist

MELZER, MORIZ (Allendorf, Bohemia) 1877–1966 (Berlin): painter

MENDELSOHN, ERICH (Allenstein/Olsztyn) 1887–1953 (San Francisco): architect

MESSTER, OSCAR (Berlin) 1866–1943 (Tegernsee): inventor, film producer and director, made his own films from 1897, the first to try and establish a German film industry, made the first experiments with sound films

METZNER, ERNÖ, 1892–: painter, film-set and costume designer and film director, made short films and publicity films from 1929, emigrated to France and England in 1933

MEYER, ADOLF (Wechernich, Eifel) 1881–1929 (Baltrum): architect

MEYER, HANNES (Basel) 1889–1954 (Crocifisso near Lugano): architect

MIES VAN DER ROHE, LUDWIG (Aachen) 1886–1969 (Chicago): architect, designer

MOHOLY-NAGY, LASZLO (Bácsbarsod, Hungary) 1895–1946 (Chicago): painter, sculptor, art historian, collage maker, made experimental and documentary films from 1921–36, emigrated via Amsterdam and London to the USA in 1934

MOISSI, ALEXANDER (Triest) 1880–1935 (Lugano): actor

MÜLLER, GERDA: actress

MURNAU, FRIEDRICH WILHELM [Friedrich Wilhelm Plumpe] (Bielefeld) 1889–1931 (Santa Barbara): actor, directed his own films from 1919, moved to Hollywood in 1926

MÜTHEL, LOTHAR (Berlin) 1896–1965 (Frankfurt-am-Main): director and actor

MUTHESIUS, HERMANN (Gross-Neuhausen, Thuringia) 1861–1927 (Berlin): architect

NEHER, CAROLA: actress

NEHER, CASPAR (Augsburg) 1867–1962 (Vienna): stage designer, worked in Berlin from 1923, in Zurich from 1945

NEUTRA, RICHARD (Vienna) 1892–1970 (Wuppertal): architect, opened his own practice in Los Angeles in 1926

NIELSEN, ASTA (Copenhagen) 1881–1972 (Copenhagen): stage and film actress, producer, worked in Denmark in films from 1910, in Germany from 1911

NOLDE, EMIL [Emil Hansen] (Nolde, Schleswig) 1867–1956 (Seebüll, Schleswig-Holstein): painter

NUSSBAUM, FELIX (Osnabrück) 1904–1944 (Auschwitz): painter

OPHÜLS, MAX [Max Oppenheimer] (Saarbrücken) 1902–1957 (Hamburg): film actor and director, made his own films from 1930, emigrated 1933

OSWALD, RICHARD [Richard Ornstein] (Austria) 1880–1963: film director and producer, made films in Berlin from 1914

OTTO, TEO (Remscheid) 1904–1968 (Zurich): stage designer, emigrated to Switzerland in 1933 .

PABST, GEORG WILHELM (Raudnitz) 1885–1967 (Vienna): stage and film director, made his own films from 1923, worked in France and the USA from 1932, returned to Vienna in 1937

PALLENBERG, MAX (Vienna) 1877–1934 (d. in an airplane accident): actor

PAQUET, ALFONS (Wiesbaden) 1881–1944 (Frankfurt-am-Main): author and playwright

PAUL, BRUNO (Seifhennersdorf) 1874–1968 (Berlin): architect

PECHSTEIN, MAX (Zwickau) 1881–1955 (Berlin): painter, graphic artist

PERI, LASZLO [Peter] (Budapest) 1889–1967 (London): sculptor, actor, architect

PFEMFERT, FRANZ (Lötzen, East Prussia) 1879–1954 (Mexico City): author and editor

PICK, LUPU (Rumania) 1886–1931: film actor and director, made "chamber-play" films

PIRCHAN, EMIL (Brünn) 1884–1956 (Vienna): stage designer, painter, architect

PISCATOR, ERWIN (Ulm) 1893–1966 (Starnberg): theater manager and producer, emigrated in 1933, founded and worked at the Dramatic Workshop and Studio Theater New York (1939), returned to Europe in 1951, with B. Brecht foremost exponent of epic theater

POELZIG, HANS (Berlin) 1869–1936 (Berlin): architect

POELZIG, MARTHA HELENE [Marlene] (Hamburg) 1894– (lives in Hamburg): sculptress, worked in Poelzig's architectural offices

POLGAR, ALFRED (Vienna) 1875–1955 (Zurich): author, emigrated in 1933

POMMER, ERICH, 1889–1966: film producer, emigrated to the USA in 1933, produced films in Germany from 1950–56

PONTO, ERICH (Lübeck) 1884–1957 (Stuttgart): actor

PUNI, IVAN ALBERTOVICH [Jean Pougny] (Konokalla, Finland) 1894–1956 (Paris): painter

REINHARDT, MAX [Max Goldmann] (Baden near Vienna) 1873–1943 (New York): actor, theater producer and manager, directed his own films in 1913–14, emigrated to Austria in 1933, to the USA in 1938

REINIGER, LOTTE, 1899–1980: film-maker, invented "silhouette" films, from 1919 made animated films with scissors art, after 1930 also made films on musical themes, worked in England after 1945

RICHTER, HANS (Berlin) 1888–1976 (Locarno): painter, film-maker, made experimental films from 1921–29, emigrated to Holland after 1933, then to Switzerland and the USA

RING, THOMAS (Nürnberg) 1892– (lives in Unter-Gruppenbach near Heilbronn): painter

ROBINSON, ARTHUR, 1888–1935: author, film director for historical and "chamber-play" films from 1914

RUTTMANN, WALTER (Frankfurt-am-Main) 1887–1914 (Berlin): director of avantgarde and documentary films, experimented with sound montages in 1929–30, after 1933 made documentary and propaganda films

RYE, STELLAN (Denmark) 1880–1914: director and scriptwriter

SAGAN, LEONTINE (Austria) 1899–1974: stage and film director, after 1932 worked in the theater in England and South Africa

SALVISBERG, OTTO RUDOLF (Köniz near Bern) 1882–1940 (Arosa): architect

SCHAD, CHRISTIAN (Miesbach, Upper Bavaria) 1894– (lives in Keilberg near Aschaffenburg): painter, graphic artist

SCHARFF, EDWIN (Neu-Ulm) 1887–1955 (Hamburg): sculptor

SCHAROUN, HANS (Bremen) 1893–1972 (Berlin): architect

SCHEFFLER, KARL (Eppendorf near Hamburg) 1896–1951 (Überlingen on the Bodensee): drew ornamentation for wallpapers, art journalist

SCHLEMMER, OSKAR (Stuttgart) 1888–1934 (Baden-Baden): painter, graphic artist, sculptor

SCHLICHTER, RUDOLF (Calw) 1890–1955 (Munich): painter

SCHMIDT–ROTTLUFF, KARL (Rottluff near Chemnitz) 1884–1976 (Berlin): painter and designer

SCHOLZ, GEORG (Wolfenbüttel) 1890–1945 (Waldkirch): painter

SCHRIMPF, GEORG (Munich) 1889–1938 (Berlin): painter

SCHÜTTE, ERNST: stage designer

SCHWITTERS, KURT (Hanover) 1887–1948 (Ambleside, England): painter, sculptor and collage maker

SEEBER, GUIDO, 1879–1940: cameraman from 1909, made his own shorts and trick films

SEGAL, ARTHUR (Jassy, Rumania) 1875–1944 (London): painter

SINTENIS, RENÉE (Glatz) 1888–1965 (Berlin): sculptress

SIODMAK, ROBERT (USA) 1900–1973: director, worked in German films from 1929–32, then in France and the USA, made films again in Germany from 1957–62

SKLADANOVSKY, MAX (Berlin) 1863–1939 (Berlin): inventor and producer

SKLADANOVSKY, EMIL, 1859–1945: inventor and producer

SKLADANOVSKY, EUGEN, 1899–1945: actor Max and Emil discovered the cinema process and were the first German film producers; they made short circus and "street" films in 1895–96 with Eugen as an actor

SPEER, ALBERT (Mannheim) 1905–1981 (London): architect

STECKEL, LEONARD: actor and director

STEGER, MILLY (Rheinberg am Niederrhein) 1881–1948 (Berlin): sculptress

STEINRÜCK, ALBERT: actor

STERN, ERNST: stage designer

STERNBERG, JOSEF VON (Vienna) 1894–1969

(Hollywood): film director, made films in the USA from 1925, his only German film was *Der blaue Engel* (1930) with Marlene Dietrich

STRAUB, AGNES (Munich) 1890–1941 (Berlin): actress

STRAUMER, HEINRICH (Chemnitz) 1876–1937 (Berlin): architect

STROHBACH, KLAUS: stage designer

SUHR, EDWARD: stage designer

TAPPERT, GEORG (Berlin) 1880–1957 (Berlin): painter

TAUT, BRUNO (Königsberg) 1880–1938 (Istanbul): architect

TESSENOW, HEINRICH (Rostock) 1876–1950 (Berlin): architect

THIMIG, HELENE (Vienna) 1889–: actress, emigrated to the USA in 1933, returned to Germany in 1946

TOLLER, ERNST (Samotschin, Posen) 1893–1939 (New York): politician, author, emigrated to the USA in 1933

TRENKER, LUIS (St. Ulrich): actor in mountain films, made his own films about Nature and the Fatherland from 1931

TRIVAS, VICTOR (Russia) 1896–1970: decorator, scriptwriter, film director, emigrated to the USA in 1933

TROOST, PAUL LUDWIG (Elberfeld) 1878–1934 (Munich): architect

UHLMANN, HANS (Berlin) 1900–1975 (Berlin): sculptor

ULMER, EDGAR (Vienna) 1904–1972: film-set and costume designer and film director, made B films in the USA from 1932, made Yiddish films in the USA and Poland, worked on films in Europe from 1964

UNRUH, FRITZ VON (Koblenz) 1885–1970 (Diez): author, emigrated to France in 1933

VALK, FRITZ: actor

VELDE, HENRY VAN DE (Antwerp) 1863–1957 (Zurich): architect and designer

VIERTEL, BERTHOLD (Vienna) 1885–1953 (Vienna): poet, director, emigrated in 1933, in the USA in 1939, returned to Europe in 1949

WAGENHEIM, GUSTAV VON: director and actor

WAGNER, ELSA: actress

WAGNER, MARTIN (Königsberg) 1885–1957 (Cambridge, Massachusetts): architect

WALDEN, HERWARTH [Georg Lewin] (Berlin) 1878–1941 (Saratov on the Volga): author, musician, art dealer

WÄSCHER, ARIBERT: actor

WAUER, WILLIAM (Oberwiesenthal) 1866–1961 (Berlin): sculptor, painter

WEGENER, PAUL (Arnoldsdorf near Graudenz) 1874–1948 (Berlin): actor, film director, worked in films from 1913 as scriptwriter, actor and director

WEIGEL, HELENE (Vienna) 1900–1971 (Berlin): actress and theater manager

WEILL, KURT (Dessau) 1900–1950 (New York): composer, emigrated in 1933

WIEMANN, MATTHIAS (Osnabrück) 1902–1969 (Zurich): stage and film actor

WIENE, ROBERT, 1881–1938 (Paris): actor and film director, worked as scriptwriter for films from 1912, emigrated to France in 1930

WILDER, BILLY (Cracow) 1906–: film director, producer, scriptwriter and journalist, emigrated to Paris in 1933, then to the USA

WILLE, RUDOLF (Hildesheim) 1873–: architect

WINTERSTEIN, EDUARD VON [Eduard von Wangenheim] (Vienna) 1871–1961 (Berlin): actor

WOLF, FRIEDRICH (Neuwied on the Rhein) 1888–1953 (Lehnitz near Berlin): doctor, author, emigrated in 1933

WUNDERWALD, GUSTAV (Cologne-Kalk) 1882–1945 (Berlin): painter, scenery painter and stage designer

ZINNEMANN, FRED (Vienna) 1907–: film director, made films in Hollywood from 1942

ZUCKMAYER, CARL (Nackenheim on the Rhein) 1896–1977 (Saas Fee, Switzerland): author and dramatist

PHOTO CREDITS

INDEX